D0058410

About Island Press

Island Press is the only nonprofit organization in the United States whose principal purpose is the publication of books on environmental issues and natural resource management. We provide solutions-oriented information to professionals, public officials, business and community leaders, and concerned citizens who are shaping responses to environmental problems.

In 1994, Island Press celebrated its tenth anniversary as the leading provider of timely and practical books that take a multidisciplinary approach to critical environmental concerns. Our growing list of titles reflects our commitment to bringing the best of an expanding body of literature to the environmental community throughout North America and the world.

Support for Island Press is provided by Apple Computer, Inc., The Bullitt Foundation, The Geraldine R. Dodge Foundation, The Energy Foundation, The Ford Foundation, The W. Alton Jones Foundation, The Lyndhurst Foundation, The John D. and Catherine T. MacArthur Foundation, The Andrew W. Mellon Foundation, The Joyce Mertz-Gilmore Foundation, The National Fish and Wildlife Foundation, The Pew Charitable Trusts, The Pew Global Stewardship Initiative, The Rockefeller Philanthropic Collaborative, Inc., and individual donors.

About the Center for Resource Management

The Center for Resource Management (CRM) is a nonprofit organization with a history of addressing complex natural resource issues. CRM's activities fall into three major categories: public policy and consensus building, demonstration projects, and environmental assessment and decision-making. The hallmark of CRM's work is the formation of unusual coalitions and alliances between different sectors and interests. These coalitions focus on resolving conflicts, creating policy, and demonstrating new ideas or approaches to environmental problem-solving.

CRM works on a broad range of issues and projects, including global climate change, integrated solid waste management, clean air, Native Americans and the environment, alternative fuels, zero emissions vehicles, renewable energy, sustainable forestry in the Russian Far East, and oil and gas development. Project partners include such organizations as the United Nations Environment Programme, the World Bank, the Native American Right Fund, Wal-Mart, S.C. Johnson & Son, Inc., Ben & Jerry's, Procter & Gamble, GNB Technologies, the Pebble Beach Resort Company, and Weyerhaeuser. CRM has offices in Salt Lake City and Denver.

Deep
Design

Deep Design

Pathways to a Livable Future

David Wann

with the
Center for Resource Management

ISLAND PRESS

Washington, D.C. • Covelo, California

ISLAND PRESS is a trademark of The Center for Resource Economics.

Graphic appearing within title type on cover and title page as well as on chapter openers used with permission of Bob Simmons, Continued Success Foundation, Boulder, Colorado.

Library of Congress Cataloging-in-Publication Data

Wann, David
    Deep Design: pathways to a livable future / by David Wann with Center for Resource Management.
        p.   cm.
    Includes bibliography references and index.
    ISBN 1-55963-420-0 (cloth)
    1. Design, Industrial—Planning.   2. Design, Industrial—Environmental aspects.   I. Center for Resource Management.   II. Title.
    TS171.4.W36   1996   95-32237
    601-dc20   CIP

Printed on recycled, acid-free paper ∞ ⊕

Manufactured in the United States of America

10 9 8 7 6 5 4 3 2 1

Contents

Foreword

David Wann and the Center for Resource Management are leading the way out of what is perceived as an intractable dilemma: how to improve environmental standards and resources without punishing commerce. There are those who say that commerce should rightfully bear the burden of past excesses, and indeed that has been, and will continue to be, a pattern with respect to mitigation and cleanups. But even then, the consumer is going to pay in the end, and more important, all the cleanups in the world will fail us if we don't eliminate the cause of degradation, waste, and pollution. This is where design comes in—a lightly regarded word with artistic overtones that has emerged as the leading integrating concept for preventing environmental damage.

Design is the only term we have to indicate that our plans, purposes, and projects must now take into account several disciplines, rather than one or two. We now know that if we are to solve ecological problems, we cannot practice architecture without knowledge of forestry and energy issues, that chemical engineering without epidemiology and biology is inexact and lacking, that transportation systems that do not take into account community, family, and climate are not systems at all. This is both the challenge and the gift of the future, the bankruptcy of traditional linear thinking coupled to its attendant professions, and the emergence of cyclical-systems thinking using integrative design approaches.

It can be said that good design never emerged from license or excess. Breakthroughs in design thinking come from limitations, problems, definitive criteria, and strictures that must be addressed by a product, a building, a process. The good news, ironically, is that we have those strictures and limitations in abundance. We have always had them, but we chose to ignore carrying capacity and the principles of this nonlinear, self-organizing system we lovingly call earth. As environmentalists, biologists, and other scientists have raised a hue and cry over climate change, forest health, species loss, and the myriad of other feedbacks caused by our industrial civilization, they are easily typecast as Cassandras, gainsayers, and worse, their concerns are perceived as annoying obstacles to growth.

Today, we know those limitations are real. Despite all the arguments, there is no denying one important fact: that all living systems on earth are in decline and the rate of decline is increasing. It doesn't matter if we have sufficient supplies of oil, coal, zinc, or molybdemum if we lack airsheds, clean water, healthy soil, productive fisheries, and biological resources. Since it is the goal of *homo sapiens* to remain as one of approximately ten million species cohabiting the planet, we need go no further in our environmental assessment to understand that fundamental change is necessary. The concept of deep design provides us with a sense that these limitations are a pathway to elegant, innovative systems changes that will change life on earth for the better; that early limits are not mere proscriptions but markers that can guide us to new techniques, products, and enterprise that not only will dramatically reduce our dependence on natural resources but expand the meaning of work and what it means to be a human being here, on earth, in the last part of the twentieth century.

Paul Hawken

Preface

We sometimes think of progress in a strictly technical sense— new medicines, new appliances, and faster airplanes. But these products are only a reflection of an underlying, more significant progress in human understanding. In this century, we've developed a deeper knowledge of subatomic reality, molecular biology, biochemistry, human psychology, and the complex patterns of ecology. We can now begin to incorporate the latest knowledge in our innovations, to make them not only "smarter" but wiser, that is, more responsive to environmental as well as social needs.

The industrial revolution was characterized by mechanical designs that didn't accommodate biology and human psychology; the post–industrial revolution is characterized by designs that are programmed to be nature compatible and, like nature, flexible enough to adapt to changing conditions. The best nature-compatible new designs—whether products, buildings, technologies, or communities—are sensitive to living systems with which they come into contact, accomplishing their missions without undesirable side effects such as pollution, erosion, congestion, and stress. These "deep" designs increase options, flexibility, cultural equity, and individual power. They are easy to understand and implement. They don't require "pampering," sky-high insurance rates, or protective equipment. Rather than being above nature, deep designs are aligned with nature—water, the sun, our genetic heritage. Their strategies often incorporate living systems, such as alternative wastewater treatment in a greenhouse environment that's designed to take advantage of lilies, snails, and fish. These living machines, as John Todd calls them, are self-adjusting and capable of improving their own performance. Rather than being "one-size-fits-all" systems, living machines can be customized to meet a particular need. They don't simply minimize wastes, they optimize resource flow, performing the intended function with the least amount of energy, material, and maintenance. Living machines are not about going back to unsophisticated technology. On the contrary, their development was possible only because of new, high-tech materials that are lightweight, light-transmitting, flexible, and waterproof. Thus, they are a synthesis of nature and technology.

Deep designers are not satisfied with the comfortable status quo because they know there are flaws in our value systems—as well as in our standard procedures. When the human population was sparse and there were seemingly limitless resources, it made quantitative sense to base economies on total "throughput" of materials, energy, and activity. Now the situation is reversed, and to play by the old rules is to court catastrophe. Instead of pumping up economies with resource flows, we need to design for efficiency and the endless cycling of materials. If our needs were met more directly, perhaps we wouldn't have to circulate so much currency in our quest for fulfillment.

Shallow designs are cruise missiles launched obliviously into the future by a culture that thrives on short-term gratification; deep designs are groves planted to benefit humankind now and in the future. While shallow designs are anonymous and generic, providing nothing but materialistic satisfaction, deep design is informed with craftsmanship and quality for lasting satisfaction. Deep design acknowledges biological and cultural wealth as well as material wealth. We can meet many basic needs with designs that consume a minimum amount of energy and material yet are culturally informed and biologically compatible. A solar-heated house keeps occupants just as warm as the shallower oil-heated home.

This book presents many different "pathways," or scenarios, for manufacturing, retail, community design, energy generation and use, agriculture, and other human activities. Each pathway strives to meet key criteria such as renewability, recyclability, and nontoxicity. The common theme of each pathway is the search for a more elegant approach in performing services and providing functions. As these divergent pathways reach their potential, they will converge in a sustainable, steady-state society.

One of the biggest obstacles to inspired design is that conventional Western economics is nature blind. It doesn't perceive the inherent value of health, intact ecosystem, or sustainably operated industries. Fortunately, there are more tangible criteria on which to base design decisions than simply return on investment. Ecology, thermodynamics, sociology, and ethics form a secure, realistic foundation for a new kind of economics, one that considers the life cycle of material and energy as well as human need and capability. Deep design is an ongoing process. Once we have "tuned up" individual products—what I call Phase I—we need to integrate them into a system (Phase II) that is capable of regeneration, and aligned with nature's momentum.

Will deep design become part of our everyday lives? If we're smart it will. If we are each aware of what constitutes good design, we will collectively insist, for instance, that newspapers use soy-based inks, or that communities be designed to accommodate walking and bicycling. The goal of this book is to demonstrate how deep designers think, so we can begin to differentiate between designs that enhance our lives and designs that degrade them. Do we want total value in our designs, or only short-term, declining gratification? It's up to us to choose.

I researched and wrote this book under the auspices of the U.S. Environmental Protection Agency while on detail at the Center for Resource Management in Denver, Colorado. However, the views and policies in this book do not necessarily reflect policies of the EPA. Special thanks to Jack McGraw, John Cross, Linda Fisher, Harry Freeman, Don Patton, Bill Murray, Rebecca Lopez, and Heng

Ouch at EPA, Meredith Miller and Terry Minger at CRM, the William and Flora Hewlett Foundation, researchers Richard Holston, Jude Proctor, and Jennifer Haley, editors Heather Boyer and Connie Buchanan, and especially the hundred or more deep designers I interviewed, all of whom made this project possible.

Chapter 1

Deep Design
From the Visionary
to the Pragmatic

Imagine you're stranded in a vast desert, becoming more dehydrated and disoriented with each second that passes. An hour ago you drained the last drops from your water bottle, and now you can feel those drops rapidly evaporating from your forehead in the form of sweat. A genie appears! While you alert yourself to tricks the mind can play, she offers you the choice between a crisp $100,000 bill and a carafe of water complete with clinking ice cubes and a twist of lime. Which would you choose?

The fact is, your choice would depend on how lost you thought you were. What good is a $100,000 bill without a life to spend it in? Yet, if you somehow survived, you could buy much more than water with that kind of money. You hesitate, even as your legs begin to buckle from heat exhaustion. The genie, sensing that you may need prompting, expands the water option to include an oasis. She even throws a bedouin tent into the deal. As you crumple to the ground, you gasp, "Okay, okay, I'll take the oasis." Suddenly, you find yourself sipping ice water in a tent that's 30 degrees cooler than ambient temperatures. You're sitting on a Persian rug in the shade of a roof woven from camel hair. You study the tent's simple yet elegant design. The loosely woven fabric is dark colored, creating a "chimney effect": the fabric heats up, the hot air rises, and cooler air circulates in to take its place. When it rains, the tent's woven strands expand to keep you dry. And when you want to move on to another oasis, you simply roll up your home and take it with you.[1]

You may be wondering why anyone would begin a book with a fable about a desert ecosystem, a bedouin tent, and an imaginary small fortune. Our fable touches on three basic kinds of wealth: biological (the oasis), cultural (the tent), and material (the money). It's a useful analogy for the options open to us as a civilization. What will we choose? How lost are we? The choices we make by design rather than default can get these three variables back in balance. One thing is certain: the preoccupation of the world's developed countries with material wealth is obliterating both biological and cultural wealth. Yet it's not too late to change paths. We can still resolve to meet our needs with innovative, conservation-oriented design rather than expensive, energy-intensive design. We can still live in a world that makes sense.

The designs featured in this book acknowledge ecological as well as sociological limits, and announce the emergence of a new way of thinking. This is not a "how to do it" book but rather a "how to think it" book. The word "design" as used here has much wider implications than living-room decor or the shape of a car. Design is much more than architectural blueprints or bright-colored packaging—it involves everything from a low-water-use landscape to planned communities. Designers need to be aware of criteria that are common to all designs, whether they are manufactured products, systems of production, or recycling processes. The challenge is to integrate diverse designs into one grand design, a sustainable culture that fits nature the way a glove fits a hand.

The contexts in which designs are produced determine their shape. Consider, for example, Western capitalism, the premise of which is to convert resources into profit. This premise was born in an era when there were relatively few people and seemingly infinite resources. Now the world faces opposite circumstances—an exploding population and dwindling resources. This hard, indisputable fact will ultimately cause us to rethink the meaning of value. As currently structured, the field of economics measures material wealth but overlooks cultural and biological wealth. It does not adequately measure the value of redwood forests, well-cooked meals, a sturdy house full of memories, clean water, heirloom vegetable seeds, elephants, crickets, and cougars, or the sound and smell of the ocean. How can we wean ourselves from our obsession with profit to embrace these more intrinsic forms of wealth? It's not likely that many of us are going to opt to live in a bedouin tent, but we can use its remarkable design as an inspiration for other designs that honor biological and cultural wealth. Like nature's, the best human designs represent interconnectedness, flexibility and feedback. By peeking behind the tent flaps—observing and emulating various methods used by innovative designers—we can begin to piece together a future that is less threatening to us all.

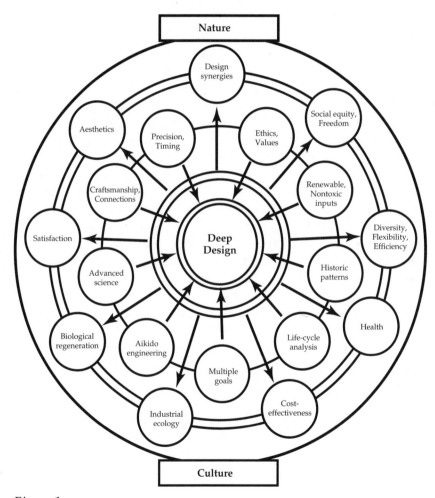

Figure 1

Deep design is the synthesis of nature and culture.

Designing with Nature Rather Than Against It

In recent years, I've talked with innovative designers in many different fields, including industrial designers, architects and city planners, transportation experts, inventors of solar devices, ecosystem modelers, and chemical and mechanical engineers. A few of these men and women are genuine sages. Their clear-headed efforts go beyond the reactive command-and-control strategy of regulatory agencies dealing with environmental problems. They are asking, What do we really want, and how do we get it by design? Instead of focusing simply on what's coming out of America's discharge pipes, stacks, and assembly lines, they are focusing on what goes into a given product or process. They are envisioning and implementing designs that enhance both environment and culture. They are confident that we can actively design a better world if we take appropriate pathways and start with the right assumptions. They live in the same world as the rest of us, yet they see it more comprehensively, perceiving how each "shallow" design makes life less worth living, while each inspired design adds value to life.

Most of them are also pragmatists. They know that passion without reason is like a plane without a destination. Before a design takes off, it should incorporate information about its life cycle: where its materials come from, how it can pay its own way, whether it's easy to understand and use, whether it dovetails with and enhances existing designs, what will happen to it at the end of its life. All too often, designers and engineers have been preoccupied with what comes out; deep designers are especially concerned with what goes in. Their products and processes are low impact from start to finish, in many cases contributing more than they take. An expertly designed building, for example, can ultimately capture more energy than it consumes, even if the full energy costs of materials extraction, building operation, and demolition are factored in.

People today are beginning to regard the world as a museum containing priceless objects rather than as a cafeteria of consumables. My daughter Libby recently posed an unsavory but intriguing question: "How big would a ball of already-chewed gum be if all wads, worldwide, were stuck together every day?" Going "upstream" from the gumball to its origins—not in the supermarket but in forests, fields, mines, and wells all over the planet—we learn that the mint fields alone for Wrigley's Doublemint gum occupy space equivalent to 30,000 football fields. Gum doesn't originate in the store, nor does aluminum with suppliers. And neither material disappears at the end of its useful life. For the first time since the start of the industrial revolution, deep designers as well as consumers want to know what a product is really made of, how it will be used, and where it will end up. In effect, they are seeing origins and consequences, and realizing that we must once again be responsible for them. Now, having begun to regain their sight, deep designers aim for more than just another marketplace transaction; they aim for a product that will deliver its service without side effects, while giving total value and satisfaction.

The products of deep designers, no matter what the field, incorporate certain common characteristics. For example, they are repairable, easy to disassemble and understand, recyclable, nontoxic, available to more than just the elite, and conducive to the good health of both humans and habitat. Deep designers imagine and then move toward designs that are steady-state and sustainable, like a climax ecosystem. They design hydrogen-powered cars, rooftop gardens in low-income neighborhoods, nature-compatible farming techniques, and closed-loop wastewater-treatment systems.

A recurring effort of deep designers is to find the best individual components for a design, then integrate those components into a system. No design is an island. Every design is a system that is part of a larger system. Take, for example, food distribution. It involves at least five key economic sectors: agriculture, transportation, packaging, retail, and consumers. The distribution network generally operates according to a conventional pattern: food is grown in one location and shipped to other, distant locations for a good profit. What if this pattern begins to change? What if we begin to grow hardier strains of crops and make more use of advanced greenhouses? What if consumers started buying produce directly from growers who received zoning approval to farm right in our neighborhoods? The food-distribution pattern would alter drastically as a result of such design changes, and our quality of life would improve.

Deep design is superior to shallow design because it looks at the big picture. An old story about two stonecutters illustrates one of the key distinctions between shallow and deep design. When asked what they are working on, one replies, "I'm cutting this rock into pieces that are 2 feet by 2 feet by 6 inches." The other replies,

"I'm helping build a cathedral." The best designers see patterns rather than fragmented pieces. They practice give-and-take because they get more value that way. Consider the design of a building. It may include state-of-the-art equipment such as computer-controlled air conditioning, windows that let light through but deflect heat, and high-performance insulation. But unless these are integrated as a system, the owner may end up paying a premium for materials and energy and still have an uncomfortable building. What if the architects and engineers consult with each other about how thick the insulation should be for cost-effectiveness, and how many windows should be the more expensive, high-performance variety? If good design can make it possible to have a smaller, less expensive air-conditioning unit, the owner will pay less, and the environment will suffer less. Fuel that remains unburned is fuel that doesn't pollute and doesn't cost anything.

Aikido Engineering:
The Environment-Design Connection

It's clear that we need more sophisticated, nature-oriented ways of providing services and performing functions. Many designers and engineers are taking an approach I call aikido engineering. Essentially, the Eastern martial art discipline of aikido seeks to utilize natural forces and succeed through nonresistance. Aikido never applies more force than is necessary. Its goal is resolution rather than conquest. We can and should use this approach to find solutions that avoid environmental and social problems.

In the past, we've tended to look at symptoms of environmental degradation such as water pollution and hazardous waste sites and think that they are the problem. Now we're beginning to look upstream from the symptoms to the root causes, making the connection between what goes in and what comes out.

Urban smog, for example, is an amorphous symptom of bad design: poor land use, inefficient fuel combustion, wasteful industrial processes, the individual acts of a million residents using low-quality paints, solvents, and fertilizers and so on. The result is a toxic miasma. The way we design and operate creates symptoms, like the extinction of a species, grossly out of proportion to the orig-

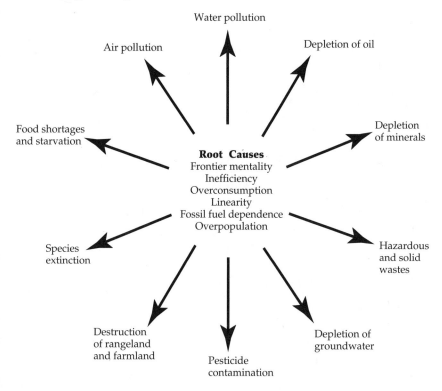

Figure 2

The root causes of environmental degradation.

SOURCE: DAN CHIRAS, *Lessons from Nature: Learning to Live Sustainably on the Earth*; WASHINGTON, D.C.: ISLAND PRESS, 1992.

inal goal. Chemicals are stronger than they need to be for a given function. Buildings don't make use of designs such as the latest passive solar, which could reduce or eliminate pollution at the mine and the power plant. Forestry practices destroy ecosystems that guard against erosion and the collapse of habitat. A list of the most significant environmental risks compiled by the U.S. Environmental Protection Agency's Science Advisory Board offers evidence that a design approach examining the way we meet needs is the only way to attack ecological and health problems at the source. The EPA list includes the following:

OVERALL HIGH/MEDIUM RISK

• "Criteria" air pollution from mobile and stationary sources (includes acid rain impacts)
• Other indoor pollution
• Drinking water from tap
• Exposure to consumer products

HIGH HEALTH, LOW ECOLOGICAL RISK

• Hazardous/toxic air pollutants
• Stratospheric ozone depletion
• Pesticide residues in or on foods
• Worker exposure to chemicals and pesticides

LOW HEALTH, HIGH ECOLOGICAL RISK

• Global warming
• Surface water pollution
• Physical alteration of aquatic habitat, such as estuaries and wetlands, and impact by mining wastes[2]

All these risks, with the exception of indoor radon, have their origins in poorly designed products, processes, and technologies. Let's take indoor air pollution as an example. It has many sources, including furniture, building materials, pesticides, and paint. Better air exchange will help reduce indoor pollution, but this strategy is shallow—it doesn't attack the causes. To eliminate the symptom of unhealthy indoor air, each of the sources needs to be better designed to emit less pollution. Only through whole-systems design can we stop the bleeding by avoiding the cut.

Design is open minded, informed, exploratory; regulations and standard operating procedures are inflexible and static. We definitely need regulations to set boundaries, but we also need to be aware that reality is not black and white—it's multicolored, a rainbow of possibilities. In addition to being strict rule setters, we need to be opportunity seekers, constantly fine-tuning regulations as reality changes and culture evolves.

America's environmental regulatory system was set up to measure industrial waste and its impact on the environment. The system doesn't sufficiently analyze what goes into the pipeline, nor does it ask what outcome might be desirable. It lets the market-place's invisible hand make key decisions, asking only that the quantity of waste be reduced. What is needed is a sweeping new approach. While the Toxics Release Inventory is valuable, having resulted in significant reductions of industrial emissions, it measures only quantity. Where are the qualitative measures that evaluate industrial products and processes on the basis of durability, energy efficiency, appropriateness for a given region, indeed, their very reason for being? Where are the inventories that measure the flow of raw materials, finished products, and recyclable materials? The basic flaw in our thinking is to assume that we can achieve quality by tinkering with quantity. As long as we think that we can control pollution, we are not likely to come up with the innovative designs to prevent it.

Ironically, the regulatory system is set up to accommodate rather than inhibit an environmentally insensitive supply-side economy. It seems to be saying no to industrial pollution, but at the same time it plays the supply side's game, failing to nurture changes that would encourage more efficient production and more moderate consumption. Both industry and the regulatory system look downstream, at finished products, at environmental impacts, at problems in conceptual "containers" such as air, water, and Superfund sites. But there is a different way of looking at environmental protection—on the demand side, where design decisions are customized, precise, participatory, flexible, and sensitive to changes in biology and culture. Demand-side management, for example, is now widely practiced by the utility industry as a way of meeting human needs like lighting and cooling. Rather than burning coal (a supply-side activity), needs are met with ingenious designs that better serve the demand side. A high-efficiency light bulb, for example, provides more light per unit of coal, saving money and preventing pollution.

Pollution prevention began in the late 1980s as an EPA and corporate nonregulatory initiative. Typically, company engineers were encouraged to ask, Is there a better way to manufacture this widget so that it minimizes pollution and also saves money? Can we substitute one chemical for another to reduce adverse effects on the environment? Deep design asks such qualitative questions within a broad context. It asks, Does this design increase ecological and cultural options, or does it narrow the field of possibilities by degrading both culture and nature? Deep design asks not only, How should the product be made? but also, What products should be made to begin with?

The environmental crisis is not simply about discharges and emissions; it is about the whole structure that underlies the discharges, the way our world is set up. In the long run, cleaning up our mess won't cure symptoms such as pollution, congestion, and erosion. They will continue to occur as long as our activities and designs are programmed wrong. Despite the legislation and technology we've deployed in the past three decades, environmental protection is not just about science and engineering. It's also about human perceptions and habits.

Patterns of Pollution

Pollution and other symptoms of environmental distress mirror the way we think and do things. The ways we mine, fish, design communities, harvest timber, grow food and fiber, clothe ourselves, and string together molecules in chemical chains are the ways we pollute. We pollute because of what we expect and how we meet our expectations. Until human activities are more closely designed to complement biological reality, we'll continue to make messes on both a local and a global scale.

We tend to think of ourselves as comic-strip heroes who can engineer our way out of any dilemma. Running out of water? Build bigger reservoirs. Oil supplies threatened? Build "smart" missiles to protect the supply lines. Agricultural pests becoming resistant to pesticides? Mix up stronger pesticides. But our solutions often have onerous side effects. And then there are the challenges that can't be engineered away, no matter how good the engineering, because they have social origins. Wendell Berry writes:

Soil loss is a problem that embarrasses our technological pretensions. If soil were all being lost in a huge slab somewhere, that would appeal to the would-be heroes of science and technology, who conceivably would engineer a glamorous, large, and speedy solution—however many new problems they might cause in doing so. But soil is not lost in slabs or heaps of magnificent tonnage. It is lost a little at a time over millions of acres by the careless acts of millions of people. It cannot be saved by heroic feats of gigantic

technology, but only by millions of small acts and restraints, con-
ditioned by small fidelities, skills, and desires. Soil loss is ulti-
mately a cultural problem; it will be corrected only by cultural
solutions.[3]

To prevent environmental problems we must absorb the right information about the world, then custom-design solutions based on that information. We must, in other words, overcome the biological blindness that has afflicted us for centuries. We need a culture that values the preservation of the systems that support it. If we continue to convert nature into dollar bills, ultimately there will be nothing left to buy.

Why are our designs out of synch with nature? Partly because we haven't agreed what kind of society we really want, or how to get it. Nor do we yet have a clear understanding of how ecosystems work. It is impossible, in these present circumstances, to reach a sustainable society. Meanwhile, nature's ability to assimilate the by-products of our disagreement and ignorance is almost exhausted. Our patterns of behavior have to change quickly.

Every day, the average American uses the equivalent of twenty-seven years of stored solar energy in the form of fossil fuels.[4] As for resource consumption, each American goes through the equivalent of 20 tons of material every year, including rock, paper, metals, and plastic. It's not just the bulk of material consumption that has repercussions; it's also the pace and manner in which the materials are shaped and used. Our industrial metabolism is hyperactive, like a teenager slam-dancing in a formal ballroom.

The way American society is set up places a heavy demand on materials and resources. For example, the population shift from urban to suburban areas requires more roads, cars, single-family houses, water and sewer pipes, and power lines. The more sprawled settlement is, the more materials it requires. The changing structure of the family also calls for more "stuff." Twenty-five percent of the U.S. population now lives alone, duplicating the need for cars, appliances, services, and power.

Style is an important factor in how much we consume and how much we pollute. For example, Americans are now buying millions of athletic shoes for general wear, causing an upsurge in the use of nonrecyclable materials. (As promoters of style change, designers carry a lot of responsibility for environmental degradation.) Short-life disposable goods encourage consumption.

If the cost of repairing a certain product is high, Americans will choose a disposable alternative. In many cases, it's not even possible to repair a durable product because the manufacturer has sealed it up to protect the warranty. The move to smaller, lighter products of comparable quality is a step in the right direction. However, when downsizing results in a decrease in product lifetime, it requires more material rather than less. A toaster with lighter, thinner walls may wear out faster.

Advertising and technical innovation create pollution by stimulating consumption. In many cases, new technologies such as compact-disc players, microwave ovens, and electronic mail don't actually replace older technologies, they simply occupy space alongside them. Most of us now have both microwaves and conventional ovens. The once-touted "paperless office" remains a fantasy; computers have been added to copy machines to breed paper.

Each American consumes something like 3 million pounds of material in a lifetime! Every day, America throws away two Super Bowl stadiums' worth of household trash, and that's just the beginning. Industries such as mining, pulp and paper, food processing, and chemical manufacturing busily extract and convert resources into mountains of biologically incompatible waste. In fact, four-fifths of the material we use never even makes it into the production phase—it's discarded as waste at the point of extraction. Meanwhile, the perceived need to consume so much stuff is running us ragged. As the typical holiday hangover after the winter consumer spree suggests, we expect far more value than we're getting. The truth is, material goods do not really meet our basic needs.

How did we get stuck in this all-you-can-eat mode that has ravaged the environment? Obviously, material consumption supplied jobs, increased investment, and yes, provided consumers with a certain amount of satisfaction. But technological capabilities outpaced understanding of how technologies worked. A good example is chlorofluorocarbons (CFCs), which have proven to be damaging to the ozone layer. Until the environment became saturated, industrial revolution strategies seemed to be working. Now, however, we can clearly see that nature sets the rules. Humans must design within those rules.

With resources abundant and technologies prolific, prices have been low, deceiving us about the real value of the products we consume. For example, we typically disregard the energy it takes to make a product. Though it's difficult to quantify, different materials represent vastly different degrees of consumption. For example, an aluminum smelter spends $1.20 on energy for every dollar spent on wages and capital, while a computer manufacturer spends only 1.5 cents. We spend fifty-six times as much energy per pound to bring aluminum into our buildings (in the form of window frames and so forth) as we spend for drywall, a material made from naturally occurring gypsum. In turn, glass, though it's made from the most basic elements, requires six or eight times more energy than drywall to be melted, shaped, and shipped to its destination in a building. The choices we make in our homes also involve "embodied energy." For example, a microwave instant dinner requires ten times the energy that a meal prepared from fresh ingredients does.

In other words, it's not just the fact that we require so many services and goods, some quite trivial, that results in environmental degradation; it's the way they are delivered by industry. But things don't have to be this way. Design can deliver services and goods more sensibly and meet our needs more precisely.

Value Added Versus Value Retained

One of the dubious bargains of our time is that we spend billions of dollars for services that used to be provided free by nature. With the approval of countless government officials at all levels and their consultants, industrial society has traded in time-tested ecological systems for imperfectly engineered substitutes that often have huge environmental and social repercussions. For example, we substitute dams and sewage-treatment plants for wetlands, and we substitute deadly, biologically blind chemicals for natural pest control.

We don't have to be "nature freaks" to know by now that nature is much more than something to dice up and sell. What our leaders have often failed to grasp is that there's more to economics than jobs and abstract Dow Jones indices. Our economy depends on a healthy global ecosystem not only to supply resources and materials but also to purify air and water, recycle waste, and maintain the beauty of nature.

From ecosystems come such benefits as food, habitat for species, natural pest control, protection from erosion and flooding, and regulation of temperature and precipitation. When ecosystems are degraded, we waste capital and create pollution by engineering artificial substitutes like dams, larger water-treatment plants, pesticides, and air-conditioning systems. Predators driven to extinction no longer keep populations of rodents or insects in check, earthworms or termites killed by pesticides no longer aerate soils, mangroves cut for firewood no longer protect coastlines from erosion, and food that's grown in depleted soil is incomplete food and no longer passes the baton of nutrition to its consumer.

Ecologists such as Paul Ehrlich and E.O. Wilson tell us that the only way to save species is to save the habitat in which they live. It's not just the "headliner" endangered species we need to protect but also the systems with which they interact. Similarly, it's not just a farm's produce we should inspect and value but also the continuity and vitality of the farm itself. It's not just lumber we should value but also the health and continuity of the forests from which that lumber came. Centuries ago, a Chinese sage, referring to the prevention of soil washing away in streams, wrote, "To save your streams, first save your forests."

Humanity benefits from a value-retained rather than a value-added approach. A value-retained approach allows direct access to the services natural systems provide. To give a practical example, if we begin to compost grass clippings, sewage, and food scraps right in our neighborhoods, we won't have to pay to ship them across the city or region. We will avoid many of the costs of trucks, pipes, waste pits, and treatment plants, and we'll end up with an excellent soil builder as well. And if wetlands are retained at the edges of our cities, we won't need expensive engineered substitutes for the extraordinary services they provide: natural water treatment, flood control, habitat, natural beauty, and groundwater recharge.

An excellent illustration of the value-retained concept is the oysters of Chesapeake Bay. According to EPA scientist and Futures Committee member Joe Abe, it is a huge mistake to overfish these environmentally friendly mollusks. They are filter feeders that provide natural purification. "In Civil War days," he says, "the oyster population was so large that the entire bay was filtered by them in three to four days. Now, fishermen are working twice as hard to make the same income because the population is only 1 percent as large as it once was—the oystermen used to pull 2.5 million bushels out, now they're harvesting only half a million bushels per year. The truth is, in many cases those oysters are too contaminated to eat anyway." Abe suggests that eating the oysters may be the worst possible use of them. "How much have we spent trying to provide an equivalent amount of wastewater treatment?"[5]

Certainly, nature is valuable for recreation, new medicines and foods, and the other quantifiable services it provides. But at a much more profound level, nature is our scaffolding, enabling our culture to paint the Sistine Chapel or consider traveling in person to Mars. Without soil microbes, nitrogen cycles, wetlands, mangroves, dense prairie root systems, and millions of other living things, there simply would be no such thing as humanity.

Incorporating Knowledge into Design

The only thing primitive about nature is our understanding of it. Yes, we know much more about biology now than we did a century ago. We know the basics of how chemicals move through living systems, from human bodies to regional ecosystems. We know that all healthy systems rely on diversity, interdependence, and flexibility. We know that the ability of many systems (including the human immune system) to cope with toxic pollution is rapidly declining, and that whole systems, suddenly reaching the threshold of tolerance, can be virtually wiped out. We understand now that each individual is part of the whole, and that each cell is a genetic holograph of an entire organism. We have a better understanding about the interplay between living things and their non-living support systems, such as the ozone layer. But we are still only pioneers. In 1990, "Sustainable Biosphere Initiative: An Ecological Research Agenda" listed ten research priorities of the Ecological Society of America:

1. Determining the ecological causes and consequences of global climate change by quantifying and modeling the links between biospheric and global change;

2. Determining the ecological causes and consequences of changes in atmospheric, soil, and water chemistry, using models of how ecological systems regulate the chemistry of the biosphere and

models for the ecological consequences of changes in regulatory processes;

3. Determining the ecological consequences of land conversion and water diversion;

4. Determining the evolutionary consequences of anthropogenic and other environmental changes;

5. Making inventories of the patterns of genetic, species, habitat, and ecosystem diversity; determining the rates of change of biological diversity and the subsequent effects on community structure and ecosystem processes. Accelerating research on factors determining diversity at all levels;

6. Accelerating research on the biology of rare and declining species, and developing the scientific information necessary to sustain populations of potentially valuable rare and declining species;

7. Determining patterns and indicators of ecological response to stress, leading to technologies that can assess the status of ecological systems, forecast and assess stress, and monitor the recovery of damaged ecological systems;

8. Accelerating the basic science of restoring damaged and degraded ecological systems, by developing, testing, and applying principles of restoration ecology;

9. Advancing, testing, and applying ecological principles for the design and use of large-scale sustainable, managed ecological systems;

10. Determining the principles that govern the outbreaks and spread of exotic, pest, and disease organisms.

While these research priorities may seem somewhat inaccessible to the lay person, they represent the type of knowledge that designs of the future should incorporate if they are to have as little impact as possible. How will science dovetail with design? Advanced information must filter into the design mainstream through the media and in curricula. Professional associations are also a key link between science and design, for they actively track relevant issues and translate the information for members. Another link is the steady upgrading of codes and standards. For example, as the health effects of materials like lead and asbestos became better documented, standards for manufactured goods and building products containing them became increasingly more stringent. Regulation drives better design.

The merger of science and design marks something new in the postindustrial age: the empiricist and the theoretician are finally shaking hands and admitting they need each other. As our science matures, so will our designs and our cultural mechanisms for assuring the quality of designs. Inevitably, designs will be overseen not just by scientists and engineers but also by an informed society.

Enough Is Enough

Nature knows that enough is enough, and that anything more is too much. Trees grow to a certain height and then stop because their vascular systems can't overcome gravity to feed water and nutrients any higher. Aquatic organisms in a lake thrive on a certain level of nutrients such as nitrogen and phosphorus, but if the lake receives too many nutrients in the form of, for example, runoff from a golf course, algal blooms occur and deplete oxygen supplies. Humans need oxygen, but only in precise balance with nitrogen, argon, and carbon dioxide. Each of these gases can be lethal by itself.

Enough means the right amount—it is not a synonym for barely adequate. We need "eco-efficient" production in balance with "eco-sufficient" consumption, to improve the quality of our lives. And we need a new definition of success, one that doesn't conceive of growth as continuing beyond the optimum.

For example, looked at from the viewpoint of total-systems, it can be argued that conventional transportation is a symptom of societal failure. In many cases, it is more expensive in real costs such as energy and environmental stress than it is worth in total-systems value. If we carefully account for the full costs of delivering a head of lettuce—road construction and maintenance, air pollution, water pollution, highway fatalities, destruction of habitat, depletion of petroleum supplies, and so forth—that familiar vegetable would cost twenty dollars or more. Or consider the fact that per capita, Americans have to transport themselves 25,000 miles a year to get what they need. This is an indicator of poor design. Our jobs are way across the city and our subdivisions are zoned to exclude businesses, farms, and open space, forcing us to travel to services.

Importing of water is a failure because the importing region is unable or unwilling to live within its so-called carrying capacity. While California continues to construct canals, pipelines, and pumps to import water, and Saudi Arabia uses fossil fuels to desalinate seawater while speculating about towing icebergs from the Arctic, Israel has pursued a more sensible design strategy. The need to use every drop of water efficiently has become ingrained in Israeli's minds, and as a result they don't consume more water than they have. This is the backpacker strategy. Backpackers know when they are carrying too much—it makes them uncomfortable. Consequently, each object in the backpack is expertly designed to perform multiple functions. Nothing is wasted.

Fine-Tuning Services

A key question designers in various sectors are now asking is, How can service be supplied in a more elegant way to minimize unwanted side effects and optimize performance? The emphasis is on service or function, rather than product or commodity. A perfect example is the utility industry. Traditionally thought of as a supplier of electricity, over the past decade the industry branched out to provide high-efficiency lighting, windows, air-conditioning systems, and so on. By making information and capital available to implement these demand-side devices, utilities reduce energy consumption and avoid the high cost of building and operating more power plants. Interestingly, what demand-side management sells is the absence of energy through efficiency. Suppliers and consumers are both beneficiaries of this revolution, and the lights still come on when we flick the switch. The fact is, it's not electricity that we want, but rather food preservation. If we provide a larger percentage of that service with advanced refrigerator design rather than with electricity, our beer will be just as cold but our utility bill will be lower.

The utilities example (dubbed "negawatts" by Amory Lovins and colleagues) has encouraged other industries to branch out and provide services rather than just products. Water suppliers are starting to encourage water efficiency rather than water consumption, and some European agricultural service companies are selling guaranteed pest control by whatever method is cheapest for specific occurrences, including natural techniques. Copy machine companies market copies, not machines, by guaranteeing machine repairs and replacement in case of malfunction.

A similar approach is gradually being adopted in the design of cars and in the design of transportation. It's not mere style that will determine the future design of cars, it's substantial qualities like aerodynamics, lightness, and strength of materials. In addition, new technologies such as hybrid engines are emerging, which incorporate flywheels to capture the energy lost in deceleration. The design information being incorporated into cars of the near future will result in cars that get 100 miles or more per gallon without any sacrifice in performance.

Another consideration is, How many people per mile per gallon? Are cars being fully utilized, or are they carrying only one person at a time? More than half the car trips in the United States are solos. An even more comprehensive question is, Can we provide better transportation if we augment our car-dominated infrastructure with other modes of transportation? Is the highway system serving us well, or are we actually serving it? Did the availability of automobile technology create the need for transportation? Certainly, cars have created distances that only they can bridge, a shopping mall mentality that only they can service. However, they don't always effectively bridge the distances they create. To paraphrase a current advertisement, The shortest distance between two points is always under construction.

We need to be asking basic questions such as, Why do we go? Let's assume that a third of our trips are for commuting, another third for recreation, and the rest for shopping and other errands. How many of these trips could be eliminated with better design? If our communities were elegantly planned for walking, bicycling, and shared transit, vehicle miles traveled would decrease, benefiting the environment, and, arguably, the quality of life. If our friends, family, jobs, stores, churches, and recreation were more accessible, nitrogen oxide and sulfur-dioxide emissions from our vehicles would decrease, there would be less acid rain, and our lakes, rivers, and forests would be much healthier. Carbon monoxide and particulate emissions would not send so many of us to the hospital.

Would we be giving up anything by changing the shape of our built environment, one neighborhood at a time, making transportation less necessary? Yes: sickness, stress, debt, environmental damage, and 50,000 fatalities a year in America alone. Assuming our alternative designs were ingenious ones, convenience would remain the same and choices would actually increase. We wouldn't have to ride exercise bikes if we rode real bikes, or walked, instead. If society manufactured fewer automobiles, there would be more capital to invest in shared transit, open space and parkland, renewable energy, highly efficient agriculture, recycling, and so on.

It's not that I'm anti-automobile. Cars are obviously here to stay, and they provide great flexibility, though beyond a certain point they become counterproductive. I'm simply antimonoculture. Any technology that dominates a culture the way cars and their infrastructure do will inevitably have adverse effects on society and the environment. Diversity, nature proves, is a much better strategy. We need highly efficient cars, and we also need good land-use planning to lessen the need for them. We need bike paths, "horizontal elevators," telecommunications, and many other options.

In turn-of-the-century America, cars eliminated one of the biggest pollution problems around—horse manure in cities. An 1899 issue of Scientific American optimistically announced the coming of the automobile culture: "The improvements in city conditions by the general adoption of the motor can hardly be overestimated. Streets clean, dustless and odorless, with light rubber-tired vehicles moving swiftly and noiselessly over their smooth expanse, would eliminate a greater part of the nervousness, distraction, and strain of modern life." Almost a century later, social critic Jerry Mander asks:

> What if the public had been told that the car would bring with it the modern concrete city? Or that the car would contribute to cancer-causing air pollution, to noise, to solid waste problems, and to the rapid depletion of the world's resources? What if the public had been made aware that a nation of private car owners would require the virtual repaving of the entire landscape, at public cost, so that eventually automobile sounds would be heard even in wilderness areas? That the automobile would facilitate suburban growth and its impact on landscapes? What if the public had been forewarned of the unprecedented need for oil that the private car would create? What if the world had known that, because of cars, horrible wars would be fought over oil supplies? [6]

The new generation of environmentally conscious designers is aware that many of our designs, from molecular compounds to communities, have occurred by accident rather than by design, and that these accidents can leave muddy footprints that need to be cleaned up. We've stumbled into entire industries. Gasoline-powered internal combustion cars were possible only because the emerging petrochemical industry made gas available. In turn, cars made environmentally damaging suburbs and accidental cities possible.

Industrialism grew exponentially, as machines and factories spun off other machines: "The machines and factories generated other machines and factories. A steel mill can make the steel to build another steel mill, a nuts and bolts factory can make the nuts and bolts that hold together machines that make nuts and bolts. More factories made even more factories possible."[7] But we overlooked an essential question: What exactly are we building?

The Value of Design:
What's Good, What's Not?

Throughout the twentieth century, an industrial alliance between physics and chemistry overshadowed the still-maturing field of biology. As we enter the new millennium, breakthroughs in our understanding of how nature works will enable a revolutionary new alliance among biology, chemistry, and physics, as well as sociology and economics, with design as a key catalyst. Fortunately, history is a library of lessons learned. Today we're smarter and we've also got some incredibly efficient file systems. We have far more complete scientific understanding to incorporate into our designs. Instead of resorting to science to help us clean up, we can use it to prevent the need to clean up. Again, the automobile is a good illustration. What do we value in a car, besides its appearance and sticker price? In a qualitative sense, our car is valuable because of the service it delivers—incredible mobility that we now tend to take for granted. The car provides destinations, friends, and recreation. More specifically, we want our vehicle to be durable, easy to maintain, nontoxic, efficient, spacious, easy to understand and operate, and comfortable. These qualities need to be cross-indexed with qualities valuable to society, for instance ease of disassembly for recycling, aggregate fleet efficiency, and materials that don't cause environmental damage during extraction and manufacturing. The overall goal is total value—a design that serves the individual as well as the system. We've come to an overlook point in our evolution—at last, we perceive that we are part of a larger organism, our culture, and that our culture is in turn part of a larger organism, the biosphere. What we do for the earth, we do for ourselves. This is the holistic pragmatism of deep design, the convergence of economics, physics, biology, and ethics.

Deep design considers the way energy, materials, and other resources are used in our society. Design approaches we take at the societal and even global scale will determine desirable approaches at smaller scales, in the design of a specific product or a chemical.

In the late 1970s, physicist Amory Lovins used needs analysis on a grand scale to select pathways—soft energy paths—for meeting various energy requirements. Asking the key question, What are we trying to accomplish? Lovins merged tangible and intangible by basing his design forecasting on the realities of thermodynamics. It doesn't make sense, he reasoned, to use electricity to heat water or buildings because the conversion of fuel to electricity wastes energy as heat and friction, and creates pollution. Why not provide all heat below the boiling point of water with solar energy?

A similar approach can be taken in the use of materials. Close to half of the materials that flow through the U.S. economy go into buildings and infrastructure, our buildings should be designed more carefully. We need to use materials that are already mined and extracted. The mandated use of recycled tires in road construction is an example of this approach. If we begin to use energy and materials intelligently rather than haphazardly, we will move one step closer to an economy that resembles a natural system.

Deep design is about thought processes and approaches. The starting point of deep design is qualitative and value oriented. It explores the question, What are we trying to do? The first consideration is, Does society need this design to begin with? If so, are ecological needs being met? We want designs to contribute to a world that is resilient, regenerative, and diverse. We want to achieve a design that contributes to our health, security, and equity. Design criteria such as durability, recyclability, and appropriate scale are prerequisites for deep design because they contribute to the overall goals.

Industrial Ecology

Although economists claim their discipline is responsive to resource scarcities, the truth is that prices don't reflect how much of a given resource is left, only how inexpensively it can be extracted. Costs are often skewed by subsidies that favor extraction and consumption over efficiency and recycling. Consumption is believed to be a good thing in and of itself because it keeps the cash register ringing. But there are no good price mechanisms to prevent the irreversible loss of natural systems. We're mobilizing more materials and energy than we need. Only immature ecological systems use more materials and energy than is necessary for their own continuation. Annual grasses and weeds dominate a landscape in the earliest phases of ecological succession. They are not conservative with resources, nor do they interact well with other species. The strategy is colonial: capture and utilize nutrients quickly, paving the way for other species to follow. There's little diversity to make the system more resilient—the weeds and grasses quickly spread and accomplish their pioneering mission. If humanity succeeds, it will be because we "succeed" to a higher evolutionary state that downplays dominance, proliferation, and consumption and moves toward partnership with other species.

In an "industrial ecology," materials and resources flow smoothly as they do in mature ecosystems. An often cited and useful example of industrial ecology is a network in Kalundborg, Denmark, that surrounds a coal-fired power plant. In the early 1980s, the power plant began to provide process steam to a neighboring refinery and pharmaceutical plant, as well as enough to heat 3,500 surrounding homes. (Prior to this, the steam had been condensed and discharged into the river.) In addition, the power plant sells reclaimed sulfur (gypsum) to a wallboard producer and fly ash to a cement manufacturer and municipal road building operation. The flow of materials and energy is two way, for the power station receives cooling water and purified wastewater from the refinery and a nearby treatment plant. In Kalundborg, as in nature, interrelationships make the system resilient.

Another useful example of industrial ecology is cited by Joel Makower in *The E Factor*. It involves a partnership between the furniture-making company Herman Miller and a local tannery that supplies it with leather. "In the tanning process, machines remove hair, bits of meat, and other organic matter from the cow hides. This waste used to be flushed into the sewer system at a cost to the tanner. But that organic material is rich in nutrients. . . . The tanner

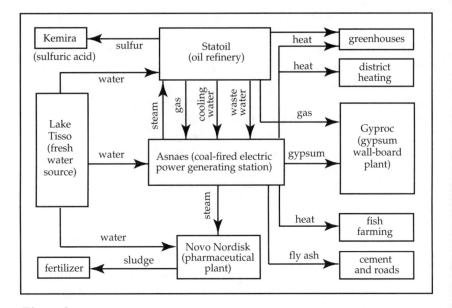

Figure 3

The flow of resources and by-products between participants in the pioneering industrial ecosystem of Kalundborg in Denmark.

SOURCE: HARDIN TIBBS, NOVO NORDISK.

has developed a process that mixes the animal sludge with Herman Miller's sawdust waste. If all goes according to plan, the fertilizer will be used on 1,600 acres of farmland to grow corn. The corn, in turn, will be fed to the cows, whose hides will eventually become part of Herman Miller's furniture."[8]

The overall goal of designing systems (as opposed to isolated products and functions) is to get the most out of resources and to deliver more quality for less effort. Like a family on a fixed income that is acutely aware of each dollar, we need to account for all of our energy and material expenditures and evaluate what we're getting in return. If our ultimate conclusion is that consumption and accumulation don't necessarily confer happiness, we'll ask the more relevant question: What does?

The typical daily needs of a typical person living in the developing world can be roughly described as follows:

1 pound of grain
2 pounds of fuelwood
fodder for animals

In contrast, the typical American consumes, on a daily basis, the equivalent of

40 pounds of oil and coal
20 pounds of other minerals
26 pounds of agricultural products
9 pounds of forest products

Many of the developed world's excesses are hidden. In the United States, if our individual share of manufacturing, energy production, agriculture, building construction, transportation, and other activities is totaled up, we each carry the equivalent of a 100-pound chunk of coal every day. If 100 pounds of coal is converted into its Btu wood equivalent, each American is carting around 150 pounds or so of firewood—compared with the third-world citizen's 2 pounds.

It is difficult for the average American to see how things are made or done, much less what quantities are consumed. We're locked out of production systems by barbed-wire fences, patent systems, and technologies too complex to understand. Gazing at the Wizard of Oz, we are told to "pay no attention to the man behind the curtain." Eventually, though, Toto will pull the curtain aside, revealing the shortcomings of our awesome supply-side Wizard.

Should we wait that long? Knowing, for example, that the building sector requires 6 percent of our primary energy for construction and another 33 percent for operation and maintenance, we can design and engineer superefficient strategies in our buildings and eliminate the need for many of our roughly 750 monster power plants. The Institute for Local Self-Reliance estimates that by striving for efficiency, Americans can lower energy consumption by 25 to 50 percent, recycle 70 percent of materials, and decrease water usage by 25 to 75 percent.

In general, knowing the potential of deep design, we can tap into Detroit's "oil fields" with superefficient car designs, into "mines" of scrap metal, recycled asphalt, and concrete, and so on.

Agricultural	Solid Waste (continued)
• Amount of fertilizer and pesticide used per acre of agricultural land or per bushel of yield	• Waste generated per dollar of value added of product or per pound of product
Energy	• Ratio of weight of packaging to product
• Consumption per capita (total, by fuel source, by end use)	• Jobs per 15,000 tons per year of materials recovered, materials disposed
• Portion generated from renewable resources	• Value added per ton of material recovered
• Consumption per vehicle mile (passenger mile)	• Portion of recovered materials manufactured into end products locally
• Industrial-process consumption per dollar of value added of product or per pound of product	**Sewage Sludge**
• Percentage of industrial-process energy recovered	• Generation per capita
• Portion of generating capacity supplied by cogeneration	• Percentage recovered for beneficial land use
• Efficiency of energy-generating plants	• Portion of soil amendments used by government agencies consisting of sludge-derived products
Solid Waste	**Water**
• Materials generated and recovered per capita and per household	• Residential consumption per household and per capita
• Recycled content of typical products sold and manufactured	• Industrial consumption per dollar of value added of product or per ton of product
• Portion of each material reused, recycled back into its original form, recycled for a secondary use, and recycled for a tertiary use	• Gallons consumed per ton of sewage treated

Figure 4
Examples of materials-efficiency indicators.

Source: Institute for Local Self-Reliance.

In direct proportion, as extractive and fuel-intensive industries decline, other industries based on recycling and renewable energy will rise. This tuning-up of society's industrial metabolism offers countless opportunities to protect our environment and enhance our culture.

The Origin of Design Species

Progress isn't always forward. Cultures evolve by trial and error just as ecosystems do, and some of our current methods and designs are failures. Asbestos, CFCs, PCBs, lead—all these are extinct or on the endangered list. Materials that continue to survive in our built environment will meet certain key criteria. They will be durable, efficient, nontoxic, recyclable, renewable, and ecologically sustainable. They will perform their services precisely, without delivering unwanted side effects.

No design is self-contained—it evolves out of previous generations. In the eighteenth century, carbon was discovered in steel. Too much carbon resulted in a brittle metal. Metallurgical lessons learned in the next century enabled the Eiffel Tower to be built. In the twentieth century, only a third as much steel by weight was required to make repairs on the French landmark, because alloys were structurally more sophisticated. A major evolutionary principle is getting the best performance with the least amount of effort.

How do we achieve such performance? First, we need a complete audit and tune-up/overhaul of existing processes, such as the widespread phaseout of chlorinated solvents in industry and the replacement of inefficient lighting in the nation's buildings. Second, we need to alter the shape and direction of human activity, integrating the earlier changes into a sustainable system.

Sources such as the World Resources Institute, the Worldwatch Institute, and the Office of Technology Assessment point to technologies progressing through both phases on the pathway to sustainability:

- Motors that cut energy needs in half yet deliver the same power;
- Gas turbines that cogenerate electricity and heat 50 percent more efficiently than today's power plants;
- Solar thermal and wind systems that produce electricity at prices competitive with nuclear;
- Steelmaking that consumes 40 percent less energy per ton than today's average;
- In the paper industry, precision timing and automated processes that can reduce variations in pulp quality by 31 percent while cutting steam use by 19 percent;
- Ethylene production that has brought down energy requirements by an average of 3 percent annually since 1960.

As we continue to steer away from an infrastructure specifically arranged to feed our energy and material addictions, new design pathways will open up, such as:

- Manufacturing detoxification (including chemical substitutes that are less toxic);
- Continued improvements in high-strength, lightweight composite materials;
- Microbial and bioengineered products that can substitute for chemical pesticides and fertilizers;
- Further innovations in electronics miniaturization, microprocessors, and computer-aided design, and in telecommunications and remote sensing;
- Cars incorporating lightweight materials and hybrid power systems;
- Fuel cells and more efficient batteries;
- Breakthroughs in light reflectivity, such as light pipes and fiber optics;
- Improved understanding of the human immune system and the chemicals it can tolerate, as well as of the assimilative capacity of ecosystems (nature's immune system);
- Continued innovations in biotechnology and genetics;
- Innovations in "nanotechnology," or microscopic machines that can manufacture at the molecular level.

Such innovations will occur only if there is political conviction behind them. In Japan, a long-term research agenda has been laid out and heavily funded to explore many such areas, even though profits may not be seen for half a century.

Can we build a sustainable society on the foundation of deep design? If that's what we decide to shoot for, yes, it is within our reach. We can overcome biological blindness, economic ideology, and social inertia to shape a new, more meaningful culture. In a sense, we've become quite proficient at "getting there," but we don't know yet where we're going—Einstein's "perfection of means and confusion of ends." We know we can make radical changes in the way we live, work, and provide services, because we've done it, haphazardly, over the past hundred years. Now we need to focus on the wisdom and visionary thinking that has a better idea of destination.

Chapter 2

The Social-
Environmental
Connection
*What Do We Want, and How
Can Design Deliver It?*

Design has always been about the convergence of information, patterns, and resources. Deep design adds a richer mix than ever before of information directly related to the environment and human needs. Because of this richness, a good design satisfies us, whether it's Scandinavian cookware, a comfortable solar-heated house, a recyclable container, or a juicy, organically grown Colorado peach.

Many designs fall short of their full potential yet still benefit us. This book describes many such "green" designs. In a useful publication, *Green Products by Design*, the congressional Office of Technology Assessment gives its definition of green design:

> *Government regulations typically influence the design process by imposing external constraints, for example, requirements that automobile manufacturers comply with the Corporate Average Fuel Economy (CAFE) standards, and with auto emissions standards under the Clean Air Act. . . . The phrase "green design" [means here] something qualitatively different: a design process in which environmental attributes are treated as design objectives or design opportunities, rather than as constraints. A key point is that green design incorporates environmental objectives with minimum loss to product performance, useful life, or functionality.[1]*

The two basic goals of green design as defined by the OTA are waste prevention and better materials management. "Do it right to begin with" is the crux of green design. The question is, What's right? What do we want, not just in individual green products, but in a much deeper sense as a society?

Architect Randy Croxton has successfully progressed beyond the standard operating procedures of conventional design. Many of his buildings exemplify a pathway from regulatory compliance through green design to deep design. "Some architects brag about being code-compliant," he says, "But to me, that's an admission that you've built the worst building the law will allow."[2] The Audubon Headquarters building in New York City was designed by Croxton Collaborative. It has low maintenance requirements and makes use of materials such as scrap iron pipe, for handrails. By incorporating nontoxic materials and six times the volume of required fresh air, the designers created a building conducive to productivity. The Audubon Headquarters capitalizes on natural daylight and incorporates buildingwide recycling, for example, a compost system that feeds into a roof-top garden. Lights are also automatically turned on and off with occupancy sensors. These attributes, though they can't be seen, can indeed be felt. Croxton comments, "The central point that's missed over and over again is that many people feel that environmental design is being driven by 'You should do it,' and, 'Save the trees,' and not by a very careful analysis and justification of what's in the client's best interest. The fact is, by pursuing the underlying potentials of the building, we ended up doing an extremely high-performance design." Croxton not only retained the value of existing resources such as the building structure, he also provided a niche for solar photovoltaics when that technology becomes economically viable in the future. "Photovoltaics will become cost-effective at different times in different parts of the country," he says, "and it's up to the architect to be ready for the wake-up call in his or her own region."

The Audubon Building exemplifies deep design because it makes full use of and integrates a pattern of variables, rather than maximizing a single variable. It promotes both environmental and human well-being, and it is infused with a sense of both past and future.

Saying the W Word

Here goes: the W word, wisdom. What do I mean by wisdom? In *The Power of Limits: Proportional Harmonies in Nature, Art and Architecture*, Gyorgy Doczi makes a key distinction between it and knowledge: "Wisdom is a pulling together, knowledge a taking apart. Wisdom synthesizes and integrates, knowledge analyzes and differentiates. Wisdom sees only with the eyes of the mind; it envisions relationship, wholeness, unity. Knowledge accepts only that which can be verified by the senses; it grasps only the specific."[3] A knowledgeable farmer using state-of-the-art agricultural science feels good about his or her yields per acre, but the wise farmer asks, Yield per acre over what period of time? Will the children be able to make a good living from the land if they choose to? Will the nearby lake and aquifer become polluted by rapidly eroding soil? Will the produce that comes from the land be nutritious because it springs from healthy soil, or nutrient-poor because it is grown in heavily fertilized, eroding soil?

Consider the difference between rational thinkers and intuitive thinkers. Those familiar with Myers-Briggs tests are aware of the theory that there are at least eight primary personality types, two of which are sensory and intuitive. Knowledge tends to be left-brained and sensory-based, while wisdom is right-brained and intuitive. Deep design makes use of all human capabilities, but in our era, the accent needs to be on intuitive, paradigm-shifting capabilities.

Deep design is active, practical wisdom, tangibly applied in the creation of ingenious, multifunctional designs. Designers don't have to be ethical to deploy deep design (although it would help), but they should be aware that shallow designs are expensive in the long run, and that someone will eventually have to pay the costs of disposal, insurance, pollution, cleanup, taxes, vigilance, and degradation of life-support systems.

Designs That Fit: Life-Cycle Analysis

Deep design is informed design, but it makes a leap of faith beyond information into imagination and intuition. It might be thought of as a catalyst that converts the visionary into the useful, or gravity that pulls untried concepts down to earth. Deep designs work because they fit, that is, they contribute to the good of society and of the entire biosphere. An analogy is natural design. Few species are soil destroyers. A soil-preservation strategy is literally a no-brainer—the planet's species have reached evolutionary consensus that healthy soil enables life to thrive. Each land-based species contributes in some way to the integrity of the soil; it pays a behavioral tax.

Deep design strives to emulate nature's rightness by converting flows such as nutrients, heat, light, and chemical reactions into precisely delivered functions and services. One of its most useful tools is life-cycle analysis, which responds to the quintessential question, Where does it come from, what does it accomplish, and where is it going? In other words, it asks whether a design will accommodate natural systems and society. An insulation called Air-Krete has a potentially cleaner life cycle than conventional insulations such as energy-intensive, abrasive fiberglass. Air-Krete's manufacturer once produced urea-formaldehyde insulation, a product that was banned because of health risks. The company hired a scientist to research alternatives. He came up with a product made from magnesium in seawater, mixed with air and Portland cement. It is made from environmentally sound materials, is a net energy conserver, and can be recycled.

In addition to environmental impact, life-cycle analyses should consider a design's effect on culture, family, and individual as well as on intangibles such as value systems. A given design may have a lot going for it, but still not quite fit in a cultural sense. A World Bank–funded project installed an apparently excellent design in an underdeveloped village, a solar-powered water pump that eliminated hand pumping at the communal well. The pump offered many advantages, in particular, renewable energy. But it lacked social perspective. Apparently, villagers missed their informal meetings at the hand-powered pump. When a component of the solar-powered system malfunctioned, the villagers eagerly went back to the old pump and applied some muscle power.

Chicken Goggles

A lot of advanced knowledge went into the invention of chlorofluorocarbons. On the surface, CFCs seemed to be the perfect refrigerant and propellant, being nontoxic and nonflammable, and offering desirable engineering properties. However, in hindsight it wasn't wise to go ahead with CFC production. If we had known more about the life cycle of CFCs, the way they destroy the planet's ozone layer as well as contribute to global warming, we might not ever have produced them.

Countless industrial processes are ingenious yet lack a larger perspective. Consider the design strategy in a particular industry, the egg industry. In *Bionomics: The Inevitability of Capitalism*, Michael Rothschild gives a history of egg-producing technology.[4] The first major innovation was simple sheds for the chickens: "With their chickens confined, farmers could find more of the eggs, and they lost fewer birds to foraging dogs. The first chicken houses were little more than enclosed dirt floors covered with wood shavings, and since the birds wound up scratching for food in their own manure, they often were heavily infested with parasites."[5] This problem found a solution in wire cages that separated the chickens from their manure.

The same man who brought layer chickens indoors on a large scale experimented with the benefits of light in the production of eggs. Electric light fools a chicken's pituitary glands into the belief that it's summer all year around. At Darwin Farms in California's Sierra Nevada range, fluorescent light is dispensed intermittently by an accommodating robot that, at hourly intervals, also delivers feed on a trolley to cages stacked ten feet high. Hungry birds are not as productive in their laying.

Darwin Farms is on the cutting edge of another innovation. It has been documented that, for some unexplained reason, the red wavelength of the color spectrum enhances egg production. Red light makes chickens more passive and less likely to peck each other through wire cages. When the robotic waiter rolls by on its conveyor, they eat less feed, saving the producer significant costs when multiplied by a quarter of a million birds. Trying to maximize profits, the producer experimented with red-lensed goggles, but the birds got their goggles tangled up in the cage wires. He has now gone to red contact lenses for the chickens, a design that the lens manufacturer, Animalens, claims could ultimately shave billions off production costs.

Chicken contacts are an ingenious innovation derived from

direct observation. But they aren't deep design. The egg producer is not asking, How good are the eggs? just, How many eggs are there per robot-fed unit of feed? He's not asking, How can we transmit nutrient through soil, feed, chicken, egg, human, and back to the soil? but rather, How can we substitute technology for nature to increase profits?

You could call it an economic success that a quarter million hens have been forced to lay billions of eggs—or you could call it a detour around quality. Isn't there a better design strategy, one that would balance such factors as health, overall sustainability, profit, choice of construction materials, and the humane treatment of animals? Many consumers are now paying a premium for eggs produced by free-ranging chickens that make their own dietary choices, live in the fresh air, and aren't required to wear contact lenses. This solution isn't limited to chicken farming. Iowa hog farmer Dick Thompson balances goals by providing small, immaculate "cabins" for his animals, with lots of sunshine and fresh water. He also feeds the pigs *Lactobacilli,* which occur in yogurt, and exposes them to composted manure to build up their resistance. These measures lower his antibiotic costs and result in meat with fewer chemicals. The approach is wiser because it capitalizes on what nature has already learned through evolution.

Designing for Social Needs: Changing the Channel

The term "status quo" has been wryly defined as "this mess we're in." Until we acknowledge the mess, we won't go out of our way to change it. Evolution is about change, and an inflexible, unchanging culture is destined to crack. Is it arrogant to believe that we're somehow more powerful or more clever than evolution, which, after all, brought us here? Our inflexible institutions, large and powerful as they seem, are like poorly designed skyscrapers on an earthquake fault. Why are we so smug about high technology, progress, and the high-speed chase that our lives have become? Because we're being paid to be smug. Smugness is embedded in our jobs, retirement benefits, and tax subsidies. We've been programmed to be smug, by marketing techniques of unprecedented effectiveness. Of course new technologies, gadgets, and designs amaze us—news of them comes directly from high-salaried salespeople and advertising agencies. "The longer one watches television," writes Jerry Mander, "the more likely the brain will slip into 'alpha' level: a slow, steady brain-wave pattern in which the mind is in its most receptive mode: information can be placed into the mind directly, without viewer participation." We are programmed to be consumers in an invasion of the mind snatchers. Fortunately, we can snatch our minds back. The world is a manufactured artifact that can be taken apart and reassembled in better ways. Deep design is about rearranging our priorities, then redesigning the world according to these new priorities. Suburbs can be reshaped by both attrition and deliberate demolition, to include stores, farms, jobs, and diverse income levels. Agricultural systems can be designed for the climactic and soil conditions of each given region. Manufactured items can be designed for durability and recyclability.

The information we include in our designs will determine whether they are benign or cancerous. This is no light matter. What takes place in the collective heads of designers will determine the fate of our world. If status quo is this mess we're in, we'd better start redesigning.

Slow Is Beautiful, Too Wealthy Is Unhealthy

Meeting fundamental needs like food, water, and shelter occupies much of our time, as it always has. Our problem lies in the way we meet these needs. Are we really a society that wants to be in a hurry, or are we trapped in the racing floodwaters? It's not just the Joneses we're compelled to keep up with, it's the technological metabolism of culture itself. Gandhi once observed that it's irrelevant how fast we go if we're traveling in the wrong direction.

Large institutions encourage speed; after all, they profit from increased transactions and travel. For individuals, however, speed causes anxiety. Never in history have humans performed so many calculations, evaluations, and adjustments in a typical day, mental activity that has little or no intrinsic meaning. Herded into a hyperactive future by society, we're too passive and disorganized to resist.

The ecological implications of cultural velocity are staggering: the faster we go, the more we consume, and in turn, the more we degrade. Information, energy, and materials circulate through Western society like a flash flood, eroding values, habitats, and most important, our ability to take care of things. We let things go because time is money and we never have enough of it to do a careful job.

Scurrying around distractedly, we neglect alarming signals such as ecological and social stress. The likely result is "overshoot," a system breakdown that occurs "if a society takes its signals from the simple availability of stocks, rather than from their size, quality, diversity, health and rates of replenishment. . . . Overshoot comes from delays in feedback—from the fact that decision makers in the system do not get, or believe, or act upon information that limits have been exceeded until long after they have been exceeded."[6]

The current pace of agricultural production is a good illustration of both superfluous speed and delayed feedback. With chemicals and more sophisticated mechanization, farmers can cultivate more acres per unit of time. But this increase in production has a cascading effect: farmers who deliver greater volume per acre create surpluses that bring prices down. Other farmers, thus, are forced to increase their output per acre just to stay in business. They are so busy increasing yields that they often neglect soil conservation and the damaging effects of pesticides, herbicides, and fertilizers. The faster our speed, the more likely we'll exhaust fundamental resources like soil.

The ecological implications of agricultural speed fan out in many directions. Consider feedlot-based meat production. Something like 80 percent of our grain crop feeds cows, pigs, and chickens, not people. Yet the nutritional value of grain is six times greater if we eat it directly, because the conversion of grain to beef or pork burns up so much of its caloric value. Instead of useful human energy, our grain gives us millions of tons of concentrated manure. If we were to eat less meat per capita and more grain, we would slow down the environmentally damaging pace of agriculture and improve our health at the same time. Nature would have a better chance to regenerate. The production system, the farm, would retain its vitality. In a very tangible sense, slow is beautiful.

The same holds for most of our industries. The speed of communication, the velocity of vehicles, the cadence of suburban development all reinforce each other, culminating in a culture that can't keep up with itself. The late Joseph Campbell believed that global civilization is currently operating without a guiding myth, because humankind is moving too quickly to create one. Few of us have the schedule of the typical Bushman, who, according to anthropologist

Richard Lee, works two hours and nine minutes a day. The Bushman's attitude is, "Why work all the time when there are so many mongomongo nuts in the world?"[7]

At the root of our global environmental crisis is the collective, futile attempt to satisfy needs with material goods: piles of clothes, fancy cars, gadgets to perform every task. Deep design substitutes contentment for excess. Affluent humans need to take the direct route to fulfillment, substituting identity, community, love, and joy for material consumption. Another human trait, adaptability, has also contributed to the environmental crisis we face. In fact, this single trait, adaptability, may be both the reason we have survived and the reason we will ultimately disappear as a species. We've adapted too readily to global changes such as major shifts in land use. Meanwhile, our quality of life has begun to slip away. The serenity of undisturbed open space has disappeared only to reappear in simulated form on our TV screens.

The Stuff of Dreams

As a culture, we are defined by what we use. A three-part PBS series called "The Stuff of Dreams" struck me as a good illustration of this. Funded by Dow Corning, the programs were beautifully produced, but they built to a dubious conclusion: that the exotic new materials now being engineered will one day propel us "beyond nature." Why would we want to go beyond nature? Aren't we part of nature?

"The Stuff of Dreams" takes viewers on a three-hour tour of the future according to Dow. New materials like Kevlar, Spectra, titanium, graphite, and ceramic-metal composites are presented in the shape of surfboards, golf clubs, football helmets, and state-of-the-art jet engines. A colorful sailboat, which contains no canvas, wood, or rope, is praised for being "built with chemistry." There's no question that these materials will prove useful, along with the robots, fiber optics, and the superchips that enable them. But shouldn't we be designing something more consequential than toys? What about compost makers, photovoltaic panels, recyclable building materials, and superefficient automobiles?

The shiny, futuristic reality evoked in "The Stuff of Dreams" extends the tradition begun back in the nineteenth century with expositions and continuing with theme parks and world's fairs. Jerry

Mander recalls that "most dramatic visions" at the 1939–1940 World's Fair in Chicago "were inside the corporate pavilions: dioramas of sparkling-clean, seven-tiered techno cities. Monorails transporting people at 200 miles per hour. Sleek, long-finned cars moving at incredible speeds on elevated roadways. Private planes and helicopters whirling between 500-story buildings. Humans flying about with little rocket packs on their backs, while robots, at street level, walked the dogs. The DuPont dream could be everyone's dream. . . . As a child of those times, I found the images thrilling and powerful. They became a kind of mental blueprint that I carried to the future, in common with most of my generation."[8] Americans in this century were taught that they could have virtually anything imaginable, but in the excitement they forgot the simple value of contentment. It's becoming increasingly obvious that our dreams have not been fulfilled.

If a person is completely incapable of meeting his or her own needs, and is totally dependent on institutions for survival, that person is either a mental patient or the typical American. In the words of Princeton scientist Robert Socolow, the supply side of our society intentionally perpetuates "consumer humiliation by breeding dependence on systems we can't understand, control, diagnose, repair or modify."[9] Do we have a good thing going, or a good thing going bad? Compare American faces of the 1950s to faces of the 1990s as documented on the covers of *Life* magazine. In the 1950s, we were upbeat, victorious, on top of the world. In the 1990s, we're tired, stressed out. We're realizing that big houses and big lawns mean big utility bills and lots of maintenance. That unplanned, accidental cities become chaos on wheels. That the substitution of petrochemicals for natural chemicals can be fatal.

Acknowledgment is the first step to combating our fatigue. Americans are beginning to raise expectations about quality, and to devise and rediscover methods of meeting those expectations. Just as we should be at this moment in history, we're changing. Best-selling Japanese writer Taichi Sakaiya traces changes brought about in the West to the oil shortages of the late 1970s and early 1980s: "The thirty years of infatuation with 'faster, bigger, more' peaked and reversed gear: consumers were suddenly anxious for 'light/thin/short/small,' and companies worked to increase the amount of variety and intelligence built into their product lines."[10] American technology scholars agree. After the energy crises of the

1970s, for example, the average weight of cars in America came down from 1,700 kilograms to 1,500. The use of iron and steel in cars fell from 81 to 69 percent, while plastic and aluminum use rose from 6 to 11 percent.[11]

In general, plastic films have become thinner and stronger, and the weight of aluminum cans has decreased by about a fourth. A compact disc holds as much music as two large vinyl records, and a hair-thin strand of ultra-pure glass can carry as many telephone conversations as 625 copper wires, with better sound quality.[12] What's driving this move toward what experts call dematerialization? At least four factors: the rising cost of materials (processing tends to be energy intensive); substitution of materials with superior qualities; market saturation (with streets, pipes, cars, consumer durables, and so forth already in place, demand now is mainly replacement); and changing consumer habits (discretionary spending focuses on streamlined, "smarter" design.[13]

GNP Versus Total Value

But dematerialization has not radically changed commerce as we know it. What is the perceived purpose of commerce? When money is the central goal, true value is lost. Shouldn't we reorient our thinking and put money back in its proper place as a symbol of quality work and service? Don't we have a basic need to be doing good work—not just for the money it brings, but for the satisfaction and inherent rightness of the work itself? If we have a passion for our work, we won't need to earn and spend as much money to try to forget about it; we'll obtain value directly from the work. "The aims of production, profit, efficiency, economic growth and technological progress imply no social or ecological standards, and submit to none," Wendell Berry claims, proposing an alternative set of goals: freedom, pleasure (gladness to be alive), and sustainability or longevity. "The standard implied by these aims is health. They depend ultimately and inescapably upon the health of nature, because a diseased community will suffer natural losses that become, in turn, human losses."[14] Berry's alternative goals are not hopelessly right-brained and unmeasurable; they can be tracked by using more holistic measures of success. Rather than crudely measuring cumulative goods and bads with GNP, we should track ratios of efficiency such as houses heated per unit of fuel, people transported per vehicle mile traveled, and employee productivity per year. Such ratios address functional performance and specific needs. The overall goal is more value and less waste per unit of energy or resource.

It's not enough to encourage new jobs or fund new research. When we design for quality, we need to ask qualitative questions: What kind of jobs? Is this valuable work? Does the 60 percent share of federal research and development that goes to the military really provide security, or are we looking for security in the wrong place? While we are preoccupied with the design of billion-dollar fighter planes, the real sources of security continue to unravel—water supplies, soil fertility, the integrity of families and communities, and so on.

GNP is a quantitative, one-dimensional measure, while total value is qualitative and multidimensional. Total value is not content with growth, but asks, "Growth of what? For whom? For how long? At what cost? Paid by whom? What is the real need here, and what is the most direct and efficient way for those who have the need to satisfy it?"[15]

Deep design aims for qualitative improvement without more material and energy consumption. Instead of stirring in superfluous resources, and in the process creating waste, deep design adds skill, talent, experience, and intelligence. Deep design aims for total value.

Kaizen: Continuous Improvement

The Japanese have a traditional saying, Pursue the last grain of rice in the corner of the lunch box. Japanese designers pool information gleaned from both production workers and customers, then, in stages, improve the design to the very last grain. This is part of their philosophy of *kaizen*, which teaches that the first step to improvement is admitting a problem exists. As long as a problem goes unrecognized, it cannot be eliminated. By applying their notions of "profound knowledge" and "continuous improvement," the Japanese strive to achieve zero-defect designs. By contrast, Americans tend to chase away defects with inspections and negative customer feedback.

"Robust quality" is Japanese designer Genichi Taguchi's term for the approach that controls defects upstream, as close to the source as possible. Taguchi, a Toyota manager since the Second World War, learned that defects upstream result in magnified problems downstream. Taguchi's solution, *poka-yoke*, or mistake-proofing of products, incorporates all inspection within the production process so that the final product emerges without the need for further inspection. The idea was illustrated in a Japanese-American joint venture at a General Motors plant in California. Japanese quality experts, given a shot at increasing production, delivered results in a way that surprised American managers:

> GM had assumed that automation and high technology were the Japanese secret and would be the company's route to higher productivity and higher quality. . . . GM was not disappointed with their joint venture with Toyota. When it reached full production, productivity was 50% higher than at a comparable plant producing the same car. But when GM executives visited the plant, they were shocked. There was no new equipment. In fact, some of the new automated equipment that GM had installed had been ripped out in favor of older technology. The same plant with the same workers and the same equipment was producing 50 percent more and with much higher quality than ever before. The difference was what quality guru Edward Deming called profound knowledge.[16]

According to Deming, an American expert on quality who gave industrial seminars in Japan, workers should be trained to understand the whole production system so that they can track defects back to their causes and propose improvements. Japanese workers are typically trained, in a process that takes up to a year, for every job on the production line. By contrast, American training periods typically last a week or less. Because it considers the whole puzzle and not just isolated pieces, the Japanese approach is more likely to satisfy both employees and customers.

Deming pointed out to GM managers that quality is only possible when employees feel secure and enjoy what they do. Quotas, he said, are prescriptions for mediocrity. Here are a few other distinctions between conventional management approaches and Deming-inspired approaches:[17]

Standard Company	Deming Company
Quality is expensive	Quality leads to lower costs
Defects are caused by workers	Most defects are caused by the system
Buy at lowest cost	Buy from vendors committed to quality
Fear and reward are proper ways to motivate	Fear leads to disaster
Play one supplier off against another	Work with suppliers
Treat employees like commodities	Treat employees with respect
Competition among departments	Cooperative efforts

Another proponent of TQM, Taiichi Ohno, is credited with perfecting the so-called just-in-time production system. Ohno believed that "underneath the cause of a problem, the real cause is hidden. In every case, we must dig up the real cause by asking why, why, why, why, why." Ohno gives the following example:

1. Why did the machine stop? There was an overload and the fuse blew.
2. Why was there an overload? The bearing was not sufficiently lubricated.
3. Why was it not lubricated sufficiently? The lubrication pump was not pumping sufficiently.
4. Why was it not pumping sufficiently? The shaft of the pump was worn and rattling.
5. Why was the shaft worn out? There was no strainer attached and metal scrap got in.

The same exercise can be applied to almost any environmental problem, zeroing in on both cause and potential solution. It can also take the careful designer in the other direction, toward, for example, the cultural origins of pollution. Consider a sudden fishkill in a large Colorado stream:

1. Why did the fishkill occur? A toxic metal was discharged into the stream from a copper mine.

2. Why was the compound discharged? A tailings pile was located behind a log retaining wall next to the stream.
3. Why was the tailings pile there? Regulations permitted this practice at the time of the mining, in the 1950s.
4. Why did regulations permit this practice? Extraction of materials was considered essential to supplying the American demand for commodities. Sloppiness was tolerated by regulators as a cost of conducting business, and toxicology was not sophisticated enough in the 1950s to anticipate a problem.
5. Why was extraction and consumption of materials so essential?

As a culture, the United States took a detour: the consumption of materials was perceived as progress, and the best pathway to fulfillment.

Envisioning a Sustainable Society

Imagine trying to piece together a jigsaw puzzle whose final scene does not even exist. Nobody ever painted it. Each piece is apparently part of the scene, but when you fit them all together, the result is chaos. Does this sound like the jigsaw puzzle of twentieth-century America? Before we can create a sustainable society, we have to have a sense of what that society will look and feel like.

Do we want a centralized society, isolated from natural systems and oblivious to the health of those systems, or do we want a diverse society that resembles an ecosystem and in which designs are intentionally integrated to provide the most service with the least effort? (Effort here means overall energy and materials expended, as well as the burden of environmental repercussions.) Do we want locally available and locally controlled renewable sources of energy and materials, or do we want to continue paying the price, economically and ecologically, for remote, increasingly less concentrated nonrenewable supplies?

We must first identify what we want—cultural flexibility rather than rigidity, diversity rather than homogeneity, decentralization rather than centralization, and so forth. We can then figure out what designs will give us what we want. Surely our ultimate goal is a cultural system that demands less in maintenance, stress, time, complexity, and resources, yet delivers more contentment.

Throughout recorded history, most nations have perceived their purpose as subduing other nations, acquiring territory, then exploiting territory to increase the production of goods while lowering the cost of distributing them. Toward this last goal, governments have carried out public works projects such as dams, irrigation networks, and highways. The result has been deforestation, massive erosion, extinction of species, desertification, and disintegration of communities. Is it possible that the implicit mission of nations can change from conquering territory to sustaining it? Many economists and social thinkers believe that the only way this will happen is if the world's corporations permit it, which will require a basic redefinition of the mission of corporations. In *Changing Course*, Stephen Schmidheiny suggests that corporations are now the world's dominant institutions and the only institutions with enough combined capital and economic muscle to prevent environmental catastrophe. If corporations continue to shift resources into efficient, nonpolluting processes and products such as renewable energy, superefficient cars, diverse agriculture, low-impact chemistry, and shared transit, they may get us headed in the right direction after all.

The Social Venture Network is an organization that tries to steer the corporate world in the right direction by focusing on:

- Creating better products and processes such as improved-quality housing, pollution-free manufacturing, preventive health care, nutritious food, and ecologically sound land development;
- Developing better business methods through employee participation in management or ownership, the creation of a more caring and satisfying work environment for employees, and production methods that conserve and replenish limited natural resources;
- Exploring innovative uses of profit, including profit sharing and corporate philanthropy; and
- Addressing community issues, because business affects community health and can foster more vibrant cities and neighborhoods.[18]

In Germany, a consortium of companies has formed the Federal

Association for Ecologically Conscious Management to promote the management innovations of George Winter. The Winter model for integrated systems of management identifies six principles directly related to deep design:

- Quality throughout a product's life cycle;
- Creativity of the work force, enhanced by a friendly environment (low noise, healthy food, good air quality, ecologically oriented architecture, and so on);
- Employee morale, which improves if corporate goals include both ecology and economics;
- Profitability, which can be increased by adopting cost-reducing ecological innovations and marketing ecologically oriented designs;
- Continuity, that is, avoiding environmental liability risks as well as market risks from decreasing demand for damaging products; and
- Loyalty, which is built when employees believe in a company's goals.[19]

A leading model for corporate-governmental partnerships is Japan's Ministry of International Trade and Industry (MITI). MITI seeks ways to integrate economics and politics for the purpose of working toward specified national goals. With the help of MITI, Japan adopted an ambitious policy in 1990: "To undo the damage done to the earth over the past two centuries, since the industrial revolution." This may sound like mission impossible, but the Japanese have already taken several major steps forward, including the establishment of the Institute of Innovative Technology, where researchers will explore CFC alternatives, biodegradable plastics, hydrogen-producing bacteria, carbon-dioxide scrubbers, and genetically engineered algae for superefficient photosynthesis.[20] MITI hasn't always been so "green." According to Taichi Sakaiya, "In the late 1970s when I worked at MITI, what captured the imaginations of our top researchers was technological research into how to achieve greater volume and speed; energy conservation research was still considered the province of second- and third-rate researchers willing to do on-the-spot fieldwork."[21]

What about American technology policy? The United States is at least finally conceding that cooperative efforts, even in a capitalistic economy, can be extremely fruitful. The government-funded consortium Sematech is a public-private partnership whose mission is to regain world-class stature in computer chips. Other consortia of private corporations have been formed to research electric cars, marketable fuel cells, energy-efficient refrigerators, and clean-car technologies. However, the U.S. government does not have the embracing vision of a sustainable society that the Dutch, German, and Japanese governments are developing. In terms of technology, the U.S. White House Office of Science and Technology listed the following as critical technologies: materials synthesis and processing, electronic and photonic materials, ceramics, composites, high-performance metals and alloys, intelligent processing equipment, applied molecular biology, high-performance computing and networking, pollution minimization, remediation, and waste-management technologies.[22]

The question that still needs to be asked is, With these and similar technologies as tools, what exactly do we propose to build? Even the development of pollution-control technologies may ultimately create more of an impact than it mitigates. After all, the more effectively we control status-quo technology, the less likely we are to replace it with Phase II designs that are more ecologically and socially compatible.

Creating a Sustainable Society

Is it biologically normal to be racing so much? Is it normal to have all our needs provided behind closed doors without our participation? Is it normal not to repair things? If everything we use is provided by machines, what do we do with our hands?

Clearly, we need to change the emphasis put on industrializing and "materializing" the world. Buildings should last a hundred years and provide three-fourths of their own energy needs with good design. Plastics should be designed to meet the mission and then biodegrade. Food should come from soil that is neither eroding nor losing its nutrients. Streets, bridges, and other infrastructure should be built from 100-percent recycled materials and waste products. Certain roads should be narrower, using fewer materials and discouraging high speed through neighborhoods. Lawns should be planted with native species. Paper should be less white and glossy, eliminating superfluous industrial activity, and food grains should be less refined, eliminating health risks. Bike paths should not be an

ENVIRONMENT

⇐   Wild salmon runs through local streams

   ⇒   Number of good air quality days per year

  ▭   Percentage of Seattle streets meeting "Pedestrian-Friendly" criteria

POPULATION AND RESOURCES

⇐   Total population of King County

  ⇒   Gallons of water consumed per capita in King County

⇐   Tons of solid waste generated and recycled per capita per year in King County

⇐   Vehicle miles traveled per capita and gasoline consumption per capita

⇐   Renewable and nonrenewable energy (in BTUs) consumed per capita

ECONOMY

  ⇒   Percentage of employment concentrated in the top ten employers

  ▭   Hours of paid work at the average wage required to support basic needs

⇐   Percentage of children living in poverty

⇐   Housing affordability for median- and low-income households

⇐   Per capita health expenditures

CULTURE AND SOCIETY

⇐   Percentage of infants born with low birthweight

⇐   Juvenile crime rate

  ▭   Percentage of youth participating in some form of community service

⇐   Percentage of population voting in odd-year (local) primary elections

  ▭   Adult literacy rate

  ⇒   Library and community center usage rates

  ▭   Participation in the arts

⇐   *Moving away from sustainability*

  ▭   *Neither toward nor away*

  ⇒   *Toward sustainability*

Figure 5

Indicators of a sustainable community. This chart represents the first 20 in a proposed set of 40 indicators currently under development.

SOURCE: SUSTAINABLE SEATTLE.

afterthought, running parallel to highways, but rather a feature designed to be a primary element of a community.

In the creation of a sustainable society, what we do is more important than what we don't do. The regulation of pollution is less likely to promote change than is the support of innovation. We need to be actively moving toward an ideal society rather than passively trying to avoid a bad one. In other words, we need to change the patterns of human activity. We need to take fewer steps to accomplish a desired end, that is, "softer" paths, for example, rather than using chemicals B and C to make D, going directly from A to D to reduce energy and waste simultaneously. In effect, deep designers will be insisting that monoliths like the chemical, energy, transportation, and agriculture industries do less of what they do, yet still provide the same level of service. Will they be happy about this? Only if they can make profits comparable to what they now make.

In *Abandon Affluence!* Ted Trainer presents his vision for a sustainable society—decentralization and enhanced productivity at the neighborhood level: "The decentralization of much production into backyards and factories within easy cycling distance of home will cut down the high distribution costs we now incur. We will cease to transport most food over large distances. We will reduce travel to centralized workplaces. We will make huge energy savings by dealing with sewage on the block rather than pumping it tens of kilometers to be thrown away through resource and energy-intensive treatment works."[23]

In Turner's future world, neighborhoods would be devoted to small-scale production in the form of gardens, workshops, craft centers, animal pens, ponds for fish and ducks, recycling systems, storage sheds, greenhouses, and solar and wind systems. Blocks of ten to twenty houses, the unit of organization, would flush waste into a common neighborhood treatment system that would in turn produce half a ton of high-quality fertilizer and energy. The neighborhood residents would make use of a house on the block that had been converted to a group workshop, craft center, library, computer terminal, store, drop-in center, and focal point for meetings and recreation. Where back fences used to meet, there might be a compact collection of jointly operated fowl pens, fish ponds, fruit trees, and greenhouses.

What would the environmental and social benefits of this alternative scenario be? Humans would become reconnected to the basic resources of life, filling the void and craving left by today's typical lifestyle. Nutrients and materials would be carefully stewarded back into productive use, and there would be no wasted transportation. Land would be tended more efficiently and carefully, delivering more value per acre, and the pace of life would be less frenzied.

The first reaction to this sort of scenario is typically, I don't want to do it myself, and besides, I don't have the time because I have to work. This is a status-quo response that assumes conditions and behavior will remain the same. Yet, what if we continue to express dissatisfaction with our current jobs and pace of life? What if many of us decide to opt for early retirement and part-time jobs? What if we decide we'd rather live our lives than try to buy them? What if we move half a step closer to the Bushman's leisurely lifestyle? The rules would be different. In fact, they are already changing. Cultural dissatisfaction and environmental disruption are driving sweeping changes in society.

While Trainer's scenario is only one alternative, it is appealing: its essential ingredients—efficiency, social coherence, flexibility, and renewability—are all deep-design criteria. As we speculate on designed transformations such as decentralized, highly productive communities, it is reassuring to realize that a lot of help will come from the convergence of circumstances. Evolution tends to pick up the check if given half a chance. Our mission is simply to go with the flow of evolutionary momentum.

One of Western civilization's primary conceptual tools over the past millennium has been the scientific method with its reductionist, experimental orientation. We took things apart to understand them. Now, equipped with our catalogue of information, it is time to start putting things together.

Benign Design

During the industrial revolution, design tended to narrowly focus on variables such as appearance and cost. Environmental and social concerns were perceived as too costly to address. Today, many designers are finding ways to make deep-design approaches pay. The design phase is where you save the money, whether it's in manufacturing, agriculture, or architecture. According to GM executives, 70 percent of the cost of manufacturing truck transmissions is determined in the design phase. A study at Rolls-Royce reveals that design determines 80 percent of the final production costs of 2,000 components.[24]

Yet there are many reasons why deep design is difficult to implement (which of course makes achieving it all the more satisfying). Probably the biggest hurdle is first cost, and who's going to pay it. For example, why should a businessperson who leases an office building care about energy efficiency if his tenants will pay the utility bills? Why should the typical American buy an alternatively fueled vehicle when gasoline is so cheap?

Paul Hawken addresses questions like these by proposing a new way of looking at economics:

> What we have now is a least-price economy, wherein we are rewarded for producing things at the lowest price. What we are going to is a least-cost or restorative economy, where we are rewarded for producing things with the lowest impact on the world around us. The least-price economy rewards you for . . . soil erosion; it rewards you for cutting down primary forests and overgrazing cattle on public lands; it rewards you for burning fossil fuels and releasing greenhouse gases. It gives incentives to manufacture products at the lowest price and to avoid paying for the downstream . . . effects of your activity. Those costs are considered a societal problem, not a commercial one, which is why we have more taxes, more government, and less money. In a least-cost economy we move to that system of agriculture, forestry, transportation, construction, and communication that has the least cost to the environment. . . . In a least-cost economy, those resources, our "natural capital," are valued at their true replacement cost. Instead of competing to produce the cheapest goods in terms of price, we compete to produce the goods and services we need . . . which have the lowest impact on those resources, and thus the lowest cost to current and future generations. . . . The lowest cost system is the most efficient, in both industrial and biological terms, and is better for the individual who is the customer, the worker who manufactures it, the habitat from which it is drawn, and for the generations unborn.[25]

In this alternative economy, we need vigorous, challenging codes, as well as creative financial tools. Prohibitive up-front costs could be overcome with pooled money that spreads economic risk among many players. We have a Superfund for past mistakes— why not create an Ultrafund to prevent future mistakes? This would make capital available at low-interest rates for the manufacture or purchase of deep designs.

There are other obstacles besides cost. Many industries are already tooled up to produce a given design. Take the car industry, where design inertia is widespread. This industry directly or indirectly affects a sixth or more of the American economy, so there's a lot of economic convenience associated with maintaining the status quo. Typically, the economics of an existing design is firmly entrenched: the market has been identified and a lot of capital has gone into capturing and holding onto it.

The story of the design revolution in watches is an interesting example of technical inertia. Several designers came up with a new kind of watch in the 1970s, the gearless, quartz-crystal watch, that was more precise, less expensive, and more durable. They tried to market it to the industry, but their sales pitch fell on deaf ears, especially in Switzerland, where fine watches had been crafted for hundreds of years. The Swiss, who at that time had a monopoly on the market, simply couldn't see the potential of watches that didn't have gears. Finally, the inventors sold the idea to Japanese and American companies, and the Swiss share of the market plummeted.

Indeed, designs can become stubborn and self-replicating:

> *The standard QWERTY keyboard was invented late in the nineteenth century to solve a problem with early mechanical typewriters—the tendency of the keys to jam when two neighboring keys were struck in succession. Revised keyboards have been shown in tests to be easier to learn and to produce significantly faster typing speeds. But such studies and tests have made no difference. The QWERTY "gene" is in the system, defended by an enormous installed base and the human inertia that resists relearning. And like a gene, the QWERTY keyboard has been passed on from mechanical to electrical typewriters and then to computer keyboards.*[26]

The way the deep designer overcomes such obstacles is through a streak of "deep" stubbornness, deep conviction, or simply deep desperation. Minds are like parachutes—they work best when they're open. While regulators and companies with vested interests are saying no, designers in the back room are saying yes to a concept that may eliminate problems altogether.

Let's look at the experiences that some designers have had. Bob Roberts, now retired from the U.S. Air Force, knew there was a better way to strip paint off jet fighter planes than spraying 10,000 gallons of highly toxic methyl ethyl ketone over them. For years, he experimented with variations of sandblasting wherever he could find an experimental room. Sandblasting pitted the metal, so he tried other materials, including walnut shells and button fragments, which were soft enough not to create pits but hard enough to remove the paint. Plastic was the material that worked best: after removing the paint with less environmental impact, the plastic was 95 percent recyclable. Roberts's persistence and inventiveness paid off after years of effort. Subsequently, other experimenters have come up with potentially superior designs, for instance using frozen carbon-dioxide pellets as the blasting medium.

Inventor Jim Lenhart produced a patented solar collector from recycled soda cans and bottles. Cut and fitted ingeniously and glued together with nontoxic silicon, the collector, with a fan powered by a single photovoltaic cell, pushes hot air through a serpentine conduit of cans inside transparent bottles. For Lenhart, the design is most significant for what it communicates: "Just about everyone in our country has touched a pop can, and this collector generates clean energy out of that American symbol of consumption."[27] Despite an initial lack of enthusiasm from bureaucratic agencies, for whom the device is not sufficiently "polished," Lenhart is attempting to market his hybrid of high and low tech to low-income housing units and for supplemental uses such as heating recreational vehicles.

Designer Sally Gurley, who perfected a technique for producing dyes from natural ingredients, illustrates how formal training can sometimes be an obstacle to innovation. With her limited knowledge of chemistry, Gurley experimented with methods to keep colors fast without the application of toxic metal solvents. Chemists said it couldn't be done. "The lucky thing is that I'm not blinded by the normal rules of chemistry," she said. "You can know too much, and that limits you. My gut instincts are usually right, and after the chemists look at the final product they can explain it. It still works within their laws."[28] Gurley had been making custom wool rugs for years and knew people who were allergic to the dyes used in the fabric. So she launched a company, Allegro Natural Dyes, using five basic ingredients: osage, derived from the bodark tree (used for yellows); indigo, from the indigo bush (blue); madder root (orange, peach, rust); cutch, sap from the acacia tree (brown); and cochineal, from the parasite of the prickly pear cactus (pink and red). So far, Allegro has come up with a hundred different colors for cotton, three hundred colors for wool, and additional colors for linen and silk. Gurley soon caught the attention of Levi Strauss, which ordered an experimental twenty thousand pairs of naturally dyed jeans. "The colors are kind of earthy, but that's the style now. You're not going to get the neons—those are highly toxic to make," says Gurley.[29]

The synthetic dye industry has $15 billion of muscle behind it. But judging from Gurley's success so far, she seems quite capable of finding a niche for her intuitive aikido design.

Environmentalist Dennis Sohocki refers to grassroots design as guerilla design. Rather than wait forever for large bureaucracies to come up with the perfect program, Sohocki advocates creative changes that get results now: "Many governments try to come up with programs that are too expensive to implement. For aluminum recycling, why not just provide free containers to put aluminum cans in—just to make sure they get separated—and the scavengers will take care of the pickup," he said. "You don't need to create a tax burden in the form of a fleet of trucks to get the job done."[30]

Obviously, it takes a certain type of person to overcome the barriers that stand in the way of enlightened design. Deep designers tend to be both rational and intuitive, and by nature they are problem solvers as well as conflict resolvers. Cultural evolution is partly driven by the tension between those who want a thing to be different and those who want it to remain the same. Designers are typically hired (or self-assigned) when a decision has been made to reinvent a design. Their professional mission is to balance multiple variables. What if we could come up with something that made everybody happy? they ask. What design will provide the most value by using the most appropriate resources? Deep designers are innately curious: they want to know why barnacles don't stick to a dolphin's skin and why eagles seem to be fatally attracted to wind generators. They want to know how air flows through a building, and how the chemicals they specify for a certain product interact.

As the design profession becomes more sophisticated, legal responsibilities will grow. Under the threat of lawsuits, each designer will have to provide a level of excellence that is equal to the best available designs. If a building becomes "sick," an architect might be held accountable for not providing what a more knowledgeable architect provided elsewhere. Similarly, companies are learning that a single environmental oversight such as minute quantities of pesticide in baby food can ruin their reputation for good.

With a few exceptions, design and engineering schools are not teaching the broader perspective of enlightened design. Their orientation is still typically maximizing output rather than customizing input. Recently released design textbooks discuss concepts such as cost per unit without mentioning more long-term questions such as, Does the design fit its environment? What's taking up the educational slack are trade associations such as the American Institute of Architects and the Industrial Designers Society of America. At conferences and in publications, among them, *The Environmental Resource Guide* and *Innovation*, these organizations are quickly spreading the word about deep design.

Deep designers fight for their designs in the belief that an environmentally sound product is more important than money. In a total value sense most deep designs are ultimately less expensive than shallow ones, though existing subsidies, tax structures, and standard operating procedures sometimes inhibit their implementation. If economics inhibits brilliant design, it is economics that must bend.

Your Money or Your Life?

All-pro punt returner Rick Upchurch was once asked how he managed to return so many punts for touchdowns. Shrugging his shoulders, he replied, "First I run towards them, and then I run away from them." Implementing good design is sort of like returning punts in a football game. Designers overcome challenges—both social and environmental—with finesse rather than mere force. Without finesse they'll never overcome the challenges that keep coming at them, such as opposition from a mainstream that mistrusts anything different.

Tom Chappell, cofounder of Tom's of Maine, is one such design champion. Chappell's small, dynamic company goes head to head with monolithic competitors such as Colgate and not only survives but continues to grow. His personal history sounds a little like George Bailey's in the movie "It's a Wonderful Life." Chappell is a crusader for decency. He envisioned Tom's of Maine as the Procter and Gamble for people who wanted natural shampoos, deodorants, toothpaste, mouthwashes, lotions, you name it.

In 1974, Kate [his wife] and I wondered why all toothpastes were full of complex abrasives, dyes, artificial flavors, preservatives, binders, fluoride, and worst of all saccharin, long suspected as a cause of cancer. Why were Americans consuming seven hundred million tubes of toothpaste every year and spending more than a billion dollars filling their mouths every day with chemicals? Had anyone ever asked if that was what people really wanted in a toothpaste? Kate and I asked—and we've ended up attracting eight million toothpaste buyers and users in America to Tom's of Maine's natural brand. We simply followed our intuitions.[31]

They designed a new baking soda toothpaste but thought it tasted awful. Still, the two stood by their natural ingredient, in the face of opposition from marketing and sales experts who had strong doubts the new product would sell. "We all know people," they argued, "who boast about their aged parents still having every tooth in their head when the only thing they brushed with their whole lives was baking soda, right out of the box. By creating a baking soda toothpaste, we were confirming a traditional belief in a natural product."

Chappell is a pioneer. He doesn't want to be like the big companies, whose buy-out offers he has consistently refused; he wants them to be like him—not just financially successful but also environmentally sensitive and socially responsible. When pioneers blaze new trails, others follow. The same year Tom's launched a baking soda toothpaste, "Arm and Hammer launched its own baking soda toothpaste with an eight-million-dollar advertising campaign and gained nearly 8 percent of the total toothpaste business. Colgate followed with its own baking soda brand, with Lever Brothers and Procter and Gamble following. Three years after Tom's of Maine became a leader in the development of the product, 20 percent of the market is baking soda toothpaste."[32]

In keeping with the kaizen philosophy of continuous improvement, Tom's of Maine bases its decisions on customer feedback.

Chappell believes the consumer is more than a statistic. "People," he remarks, "have a curious habit of coming up to me to talk about my products. 'I was thinking about you this morning as I brushed my teeth and put on my deodorant,' they'll say, without so much as a blush." As a result, Chappell and his creative team came up with a new policy: When you're developing a product or packaging it or writing copy for it, . . . imagine yourself talking to a customer who is standing absolutely naked in his or her bathroom. . . . They bought your product, they trust you, and they're going to use it in that state of absolute vulnerability. Naked. And you're the only people who can determine the safety and total integrity of that product in that moment."[33]

Tom's of Maine is a good example of how deep design can deliver total value. Not only are sales continually growing (now $20 million annually), but most of the participants are satisfied—manufacturers, consumers, and the environment.

Chapter 3

Design at the Molecular Level
Pathways to Chemicals That Fit

When nineteenth-century chemists began tinkering with the molecules contained in newly discovered deposits of fossil fuel, it was like the opening shot in a game of billiards: new compounds scattered in all directions. According to David Morris and Irshad Ahmed at the Institute for Local Self-Reliance, "Early in the 20th century, a petroleum-cracking process was invented that yielded as much as 50 percent gasoline, up from the 10 percent or lower yields previously achieved. Cracking not only produced more gasoline but a variety of byproduct chemicals that became the basis for new products and industries. These included vinyl chloride, nylon, and lucite. Teflon, neoprene, synthetic rubber, Orlon, Dacron, polyester, and Mylar quickly followed."[1] Chemistry became a sophisticated new language, its grammar encoded in molecular structure. But future generations may regard our first primitive experiments as baby talk. So far, the field of chemistry has been an infantile, exploratory science, expanding largely by accident rather than design. Molecules were combined simply because they were there. Consider, for example, industrial uses for arsenic developed by Swedish researchers anxious to use the waste products of their indigenous copper ore, which is particularly high in this element. The mission developed for arsenic-containing products was to kill pests and preserve wood. Unfortunately, arsenic is toxic to most forms of life.

57

Over the past few decades, scientists have intensified their focus on chemistry. A hundred years ago, industry utilized only about twenty elements of the periodic table; today it draws on virtually all ninety-two naturally occurring elements. Seventy to eighty thousand compounds have now been synthesized, more than ten thousand of which are produced in commercial quantity. In 1900, production of synthetic organic chemicals was negligible; now it amounts to 225 billion tons per year. As recently as 1955, almost three-fourths of the materials Americans used were made from renewable sources. That figure has since been inverted—roughly three-fourths of the materials of everyday life are now made from nonrenewable resources.

The 1950s television slogan "Better living through chemistry" has become a fait accompli. The question is, Better living for whom? The chemical producers? Are we getting 225 billion tons' worth of value out of this avalanche of chemicals? In fact, the $50 billion or more spent in the United States annually to dispose of hazardous waste is only one of the disadvantages that have to be accounted for in a total-value sense. The health implications, from allergies to immune system dysfunctions like cancer, are frightening. On a case-by-case basis, it's time for us to examine exactly where these chemicals are being used and how well they're being used.

Having learned the basic vocabulary of chemistry, we have to decide what we want to say. What exactly do we want chemicals to accomplish? Which chemicals and production processes do we want to hold onto, and which do we want to discard?

This chapter focuses on various pathways to targeted end uses for chemicals. What is the most efficient, cleanest way to put ink on newsprint? Clean clothes? Produce the intermediate chemical from which a nylon comb or gear is made?

Obviously, chemistry is one of the primary bonds keeping our present economy together. The way we dress, eat, control pests, transport and shelter ourselves—all these fundamental activities are dependent on (addicted to) chemicals. Conventionally produced cotton, for example, contains plasticizers, defoliants, pesticides, and dyes; shoes are tanned with chromium and shoe soles contain lead; silk blouses contain zinc, tin, and toxic dyes.[2] But the heaviest application of chemicals occurs behind the curtains of industry. Huge volumes of intermediate chemicals are manufactured so that other products can be made from them. The manufacture of phosphate fertilizer, for instance, creates mountains of calcium sulfate waste that contain trace contaminants, making it difficult to use elsewhere. And what about the production of a simple nylon comb? It follows a hidden pathway of extraction and chemical transformation with branching paths that lead to landfills and incinerators.

Our challenge is to develop a sophisticated, multidimensional language for chemistry, in which precision and biocompatibility are grammatical rules. We need to incorporate knowledge about toxicology, immunology, and the environmental fate of chemicals into the design process, while avoiding compounds with properties similar to those of PCBs, CFCs, and the other extinct species in the evolution of chemistry.

Nineteenth-century chemists and the alchemists who preceded them knew little about the environmental and health effects of chemicals. Sir Isaac Newton wrote a letter to colleague John Locke complaining about severe insomnia, poor digestion, depression, and paranoia. He blamed these maladies on "sleeping too often by my fire," not even suspecting the real cause:

> Over the years before his breakdown, Newton did many experiments in alchemy with a wide variety of metals, including lead, arsenic, antimony, and mercury. Most of the experiments involved heating the metals in large open vessels, in furnaces and over candles, undoubtedly exposing him continually to toxic vapors.
>
> Newton also had the early chemist's penchant for tasting the products of his experiments. On 108 separate occasions he recorded that he had tasted materials, whose flavors he described as ranging from "tasteless," "sweetish," and "saltish," to "strong stiptic vitriolique taste."[3]

Newton's experiments were the baby talk of a prodigy. Three hundred years later, several locks of the great man's hair were analyzed by sophisticated instruments and found to contain the heavy metals that had made his life so unbearable.

New insights into the intersection of biology, ecology, and chemistry tell us more certainly which chemicals and industrial processes to avoid altogether. According to scientist Robert Ayres, we need to "eliminate many of the widespread uses of toxic heavy metals (arsenic, cadmium, chromium, copper, lead, mercury, nickel, silver, and zinc) and of halogenated hydrocarbons. All of these materials have been implicated in environmental problems, and in the long run it appears likely that all of them will have to be replaced or used only in applications permitting an extremely high degree of recycling."[4] The EPA is well aware of the metals problem. In its "33/50" project, industries were asked to reduce their use of seventeen high-risk chemicals by 50 percent by 1995. In addition to highly toxic solvents such as trichloroethane and intermediate chemicals such as benzene, the list includes the metals cadmium, chromium, lead, mercury, and nickel. And Clean Air Act amendments of 1990, which target 191 chemicals for reduced emissions, include lead and mercury.

If substitution is the first step toward the deep design of chemicals, process change is the second. EPA scientist Ivars Licis and colleagues have identified a number of industries that present opportunity for the elimination of high-risk chemicals, including textiles (recovery of dyes and scouring agents), pulp and paper (increased strength of recycled fibers), printing (use of computers in pre-press photography), chemical manufacture (more efficient synthesis), dry cleaning (solvent recovery), and paint manufacture (low-emission products, improved application techniques). More radical steps involve changing what chemicals are made of, and how they are made. While a certain chemical may be benign, producing it may be toxic. Typically, chemical manufacturing involves extremely high temperatures and pressures, acids and caustic chemicals, and heavy-metal catalysts, and it creates abundant waste. According to Fred Leavitt, executive director of the industry-based Council for Chemical Research, "We typically get only half a pound of product for every pound of reactant we put into a process to create a chemical product. The new challenge is to improve the efficiency of chemical manufacture by finding new reactions, new catalysts and more appropriate end products. Rather than putting molecules A and B into byproducts, we want them to go into the products themselves. Green chemistry is about getting the best performance from each molecule."[5]

Stalking the Wild Molecule

Applying deep-design criteria, we need to decide on whether chemicals are even necessary for a given function. A Danish cotton producer, Novotex, has eliminated chemicals throughout the life cycle of cotton production—growth, harvest, spinning, knitting, dyeing, finishing, garment production, packaging, and transport. Dying is done in enclosed, high-pressure jet machines that reduce water consumption and eliminate pollution. There are no chemicals such as formaldehyde used in the drying process, and the result is an improved quality of cotton. As Novotex managers are aware, clean cotton production has many benefits, including reduced erosion, improved worker health, and the protection of habitat. Why create molecules that cause environmental damage when nature has already provided them?

Researchers are looking carefully at many natural molecules, assessing their potential to perform as well or better than petrochemicals. At the University of California, Santa Barbara, Dan Morse and his students are exploring the incredible strength-to-weight ratio of abalone shells, which are made from paper-thin templates of protein. Scientists at State University of New York, Buffalo, are delving into the natural chemistry of dolphin skin, designed by evolution to prevent barnacles from becoming attached. Many chemicals now in use can be effectively replaced with existing materials whose extraction and manufacturing won't adversely affect the environment, such as rice hulls for insulation or cornstarch for biodegradable polymers.

Chemistry in the next century will undoubtedly follow up on the promise of such research. Meanwhile, petrochemistry will become increasingly frugal and efficient, getting the most out of each molecule and minimizing environmental damage with techniques such as on-site generation of hazardous production chemicals to avoids the risk of transport.

One intriguing yet potentially problematic technology is slowly being transformed from science fiction into fact. Known as nanotechnology, it will deploy machines capable of self-replication of building large volumes of material atom by atom. Theoretically, this will allow for great precision, moving materials production beyond waste minimization into resource optimization. Ralph Merkle of Xerox's Palo Alto Research Center explains nanotechnology this way: "Nature has given us a wonderful Lego set. The only problem is that today we can't pick up and put down the individual Lego bricks—we don't know how to snap them together. We have boxing gloves on our hands—we have to scoop them together in large numbers and pile them up and it doesn't quite give us what we want. In the future, with molecular manufacturing, we'll be able to snap together the bricks in exactly the way we want, and get precisely what we want: materials that are lighter, stronger, and less polluting."[6]

In the near future, chemists will continue their research into renewable resources as suppliers of chemicals. David Morris of the Institute for Local Self-Reliance, who has done extensive research in this area, calls it the carbohydrate economy. This involves the direct use of plant molecules for industrial purposes, rather than petrochemicals. Morris reasons that anything that can be produced from hydrocarbons can also be produced from plants, often with fewer environmental impacts. Plant molecules contain less sulfur and nitrogen, thus creating less acid rain. Carbon dioxide emissions that contribute to global warming are also reduced, since during growth, plants absorb carbon dioxide. Using plant molecules directly, rather than waiting millions of years for them to appear as petroleum, also avoids the high temperatures, pressures, acids, and heavy metals typically required to break the tight molecular bonds in hydrocarbons, saving energy and avoiding pollution. Essentially, what this is about is the cost-effective, methodical use of naturally occurring molecules.

What will make the carbohydrate economy viable? The convergence of green consumerism, environmental-legislative incentives, and technological breakthroughs. In fact, biological strategies have already penetrated the marketplace in a significant way. Genetically engineered microbes (fungi, yeast, and bacteria) function as natural catalysts in the manufacture of enzymes. Because of a 75-percent drop in cost of manufacturing these enzymes, half of the detergents made in the United States, and more than 90 percent of those made in Europe and Japan, use them. This trend accompanies a 50-percent decrease in the use of phosphates, which cause ecological damage in lakes and other waterways. Enzymes in detergents dissolve protein and starch particles. According to the OTA, an entirely new range of nontoxic, renewable, and biodegradable materials may be on the horizon because of the potential of such "industrial-strength" enzymes. For example, researchers are looking at how they might be used for applications as diverse as artificial skin, superabsorbents, and permeable coatings for agricultural seed. Is the carbohydrate economy more than just a good idea? Emphatically, yes. If current growth rates in the industry continue, plant matter–based products will rapidly capture significant shares of the U.S. economy. Already, plant-derived paints have captured 3 percent, and plant-based detergents more than 10 percent, of their respective markets.

How a Deep Design Came into the Mainstream: The Rise of Soybean Ink

Vegetable oil–based inks such as soybean ink are another part of the carbohydrate economy. Soybean ink, which has 3 to 15 percent VOC (volatile organic compound) emissions, compared with petroleum-based ink's 36 to 40 percent, has captured 6 percent of the printing-ink market in the past few years. In fact, over the past seven years, 75 percent of America's large daily newspapers have switched from petroleum-based ink to soybean ink, a small but significant step toward a carbohydrate economy.

How did this happen? "Back in 1979," recalls George Casheau, research director of the Newspaper Association of America, "we were having trouble getting high-quality ink supplies, because of the petroleum shortages. We were as concerned as car drivers were that we wouldn't be able to fill up our tanks. We didn't want to be held hostage to overseas oil. The buy American sentiment was definitely on our minds. We started looking around for alternatives to petroleum-based ink, and formed a technical committee to evaluate them."[7]

Their evaluations were based on one essential question: What did they want in an ink? In addition to being cost effective, the ideal ink had to have certain specific engineering and environmental properties. Pressmen wanted an ink that would stay liquid and be absorbed quickly by paper, yet not bleed all the way through. They wanted an ink that produced less dot gain, that is, that didn't spread as much and that yielded more impressions per pound of ink. And they wanted fewer harmful volatile emissions in the workplace. Newspaper managers had additional concerns such as resource renewability to ensure reliable supplies, decreased consumption, compatibility with existing equipment, good public relations, and bright color. As "brokers" for the environment and providers of a healthy workplace, they also wanted biodegradability, low toxicity, and waste reduction.

The newspaper industry has felt the heat of state and federal regulations. In states such as Florida, California, and Pennsylvania, environmental regulations are becoming more stringent about volatile emissions, and the federal Clean Air Act requires large facilities to monitor them. *The Los Angeles Times* switched to soybean ink to comply with South Coast Air Quality Management's regulations, and the *St. Petersburg Times* switched after being cited by the State of Florida for excessive "fugitive emissions." The newspaper that pioneered the use of soybean ink and proved that the ink had "the right stuff" was the *Cedar Rapids Gazette*. Joe Hladky, its publisher and chairman of the Newspaper Association committee, brought environmental concerns to the table knowing that the printing industry was under scrutiny by environmentalists and regulators.

Because newsprint made up something like 5 percent or more of the solid waste going into landfills, the industry was a target for heated criticism. The idea of reducing in-plant paper waste, using a better-performing ink, and making it easier to recycle newspapers because of the biodegradability of that ink was appealing.

The committee considered various alternatives. One of the first candidates was "tall oil," a by-product of the lumber and pulp and paper industries. Early experiments were promising, but tall oil didn't store well, and supply was uncertain because of potential changes in the pulp and paper industry. In partnership with ink manufacturers, then, the committee looked at other alternatives, mainly vegetable oils such as linseed, canola, cottonseed, and soy. Initial performances were roughly comparable and somewhat lacking in qualities such as ruboff and print run per volume of ink. For instance, linseed oil, used in ink ever since Ben Franklin ran his presses, took around four hours to dry, an unacceptable delay in today's high-speed economy.

Hladky explained why soy ink won out:

At one of the meetings, they mentioned soy ink and my antennae went up, since we grow so many soybeans in Iowa. I remember when we first brought soy samples into the pressroom, the pressmen said, 'Do you know that we used vegetable-based oil back in World War II days?' We [the Cedar Rapids Gazette*] started running it, and although there were some bugs to get out, we noticed the colors had a lot more zip; they were brighter than traditional colors. We were getting better runnability—about 10 to 12* *percent more copies for the same amount of ink. And we used less paper in start-up every day—typically, we ran three hundred papers that had to be thrown away, but with the soy inks, the presses were ready to print sooner than that.*

We decided to pay the slightly higher cost for the ink, because we were committed to giving it a real shot. Since we were located in an agricultural state, it seemed to make sense for us to do it. When we started experimenting with soy ink, it sent the right signal to our readers and readers of another paper we publish called Iowa Farmer Today. *More than just writing to them, we were writing on their product.*[8]

Soon after the paper began using soy ink, Kodak sponsored a contest for excellence of color quality. "The minute we ran the soy ink everyone knew we had a winner," Hladky said. "The colors were brighter and more in focus." If there were any remaining doubts about soy ink, they were erased when the *Gazette* won that contest along with another. Ink chemists told Hladky that the difference in color had to do with the molecular structure of soy oil. Carbon chains in petroleum-based ink are different sizes, up to forty carbons long, but in soy oil they tend to be the same length, sixteen to eighteen carbons long. Soy ink had other advantages. The pressmen could actually smell the difference between petroleum ink with its volatile ingredients and the nature-based soy ink. And because soy in nontoxic, moreover, the paper didn't have to pay a premium to haul hazardous-waste ink.

The next step for the *Gazette* is to recycle the ink. Soy ink is not yet 100 percent soy oil. It still contains resins and pigments with petroleum and metal in them. However, the U.S. Department of Agriculture is at work on an ink that is completely soy, and the *Gazette* is anxious to give it a try.

The adoption of soy ink throughout the newspaper industry illustrates several points about deep design. One is that cost is not always the deciding factor. Publishers still pay a slight premium for soy inks because of the variables that make it preferable: lower emissions, better color, dependable supply, and the positive public relations of using a quintessentially American product. Another point is that soy ink has diverse champions: farmers, publishers, pressroom foremen, environmentalists, and an energetic consortium including the Newspaper Association of America, the Soybean Association, the *Cedar Rapids Gazette*, and the National Association of Printing Ink Manufacturers.

Soybean ink would never have emerged as the winner had soybeans not already been an integral part of the American economy. Their adoption as a design species has its own story. In the post–World War II period, various socioeconomic factors converged to make them a viable crop. Demand for meat products increased, creating a sudden demand for high-quality livestock feed. Tractors continued to replace horses, and synthetic fibers began to replace cotton, driving down the price of both oats and cotton; as a result, acreage was available for the high-protein soybean. Another factor was government support for improved soybean strains as well as improved processing technologies. Since 1941, the crop has been covered by the commodity price–support program, ensuring continued production, supply, and research.

A Better Pathway to a Nylon Comb

If a manufactured chemical is a misfit in our world, it is because it has not been properly designed. Like a house in a poorly designed community, misfit chemicals are not in synch with their surroundings.

According to EPA scientist Joe Breen, "The moment a chemist puts pencil to paper to design a chemical substance, he/she is also determining whether or not that process will use or generate hazardous substances that need to be treated, recycled, transported, or disposed of. The traditional approach to chemical design has been to search for synthetic pathways or reaction steps that produce the greatest yield at the least cost. The new approach is to use total-cost analysis to cost-justify more precise, environmentally sound methods of chemical synthesis."

A few innovative chemists are beginning to strive for cleaner molecular genealogies. To arrive at the same end products and services, they are following alternative synthetic pathways that consume less energy per unit of product yet deliver more product (yield) per unit of material. Using natural forces such as light, naturally occurring molecules and microbial catalysts, researchers are subtracting negative side effects from chemical-making processes. One such researcher is Dr. John Frost of Michigan State University, who has experimented with cornstarch as a starting point in the production of nylon.

Before seeing what he's been up to, we should look at the benefits and disadvantages of various methods of nylon production. Nylon is extremely useful. It can be formed in sheets, rods, fibers, bristles, tubes, coatings, and powder because of its diverse physical and chemical characteristics, including tensile strength, flexibility, elasticity, solvent resistance, durability, impact resistance, low gas permeability, stability, molecular symmetry, and the hydrogen bonding strength necessary for polymerization. If you look at a microscopic photograph of nylon fabric, you'll see one reason why it's so durable—the strands are interwoven like an oriental hammock. Research chemists and engineers like nylon for the many things that can be done with it. For example, nylon 66 can be molded into diverse objects such as gears, bearings, pipe fittings, and combs.

However, the conventional pathway to such products is littered with adverse effects. When Du Pont chemists Carothers and Hill first synthesized a nylonlike compound in 1932, they were not expected to think about environmental matters—it may not even have occurred to them. They were more concerned about smoothing out wrinkles such as the relatively low melting point of their prototype, a poor characteristic for fabrics that would be ironed. They could not have guessed that by 1993 over 4 billion pounds of nylon would be produced from petroleum feedstock. Nor did these chemists have any idea that the intermediate chemical benzene would ultimately be classified as a carcinogen and hazardous substance under the Safe Drinking Water Act, the Clean Air Act, and the Toxic Release Inventory, ranking in the top hundred chemicals on the Superfund list of most significant hazardous substances, or that it could cause leukemia, tumors, anemia, and dermatitis. Benzene is known to degrade the blood-forming organs and cause chromosomal damage, and it can be fatal at high doses. The effects of short-term exposure include dizziness, lightheadedness, headaches, vomiting, and eye, nose, and throat irritation.[9]

Benzene's impacts are by no means limited to human health. Contaminated waterways and land can affect flora and fauna. Benzene pollution has been implicated in decreased and contaminated crop and fishing yields. Among the most severe impacts are pollutants released in benzene's manufacture, one being nitrogen dioxide, an ozone depleter.[10] Nitrous-oxide emissions are already limited under the Clean Air Act, and major producers are developing the technology to reduce their emissions. But the process is difficult and expensive to implement. The benzene pathway results in numerous other environmentally hazardous substances, among them acids produced from cyclohexane conversion. In addition to all this, the benzene pathway depletes a nonrenewable resource, petroleum, which is used as both a feedstock and an energy source.

Still, benzene is spewing into our world. Of the top fifty chemicals in U.S. production, benzene ranked seventeenth in 1992, exceeding 12 billion pounds. Nylon would be considered a useful material if we didn't have to take the benzene highway to get to it.

Fortunately, there's another pathway. If it proves cost effective and ecologically benign, it could help move the field of chemistry in a revolutionary new direction toward nature-compatible synthesis of products. This is the area Dr. Frost of Michigan State University is exploring. He calls it the sweeter route to nylon. Genetically engineered *E. coli* bacteria convert glucose from cornstarch into such compounds as adipic acid, catechol, and gallic acid. The alternative pathway to adipic acid could have enormous environmental benefits because it eliminates the need for benzene feedstock. Frost elaborates: "If biocatalysis is to be a truly low-impact alternative, we have to use fewer agricultural chemicals to grow the corn. Ultimately, if we're really looking at making chemicals from plants, the day will come when you don't use corn but grasses or regenerative trees such as certain poplars that can give you multiple harvests per year, and that are perennials rather than annuals. With this kind of crop, you don't fertilize, spray pesticides, or cultivate."[11] The end product, such as the comb, will have a far cleaner life cycle. Biosynthesis involves no extreme conditions or toxic reactants. As long as we have sun, soil, and water, the molecules will keep coming.

Frost is very pragmatic when it comes to the marketing of end products. He wants to demonstrate that his alternative pathway is cost effective. "The market price is estimated at twice the manufacturing cost, so to be competitive with current prices a given process should have manufacturing costs no more than half the current market value. We've documented that we are right in the ballpark."

We're not all that distant in time from Isaac Newton's chemical tasting. But we've come far enough now to be practicing a more

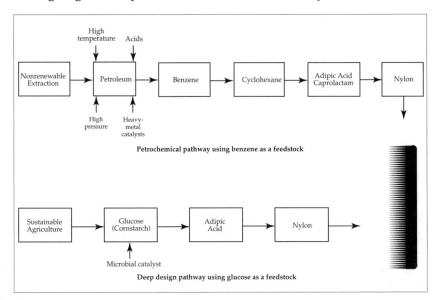

Figure 6
Alternative pathways to a nylon comb.

sophisticated kind of alchemy, turning corn into nylon instead of trying to turn base metals into gold. The pathways being discovered by biochemists such as Frost may ultimately reduce the occurrence of life-threatening diseases like cancer as well as the need for excessive government regulation.

"Designing" Healthy Air at the San Francisco Library

If we had natural microscopic vision, we'd be more than a little concerned about spending 90 percent of our time inside. We'd see dust-mite corpses, bits of plastic, and traces of pesticide disappearing into the nostrils of family members and coworkers. No doubt we would listen a little more carefully to scientists who tell us that indoor air is worse than outdoor air, even in a city like Los Angeles. The EPA estimates that the total bill for indoor pollution in the United States is up to $60 billion annually because of illness, lost productivity, legal fees, and other expenses—an economic tapeworm. The small but apparently growing sector of the population that has acquired multiple chemical sensitivity (MCS), a syndrome in which the body becomes allergic to everyday materials such as chemically treated rugs, should act as a warning. One woman described MCS as being allergic to the twentieth century. MCS is now acknowledged by agencies like the Social Security Administration and Housing and Urban Development as a legally defensible disability.

Since there are not yet set standards for using building and design products that are chemically benign, sometimes finding the safest products is a matter of trial and error. "I had a friend whose son was allergic to just about everything," explains interior designer Jennifer Haley. "They were building a new home and trying to get the contractor to use materials that would minimize his allergies. The parents would bring home small pieces of carpet and finished wood and let Max play with them and see what happened. They wanted to use wool carpet, but couldn't find a product that didn't have mothproofing applied to it. They wanted to encapsulate the studded frame of the house in foil to seal out pollution from outside sources, but the builder refused to do it, since the house was in a hot real estate location and the builder could sell the house without taking the extra trouble. So they ended up making compromises: before they moved in, they made double payments for a month so they could stay in their old house while the new house off-gassed pollutants."[12] Only deep design can provide solutions to the problem of indoor air pollution, which requires sophisticated understanding of system dynamics and the life cycle of pollutants. In this case, design is concerned with the interaction of people, materials, technology, and nature—what indoor air expert Hal Levin calls building ecology.

The dynamics of indoor pollution are complex, involving the physics of airflow, humidity, vapor pressure, boiling point, ambient temperature, molecular activity at surface and cross-sectional levels, and many other variables. To cite just one example, benzene from cigarette smoke absorbed by "sinks" such as carpeting in a room, can be reemitted when the temperature goes up or the molecular concentration in the air goes down.

In effect, buildings are extensions of our lungs. The design pathway that protects indoor air quality and lungs begins in the product manufacturing plant and continues through the building stage. A Phase I method is to increase the amount of ventilation that flows through a building, flushing harmful chemicals to the outdoors. A Phase II approach is to understand the origins, dynamics, and health effects of chemicals found in buildings and to manufacture and specify products that don't contain them.

A good example is how indoor air quality has been programmed into the design of the San Francisco Library, slated for completion in late 1995. Anthony Bernheim, an architect with Simon Martin-Vegue Winkelstein Morris, headed the team of architects, engineers, consultants, and contractors who handled this aspect of the building's design. At first, the Library Commission and the city architect were unwilling to incorporate indoor air quality into the design budget, but after Bernheim gave the library staff a presentation on indoor air quality, they changed their minds. For security reasons, the new library would not have windows that opened, and the library staff was not confident that mechanical ventilation would remove pollutants such as volatile chemicals emitted by the carpeting. They went to the city with a local official who was defending the rights of chemically sensitive people to have access to the library. The city began to listen, eventually challenging Bernheim to get the best air quality possible without putting a huge dent in the project's budget.

Bernheim rose to the challenge with an approach that gave preference to preventing pollution over trying to control it with ventilation. Because scientific data on indoor air quality are still sketchy, Bernheim made decisions based on viability and deals he was able to negotiate with suppliers of building material. First, he analyzed the total area taken up by each material. How many square feet of carpet? How much wallboard, ceiling tile, and furniture? Of the materials to be used most, which presented the greatest opportunity to prevent air pollution? Bernheim called this phase of quantity-based calculation prudent avoidance. Even without rigorous data, some pretty good guestimates could be made that would ultimately translate into better-quality air.

Formaldehyde was public enemy number one. Bernheim's team, after seeing emissions data that correlated particleboard with high levels of formaldehyde, decided to prohibit the use of this material. In fact, the team broke new ground by requiring suppliers to submit test data at their own expense on emissions from their products. Because so many product ingredients were proprietary, Bernheim examined not what was going into products, but what was *not* coming out, such as VOCs.

Other decisions the team made included specifications for

carpeting, paints, and furniture. Stone floors (granite and limestone) were specified for the entry-level floors so that particulate matter would not be deposited on the carpet, which began 100 feet into the building. The architects worked with a mill to develop carpeting that would not emit detectable levels of the toxic compound 4-PC and that would require less adhesive backing. The contractor, moreover, would be required to air out the carpets for forty-eight hours prior to installation. Another innovative specification addressed maintenance of the carpets, which were to be cleaned regularly with high-efficiency particulate-arrestor vacuums. As for paint, only solvent-free products were specified for the project; this excluded paints with high VOC emissions, preservatives, and antifreeze. Furniture suppliers were instructed to use low-VOC adhesives, to stay away from particleboard, and to apply a solvent-free agent to clean office components before occupancy. At first the team wanted hardwood-veneer furniture, but they came across an alternative material, Medite II. This medium-density fiberboard (MDF) is made out of tiny bits of sawdust bound with an inert, nontoxic glue. Woodworkers and cabinetmakers like it because it's easy to saw, doesn't produce chips, brittle edges, knots, or grains, making it easy to create shapes and relief designs.[13] Museums including the Smithsonian have used it because it doesn't contain formaldehyde, which can hurt their exhibits by degrading paper, woven fabric, and metal. Medite II brought other advantages besides versatility and the fact that it contained no formaldehyde. Bernheim estimated that when all the costs were tallied, it would be $25,000 cheaper than hardwood veneer. He and his crew were sold on the product. Still, they required the company to perform emissions testing before specifying it.

There were several last-minute challenges that came up as library construction proceeded. For acoustic reasons, fiberglass tiles had been specified for the ceiling, but they were found to emit formaldehyde, and because of their porous surface they served as a sink for toxins. Bernheim's team came up with a low-cost, high-return solution: encapsulate the fiberglass tiles in a mylar coating. The mylar, very thin, still allowed good sound absorption, and its smooth surface was much easier to clean, discouraged bacterial growth, and reflected more light.

Another challenge involved floor materials. The architectural team had decided to install a natural material, linoleum, under the auditorium seats, but when the linoleum arrived, it was offgassing volatile compounds. The team decided not to use it, opting instead for a cement product, Dex-a-tex, that dried quickly and was durable as well as stain-resistant.

Such mid-course corrections at the San Francisco Library demonstrate that choosing materials is not a black-and-white issue. Ideally, we want to put our science in the right place—the design rather than the environmental cleanup phase. But with scientific data still scarce and the economic status quo powerful, this is not always possible. Several years ago, the Formaldehyde Institute asserted that up to 8 percent of the U.S. economy was linked to products containing formaldehyde. Deciding to avoid this chemical entails both detective work and negotiations, as Bernheim found out. It will be interesting to see, when the library is complete, whether visitors will subliminally sense the salutary effects of Bernheim's efforts.

Chapter 4

In Search of the Soft Path

Efficiency and Renewable Energy

Recently, I felt the same sense of awe standing under the huge whirling blades of an Altamont Pass, California, wind generator that I once did as a boy standing under the massive skeleton of a *Tyrannosaurus rex*. I craned my neck to look above the Eiffel Tower–shaped base at three 50-foot-long, 2-ton blades wheeling in a steady breeze at about one revolution per second. The sound the machine made was much closer to a delivery truck's than a helicopter's. Across rolling hills of pasture, there were hundreds of other turbines, a whole Jurassic Park full of them. Cattle on the wind farm, unimpressed, grazed lazily among the generators.

Critics have called wind farms a visual blight, but to me the 7,500 turbines at Altamont, the largest such collection in the world, are aesthetically pleasing, a marriage of form and function. The single turbine that towered above me was more than a novelty; it was cranking out eighty houses' worth of clean electricity. At any rate, I'd rather see the steady signature of wind through turbines than the scrawled signature of fossil-fuel power: strip-mined pits, smog-choked skies, forests damaged by acid rain, and disposal sites filled with fly ash. The fact is, each of the thousands of turbines at Altamont provides a small yet significant piece of Pacific Gas and Electric's pie chart, helping shrink the fossil-fuel signature. The wind farm, located thirty miles east of San Francisco, cranks out enough electricity to power more than a third of that city's homes. On a recent day, its cumulative output was measured at 8 percent of PG&E's load. On average, 1 to 2 percent of California's total energy needs are now met with wind power.

Altamont is the effective proving ground for twenty different turbine designs from all over the world, generating one billion kwh of electricity each year, roughly equivalent to 5 million barrels of oil. By avoiding the combustion of fossil fuels, the Altamont turbines offset the emission of more than 2.5 billion pounds of carbon dioxide and 15 million pounds of sulfur dioxide and nitrous oxide annually, according to Randall Swisher of the American Wind Energy Association. He estimates that from 90 to 120 million acres of forest would be needed to provide the same air quality benefits as this wind plant.[1]

I was curious why whole hillsides of machines sat idle while others pinwheeled productively. My guide, an expert from Kenetech Windpower (formerly U.S. Windpower), explained that different machines have different cut-in speeds. Some begin generating in 14 mile-per-hour winds, while others are designed to wait for higher wind speeds.

The wind machines at Altamont are oriented toward the southwest, where 70 percent of the wind comes from. In daytime the foothills heat up faster than the land along the coast. When the hot air rises, cooler air rushes in from the ocean to fill the void, creating a natural, reliable wind pattern. The turbines are an example of human design adapted to natural design.

Scattered among Altamont's high-tech turbines are a few antique windmills that produce not electricity but mechanical power to pump water for livestock. One of the best of these old-time machines was manufactured by Aermotor Windmill Company in San Angelo, Texas. Founded in 1888, Aermotor claims its machines will run for eighty years with routine maintenance. Company president Frank McQuerry recalls a recent phone call from an appreciative rancher who bought a machine in 1902. "His machine had just set out there and pumped its heart out for ninety years," McQuerry commented.[2] The new breed of wind machine has a much higher IQ than the old windmills, incorporating electronic features, custom-designed airfoils in the blades, and many other refinements. It's reasonable to expect these machines will still be making electricity twenty to thirty years from now, each revolving something like 100 million times during its life cycle.

They are the most highly developed of a design species that has been evolving for at least a few thousand years. As early as 200 B.C., vertical-axis windmills were used to grind grain in Persia and the Middle East. Introduced in Europe in the eleventh century by soldiers returning from the Crusades, windmills were improved in Holland and England. In the eighteenth century, there were more than ten thousand in the Netherlands alone, to grind grain, pump water, and saw wood. As the industrial revolution gained momentum, the windmill was replaced by the more convenient and reliable steam engine. Now we're coming full circle: the same fossil fuel–based industrial revolution that wind machines helped spur has culminated in the high technology that makes Altamont-type machines possible. The computer has been a critical tool in the design of the most advanced turbine to date (Kenetech's 33M-VS model). Even more fundamental to its success is state-of-the-art electronics that enable the turbine to feed smooth, noise-free power into an electrical grid.

High-tech computer modeling and increasingly sensitive detecting devices have enabled surveyors to find exploitable new reserves of oil, coal, and gas, but that doesn't change the fact that the wind-power industry is coming of age, piercing a strategic hole in the petroleum industry's armor. After a decade of experiments in California, Denmark, Hawaii, and elsewhere, turbine clusters like Altamont's are likely to become more common. Eighteen thousand turbines worldwide are already hooked up to electrical grids, and at least three times that number will be installed in the United States, Europe, and Canada over the next decade.

A marriage of aerodynamics and electronics has enabled wind power to take a huge leap forward. From its origins in wooden gears and leather harnesses, wind technology has come steadily down the design pathway into the electronic age.

Stationary Flight:
Wind Power Enters the New Millennium

How exactly did the Altamont machines get here? What factors are coming together to make wind a viable energy source?

"Performance of the new wind turbines is up, and costs are down," summarizes Robert Thresher, director of the National Renewable Energy Laboratory's wind division. "Increased energy capture, reduced hardware costs, reduced operation and maintenance costs, and improved wind farm design/operation now make wind power the best choice for many niche applications."[3] Wind power is also benefiting from regulatory mandates, tax incentives, and even peer pressure at the international level. The Clean Air Act amendments of 1990 limit sulfur-dioxide emissions, forcing utilities to switch to cleaner fuels and technologies such as wind or else purchase emissions allowances from utilities that are cleaner than the standard requires. The value of wind-produced electricity is likely to increase with the approach of Clean Air Act compliance deadlines in the year 2000. Meanwhile, the National Energy Policy Act of 1992 provides a tax credit of 1.5 cents per kwh of electricity generated from wind, an incentive that helps the industry compete with heavily subsidized fossil fuels.

Over the past decade the reliability of wind turbines has increased by 30 percent or more as the industry learned how to manufacture and maintain them to prevent problems. Refinements in the aerodynamics of blades have significantly increased performance, as have innovations in variable-speed operation. Wind now represents an inflation-free, zero-emission source for utilities as well as a cost-effective hedge against increasingly tough environmental legislation. And the wind machine's typically short construction period minimizes startup delays and cost overruns.

In recent years, companies like Kenetech Windpower have been on a focused quest for a machine that can produce electricity for five cents per kwh, making it cost competitive with fossil fuel. But the underlying mission goes beyond conventional economics into deep design: creating a clean source of limitless power. What is emerging from wind laboratories is a technologically ingenious design packed with information, feedback, flexibility, redundancy, and precision. The design is more valuable than petroleum, coal, or uranium for one simple reason: it can provide the same end uses (such as lighting, cooling, and industrial power) without making a mess.

The story of twenty-first-century wind generators will be a David and Goliath account: rotors whirling in the wind versus massive power plants. Wind, as a deep design, must prove its economic viability in a world set up for cheap fossil fuels.

And it is doing just that. From 15 megawatts in 1981, global capacity grew to 2,652 megawatts in 1992. Though many Americans don't yet realize it, wind turbines have recently become cost competitive with newly constructed coal, oil, and nuclear plants.

There are several key indicators of success: the average annual productivity of a turbine, 36,000 kwh in 1983, had risen to 160,000 kwh in 1989; the average turbine, in operation 60 percent of the time in 1980, was operational 95 percent of the time in 1990; and the cost per kwh, 25 cents in 1981, was down to 5 cents in 1994.

The wind industry has tried harder than conventional energy suppliers, receiving just enough support from government and forward-looking utilities to persevere. For example, the alternative-energy incentives of the Carter years, combined with state incentives fostered during Jerry Brown's tenure as governor of California, were attractive enough to incubate scores of wind-power designs. Since then, all but the best designs have been weeded out. Utilities such as Niagara Mohawk, Iowa-Illinois, PG&E, and the utility-funded Electric Power Research Institute have nurtured the technology out of enlightened self-interest.

They know that more untapped energy blows across the country than lies beneath it. They know that despite California's dominant position in the industry, there are sixteen states with wind-energy potential equal to or greater than that state's. They know that wind energy designed for specific niches is here to stay.

The American Wind Energy Association has expressed lofty goals for the industry to kindle yet more interest from utilities and politicians:

- Build a $4-billion domestic-wind-industry base capable of delivering at least 3,000 megawatts per year;
- Create 70,000 long-term, skilled jobs, primarily in the wind-machine-manufacturing sector;
- Bring costs below 4 cents per kwh;
- Make wind power a major option in achieving the federal government's global climate change objectives; and
- Make the United States the world leader in wind-power technology and the lowest-cost supplier.

If the American Wind Energy Association's goals were met, wind would provide 15 percent of new U.S. energy-generating ca-

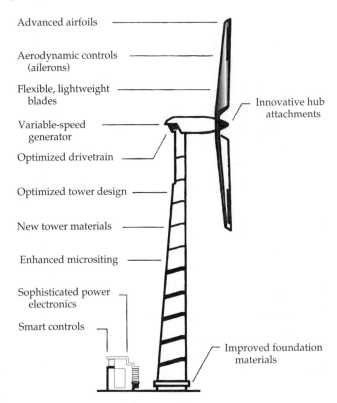

Advanced airfoils

Aerodynamic controls
(ailerons)

Flexible, lightweight
blades

Variable-speed
generator

Optimized drivetrain

Optimized tower design

New tower materials

Enhanced micrositing

Sophisticated power
electronics

Smart controls

Innovative hub
attachments

Improved foundation
materials

Figure 7
A new generation of wind turbines.

pacity between now and the year 2000, representing 1.3 percent of the nation's total capacity.

Energy experts have calculated that to provide a full 20 percent of America's electricity, a goal that is probably decades away, 18,000 square miles would have to be developed in promising locations—an area about the size of four large Montana counties. Less than 5 percent of this land, 2.5 acres per megawatt, would be occupied by wind turbines, electrical equipment, and access roads. And most of the land could still be used for farming and ranching, as it is now.

To expand further, the wind industry has to find new niches and partnerships. It also "has to capture every electron of available energy that a given breeze offers," Robert Thresher says, adding with a smile, "Fortunately, wind power is compatible with almost all human activities except for hang gliding."[4]

In many locations with the greatest wind potential, grazing, mining, forestry, and recreation would be compatible uses because generators themselves don't require much land. Wind energy could provide pollution-free energy in areas that don't meet air-quality standards. Or machines could be sited along existing power grids to add capacity quickly. In wind-wealthy Wyoming, for example, power is currently transmitted to Portland, Oregon, from Wyoming's Jim Bridger power plant. Wind plants can also reduce the risk of power outage by being redundant many times over. At Altamont, when one machine goes down, there are another 7,000-plus machines as backup.

The value of wind-generated power depends on much more than total output—it depends on where and when that output occurs. Does the wind in a given location blow when electricity is needed? The Solano wind plant in northern California generates power at the right time of day as well as the right time of year to meet peak demands. In Texas, the wind is strongest in the winter, but demand peaks in the summer because of the air-conditioning load. Wind generators there provide energy when the power plant already has a surplus. "Wind is an intermittent source: you can't count on it being there when you turn the light switch, unless you use storage or interconnect the load with the grid," Robert Thresher explains.[5] Thus wind power has to be used in conjunction with other power sources to provide reliable service. Battery storage is too expensive except in isolated areas where fuel has to be trucked in anyway. The best, cheapest option is to add wind power to a utility system already using a fair amount of hydropower and to coordinate the two sources. When there is wind, outlet valves at the hydro plant can be shut off and the reservoir's water stored for later use. It's best to have a wind resource at the time of year when the reservoir needs filling, because that increases water-storage capacity.

Another niche that wind energy can fill is distributed power, that is, energy generated with small turbines at the end of feeder lines. If the generator is located close to the load or point of use, transmission losses are minimized. As with so many deep designs, the question is one of fitting. The best wind sites need to be discovered and then fit into existing systems.

For example, North Dakota and Texas are virtual Saudi Arabias of wind energy, hypothetically capable of meeting 40 percent of current electrical needs in the United States. In those states alone, wind potential is over 2 billion barrels of oil annually. Wind prospectors use computer modeling to explore areas with the most potential: plains, tablelands, hilltops, ridgelines in mountainous terrain, and large clearings in forested areas. Factors such as remoteness of the wind source, turbulence, county zoning restrictions, and the presence of transmission lines help prospectors determine the value of a wind source. Is the area prone to snow, ice, heavy rainfall, tornadoes? Are there endangered species nearby? Houses? All these variables have to be pieced together within the larger context of both nature and culture. The wind industry needs to be clever in an area dominated by fossil fuel. Will it ultimately succeed like the computer upstarts that challenged an industry dominated by IBM? Maybe so, if wind-power strategists tap into and market the resource's inherent assets, and if the industry receives support from taxpayers.

I showed Thresher a public-service bill I had received offering customers the opportunity to support renewable energy voluntarily. "Are they kidding?" I asked. "Or are they trying to prove to us that alternative energy still can't compete?"

"No, they're completely serious," he said. "That's their 'green marketing' initiative. What they're not saying, of course, is that there are subsidies for fossil fuels built into our tax structure as well as into our utility bills. In Germany, where they're committed to making wind power an option, there is a tax subsidy for wind of about 4 cents per kilowatt-hour. If we had that, maybe wind would become 'too cheap to meter.'" Thresher was alluding, facetiously, to a slogan once used by the nuclear industry.

What are the technological features that will emerge to make wind more competitive than it is now, without having to rely on subsidies? The answer is a tool-kit of strategies, including advanced airfoil design, power electronics that enable blades to keep turning in higher winds while still delivering a steady power supply, easier maintenance to reduce downtime, and taller towers that can capture 20 percent more energy.

Thinking Like an Eagle

One of the biggest challenges facing the wind industry is birds of prey, or raptors, which fly into turbine blades and towers and die like kamikazes. In 1993, the Audubon Society, a group that was previously an ally of wind power, announced that wind-power technology should not be further implemented until the bird problem is solved.

The issue emerged after a comprehensive wildlife study, performed by the California Energy Commission, estimated that annually about four raptors were being killed at Altamont for every hundred turbines, including golden eagles, red-tailed hawks, and American kestrels. One puzzle is that although at Altamont a lot of raptors are being killed, similar installations in California don't seem to pose as severe a threat.

Will avian mortality stop the wind industry's gathering momentum? Are the adverse effects on bird populations worse than the damage from fossil-fuel plants from extraction to consumption? Kennetech bird expert Dick Curry points out, "There are always going to be birds killed, but we can surely learn to kill fewer. In the Netherlands, they did a study that showed that the number of sea birds killed was roughly equivalent to the number killed by powerlines and highways."[6] While that study didn't precisely reproduce conditions at sites like Altamont, it does raise the issue of total value. Which is worse in the long run to the birds and other animals, wind farms or the fossil-fuel superstructure?

The bird problem challenges designers to think like a raptor. Kennetech, which has already spent $2 million on research into the behavior of raptors, is confident the bird problem can be solved. At Kennetech's request, Thomas Cade, founder of the Peregrine Fund, assembled a panel of experts in avian flight, sensory perception, and population ecology to find out exactly what's happening with the birds. Why are they flying into the blades and towers? What do birds see when they look at wind towers and turbines? How can design modifications such as changes in color and pattern decrease mortality? Would better location help mitigate the threat?

According to Cade,

> It's helpful to start with what we do know about these species. We know that eagles in this area don't have predators, and therefore they don't have a sense of fear. We know that eagles and hawks are not social animals—there's no such thing as a flock of eagles. They are very solitary, and very independent. Unlike finches, for example, raptors don't seem to learn from other individuals outside the family. . . .

We know that at Altamont, eagles and hawks are in direct competition with turbines for wind: they like to hunt when it's windy because they can use updrafts to glide and soar. The Altamont area has a high population of prey species.[7]

Ground squirrels are a favorite prey of the eagle. There are lots of squirrels at Altamont, and they're highly visible because the terrain is grazed by cattle. Consequently, raptor populations are high, but sites for nests are scarce. According to Curry, fatalities seem to occur to "overflow" birds that don't have nests. Some observers have proposed that areas removed from the wind machines be baited with prey to draw raptors away, but the general inclination is not to start tampering with variables in the food chain, which might lead to other problems. The experts agree that the problem has to be looked at holistically, with raptors regarded as populations within a habitat, not just as individuals colliding with the machines. So far, research indicates no evidence of whole populations being affected, with the possible exception of eagles.

Some progress has already been made. For example, Cade's panel found a solution to the problem of fatally attractive lattice towers that birds were using as lookout perches: using tube towers, which resemble thick flagpoles, instead. More progress is expected. Thirty raptors have been radio-tagged to help scientists learn more about their behavior, and the team has mounted video cameras on site. Already, the tagging and video technology are paying off. After tracking three recent mortalities, the research team discovered that one was completely unrelated to the turbines (a female hawk killed another female), and that a second was potentially unrelated (the bird had high levels of toxins in its body).

Until recently, nobody thought much about birds when siting generators. Now a lot of attention is being given to determining location based on resident populations. At one southern California wind farm, the potential threat is to songbirds migrating to Central America. In Holland, the major threat is to waterfowl and shorebirds. Potential sites there won't be considered until regional avian experts have been consulted. Thomas Cade feels that the bird problem can be reduced simply by locating fewer turbines per square mile, resulting in fewer birds per turbine.

Cynthia Struzik, special agent for the U.S. Fish and Wildlife Service, has the difficult role of legal watchdog in the case of wind turbines versus birds. Under the Migratory Bird Treaty and Bald Eagle Protection Act, anyone who "knowingly or with wanton disregard" kills a bald or golden eagle is committing a crime. At hearings and in testimony, Struzik has been outspoken in pressing for mitigative measures. She was particularly critical of the Cade team's strategy of studying homing pigeons to learn about bird behavior. "That's like comparing apples and beefsteaks," she comments. "The only similarities between the species are they both have feathers and fly."[8] Struzik has been a strong advocate of alternative towers for the turbines, an issue closely linked to cost and aesthetics. Tube towers are slightly more expensive than lattice towers, but this may be offset by reductions in maintenance over a facility's lifetime.

Kenetech's 130-Patent Nickel Machine: Power for 5 Cents a Kilowatt Hour

For the past twenty years, Kenetech Windpower has had a mission: to produce clean wind power at costs comparable to those of conventional energy sources. In the late 1970s, the company was one among many others in the pack, but since then it has outspun the competition to become the world's leading producer of wind energy. Annual revenues for the company, now on the NASDAQ exchange, exceed $350 million dollars, and it has logged and analyzed more than 79 million hours of operating time for its turbines since 1982.

What went right? According to Robert Thresher, "From the beginning, Kenetech took the approach that they were going to design, manufacture, install, and operate the machines birth to death—cradle to grave. In other words, they decided to be involved in all steps, and this enabled them to learn from their mistakes in a whole-systems kind of way, making continuous improvements to eliminate flaws."[9] The company was started by entrepreneurs in 1974, following the first energy crisis. An engineer and a financial expert joined forces and built a garage shop operation with the goal of putting generators on barges off the Massachusetts coast. Although the company has not yet tapped into offshore opportunities, today it "flies" 3,600 of the machines at Altamont as well as operates Europe's largest wind farm, in southern Spain. Kenetech has also signed sales contracts throughout North America and Europe. For example, a joint venture with Iowa-Illinois Gas and Electric will result in the manufacture and installation of another six hundred or so machines. Other contracts have been signed with the Sacramento Municipal Utility District and with investors in Canada and the Netherlands for smaller wind plants.

One of the financial advantages of Kenetech's wind plant at Altamont is centralized maintenance. "Wind riders" or "windsmiths" go out and do yearly maintenance such as oil changes, and they are able to cover all the machines at the same time. The facility's machines can also be monitored and controlled centrally. Vital statistics about operational turbines are updated every two minutes.

Over the years, Kenetech management methodically exploited every financial and engineering opportunity, and as the company's expertise expanded, so did its pool of venture capital. Energy revenues from the first installations supplied a steady cash flow that paid investors and kept research and development going. Kenetech retrofitted turbines with innovations of its own, thus acquiring parts cheaply.[10] Above all, Kenetech gained experience in all aspects of the industry, such as wind surveying and developing wind farms. Gerald Alderson, who has been with the company more than ten years, has supplied much of the vision. His engineering team knew that reduced maintenance, increased energy output, and greater availability of machines would all lead to lower installed cost. They imagined the qualities a good machine would have and guided the company down the pathway of deep design.

What has emerged from their ten-year, $20 million research and development effort is a new species of utility-grade wind turbine that provides four times the energy at two-and-a-half times the cost of conventional turbines. From capital investment through operations and maintenance, the 33M-VS model costs about 5 cents per kwh, making it competitive with most sources of conventional energy. Designed to run for thirty years at one revolution per second, the 33M-VS is a hybrid workhorse-racehorse, producing three times the power (300 kwh) of earlier models with its longer, lighter, more aerodynamic blades and its variable-speed drive. The turbine's range spans from 8 to 65 mph, while earlier machines produce power from 12 to 45 mph. Almost all other generator models must operate at a constant rpm to produce utility-grade power, which means that above a certain speed a lot of potential energy, roughly 15 percent, is wasted. The 33M-VS captures that wasted energy. An advanced-power electronic converter allows the rotor and generator to accelerate with higher winds while maintaining a constant frequency output. Operation and maintenance costs could eventually prove cheaper, too. The drivetrain has lighter, more predictable loads, which means the support structure can be less weighty and costly to manufacture.[11] According to 33M-VS technical literature, the turbine uses stronger materials that relieve stress by flexing. Rather than just standing there and taking wind gusts "on the chin," the machines roll with the punches, converting previously damaging gusts into watts. The machine is aikido engineering at its best.

State-of-the-art wind technology like Kenetech's 33M-VS is a perfect example of deep design because it incorporates qualities such as feedback, flexibility, precision, variability, prevention, and renewability. It's a low-impact, high-return technology that supplies energy with minimal disturbance of the environment and society. A recent study by New York State's energy office found that per unit of energy, wind power creates 66 percent more jobs than natural gas and 27 percent more total jobs than advanced coal. In the fossil-fuel industry, the tasks of mining and fuel extraction are rapidly being taken over by machines. In the wind-power industry, manufacturing, installation, and maintenance jobs are still performed by people.

By meeting social and environmental needs while remaining economically viable, the wind industry is emerging as a partial but strong solution to the world's energy problems.

Harvesting Light

Light, we learn in school, is critical to the photosynthesis of plants and thus to the sustenance of life on earth. What we don't all learn is that light is also directly involved in the functioning of the human immune system, in maintaining blood levels of amino acids, in vitamin D synthesis, in carcinogenesis, and in preventing disorders such as seasonal affective disorder. Lighting expert Nancy Clanton believes that the quality of light is far more important than the quantity, and she has been actively lobbying for better lighting codes based on human need rather than on blind numbers. The amount of artificial light should depend on who needs it, and for what purpose.

"Picture a person" Clanton says, "working late in an office building. Typically, a quarter of an acre of lights are on overhead, to light an 8-by-11 inch sheet of paper. That's very imprecise." In her campaign for quality over quantity, Clanton advocates continued research on projects such as the illumination of streets at ground level. "Why should we light up the sky with streetlights when what we really want to do is light up the ground?"[12] A futurist, she predicts that light will soon be distributed in highly reflective, fiber optic–like cables that channel photons the way today's power cables channel electrons. The light source for a commercial building could then be located outside the building to reduce heating load. Diffusers at the end of the cable would make the light available to end-users in the building.

Companies such as 3M and General Electric have research teams at work on such concepts. Their technologies probably won't enter the mainstream until fiber optics itself comes of age and breakthroughs occur in reflectivity and light leakage. However, the past decade has already seen mainstream acceptance of designs that revolutionize indoor lighting: low-E glazing and superwindows.

Separating Light from Heat

Harvesting natural daylight with the superwindow is a big technological step forward. The age-old challenge of getting natural light into buildings has been a trade-off among light, heat, and appearance. The goal is transparency without glare and unwanted heat gain or loss. In houses, designers try to minimize heat loss by keeping window area small. In commercial buildings it's the opposite—architects need to minimize heat gain from occupants, machines, and lights.

Over the past fifteen years, focused efforts by industry and technology think tanks such as the Lawrence Berkeley Laboratory (LBL) have brought the highly sophisticated superwindow into the market. This window outperforms the conventional wall by regulating heat loss and gain. According to Brad Davids of E-Source, an energy-efficiency company in Boulder, Colorado, these advances are "the biggest thing in windows since the Venetians invented blinds."[13]

Glass is highly conductive. Single panes transmit heat in the form of infrared wavelengths and light in the form of ultraviolet wavelengths. The first step in the selective separation of light and heat was the double-paned window unit invented about the time of the Civil War. This innovation trapped insulating air between layers. But nothing major happened in window design until perfection of low-E, or low-emissivity, coating in the 1980s. By reflecting long-wave (infrared) radiation, low-E coatings separate light from heat. The typical low-E coating consists of a very thin layer of silver sandwiched between two layers of nonconducting material such as titanium dioxide. It has gaps that are wide enough to allow ultraviolet wavelengths through but are too narrow to let in infrared wavelengths.

LBL, under the direction of Building Technologies director Steve Selkowitz, deserves credit for developing the low-E concept. Spurred by the energy crises of the 1970s, LBL used federal funding to work shoulder-to-shoulder with private industry. Selkowitz's approach was to perceive the problem as concentric systems: the window within the context of the building, within the context of the building industry, within the context of an energy-intensive society. He knew that the opportunities were huge. In the typical commercial building, for example, 50 to 70 percent of energy goes to lighting and cooling, a situation that results in discomfort, pollution, and wasted money. America's homes presented an equally large target. As Selkowitz points out, 5 percent of the energy Americans consume annually is energy that escapes through the windows of their homes. That is the equivalent of burning 1.7 million barrels of oil every day. The challenge as Selkowitz saw it was embodying energy efficiency into the form, material, and orientation of buildings.[14]

He strove to match evolving low-E technology with the realities of the window industry. Collaborations with industry revealed that it was not equipped to perform the high-tech physics research required to develop the coating. So LBL did the initial research and then contracted manufacturing out to a small company called Suntek (later Southwall Technologies). The resulting prototype had twice the insulating capacity of a conventional window. Not satisfied with doubling the performance of the typical window, LBL set out to quadruple it. The laboratory worked with industry in the development of a double-paned, low-E-coated window that, instead of air, would seal in argon or krypton gas, which doesn't conduct heat as readily. The researchers made window casings more efficient by using less metal and more wood and vinyl, materials that are comparatively poor heat conductors. The window system that resulted from their efforts, the superwindow, outperforms a conventional wall for two reasons: it is a good insulator, and it collects solar energy, even on the shaded north side of a building. While it looks like a conventional double-paned window, the superwindow is about six times as efficient.[15]

Aware of the complexity of designing window coatings to meet specific needs, LBL's next move was to develop a software package that helps architects and engineers find the right window for the job. The window of the future will have what Selkowitz calls adaptive intelligence. That is, it will respond to different forms of feedback, including temperature, light, and power consumption. The "photochromic" window, for example, will automatically become darker (like changeable-lens eyeglasses) when light and heat reach certain levels. Ultimately, the superwindow system will bring the best of outdoors inside—ultraviolet light, plants, an expansive feeling—while excluding such undesirables as extreme temperature and glare.

The Way Station: A Building That Heals with Light

Tena O'Rourke is director of the Way Station in Frederick, Maryland, a facility that treats emotionally and mentally impaired patients. When the Way Station was preparing to expand in 1990, she solicited bids from architects. The proposals were disappointing. "We needed a very special kind of building," she points out, "one that would help us accomplish our mission of healing. The kind of plans we received at first were just conventional, dark buildings with long hallways that would have confused and isolated our members."[16] One of the Way Station staff happened to read an article on designer-engineer Amory Lovins in the *Washington Post*. She brought the article to work, and Tena promptly got on the phone to Lovins, who happened to be scheduled for a talk in the area a few weeks from then. Lovins met with the Way Station's management and explained the advantages of buildings that were full of light and fresh air yet still energy efficient. He recommended a top-quality architect, Greg Franta, for the job. The Way Station's management liked Franta's proposal, which called for sunny spaces, lush jungles, round walls for a softer feeling, and wood beams and stair rails to give occupants a feeling of security. They hired him.

Franta and his architectural team developed a strategy that provided even, natural lighting to reproduce conditions outside. Translucent banners hung from the ceiling to soften glare. Franta calls them "clouds" because they diffuse direct sunlight in the building's "sky."

Way Station activities are organized around the "light court," a green space with running water, a place for staff and members to mingle, and a pedestrian circulation system. Whenever people leave a room, they're in the light court where they can see every other part of the building.

Franta and his colleagues used "light shelves," flat, white-painted surfaces perpendicular to windows, to bounce light into the building and onto the light-colored ceiling. They also designed long window slits called clerestories that allow soft light in at the top of the high walls. The building requires virtually no electric lighting in the daytime, except, occasionally, in nooks such as closets. High-efficiency lights are designed to complement natural daylight. As natural light gets brighter in the morning, the electric lights automatically dim, and as natural light wanes in the late afternoon, they gradually intensify. This and other design features have reduced energy consumption to about one-third of what it would be in a structure built to Maryland's energy standards.[17] Because energy savings translate to overall cost savings, the operation of the 30,000-square-foot facility is economically attractive.

The most gratifying proof of Way Station's success is not energy savings or award-winning aesthetics but the way patients feel. The building has become an organic part of their lives. "I change from one seat to another during the day," explained one Way Station member, "so I can follow the sunlight as it moves through the building." Another member said that the building made him feel secure, and gave him hope.

The famous designer Le Corbusier referred to well-designed buildings as "a magnificent interplay of light and mass." Certainly the Way Station qualifies as that.

Chapter 5

Re-envisioning Agriculture
Pathways to Regenerative Systems

Homo sapiens is not the only species that relies on agricultural skills to survive. Consider the leafcutter ant. It farms by composting leaf fragments and planting fungus spores. Other ant species "milk" aphid livestock. By all appearances these systems work, for ants have been farming for millions of years. Not humans. Our agriculture is a relatively new development, and it doesn't match the ants' for life-cycle efficiency. Yes, we've made some progress. Ten thousand years ago a family required 2,500 acres of hunting range to meet its nutritional needs. A thousand years ago, a peasant family could eke out a living on one-and-a-half acres. Twentieth-century Japanese rice growers can provide a family's staple diet with a quarter of an acre or less, growing not only rice but fish, ducks, and vegetables. But Japan's intentionally diverse system is far from typical. Today, most agricultural systems cannot be considered deep design. They aren't permanently in balance: inputs exceed outputs, when accounted for thermodynamically, and inputs such as pesticides, fertilizers, and antibiotics are often inappropriate. On average, crops use only 50 to 70 percent of applied fertilizer; the rest is lost in erosion or runoff that contributes to environmental degradation. Conventional agriculture maximizes a single variable, crop yield, at the expense of other critical variables such as soil vitality, nutritional value, and social integrity.

By focusing on how much rather than how well, agribusiness compromises the health of the soil, the health of surrounding ecosystems, the health of farm workers and consumers, and the health of communities. It doesn't ask critical questions such as, Where does a healthy agricultural system begin and end? Where do the inputs originate and how effective are they? What are the benefits and costs of outputs? In a healthy culture, quality has intrinsic value. In a healthy culture, farmers enjoy providing the best possible food with the best possible farming techniques, as long as they can make a decent living. The problem with agribusiness is that its bottom line is profit, not product.

High Tech and Horse Sense

What do we want agriculture to be? Half-nature, half-culture, integrating the fundamental needs of each? The agricultural system we've created in the United States is based on acquisition and consumption of resources, which serves neither nature nor culture in the long run. In agriculture, as in all other sectors, deep design begins with an evaluation of the existing system followed by a process of re-envisioning. At the most fundamental level, we know we want our farms to be less like battlefields and more like gardens. In a sense, we want to let gardens "escape" into our fields by using techniques familiar to millions of backyard growers: crop rotation, composting, companion planting, raised beds, biological and mechanical control of pests, planting seed and stock varieties with superior traits, and so on. Gardeners are intimately familiar with their plants, and their informed care is exactly what's missing in agribusiness. Rather than providing produce high in nutrition and rich in taste, agribusiness aims for high production and profit, never mind the rest.

Cheap food is not really inexpensive when total costs are accounted for. Cheap food must be paid for many times: at the market, and in taxes, insurance premiums, and doctor bills. Factory farming is encouraged with tax-based subsidies and price supports as well as by the transportation infrastructure. Along with cheap food, factory farming depletes soil and water supplies. American society spends more than $4 billion for pesticides annually, but that figure doesn't include indirect costs such as human poisoning,

Table 1

**Annual Hidden Costs of Pesticides in the
United States (millions of dollars)**

Public health impacts	$ 787
Domestic-animal deaths and contamination	30
Loss of natural enemies	520
Pesticide resistance	1,400
Honeybee and pollination losses	320
Crop losses	942
Fishery losses	24
Bird losses	2,100
Groundwater contamination	1,800
Government regulations to prevent damage	200
Total	**$8,123**

Source: David Pimentel, Cornell University, 1992.

reduction of fish and wildlife populations, livestock losses, and destruction of susceptible crops and natural vegetation.

Leafcutter ants, in culturing pure strains of their fungus crop, practice an agriculture based on the meticulous maintenance of and interactions between living systems. In contrast, much human agriculture compromises the life in soil, in water habitat, and in crops. We let living things die, cutting against the grain of evolution. With acidic fertilizer, toxic pesticide, and monoculture (single crops), we kill the soil microbes that have evolved over the course of 2 billion years to deliver just the right nutrients to plant roots. And when microbes die, the agricultural system begins to unravel.

Agricultural deep design is focused whole-systems thinking. Its goals are multiple and balanced: continuous regeneration of the farming system, a decent profit for good work, healthful food, and human connection with the Earth. It aims to take fuller advantage of biological assets such as solar energy, natural nutrients, and natural pest control. It strives for a more mature understanding of complex meteorologic, hydrologic, and other systems. It is not a regressive agriculture that goes back to the old ways, but a progressive agriculture that moves forward to a closer alignment with natural patterns. Until now, we haven't been smart or well equipped enough to farm with this degree of sophistication.

The Twentieth-Century Shallowing of Agriculture

According to John Perkins and Nordica Holochuck, the "shallowing" of agriculture hit its stride in medieval Europe when subsistence agriculture made the transition into commercial agriculture: "Landowners saw possibilities to use their lands to produce goods for trade, often in far-distant markets, rather than merely for food and fiber for local consumption." This transition was "deeply dependent on the accompanying expansion of trade, the rise of mechanical philosophy and science, and the replacement of feudalism with liberal capitalism."[1]

The introduction of synthetic fertilizer in the nineteenth century accelerated the speed of this transition. German chemist Justis von Liebig analyzed the ash residue of burned plants and discovered their primary components to be nitrogen, phosphorus, and potassium. Thus was the fertilizer industry born. Farmers began adding these three elements to their soil and getting dramatic increases in yield. But Liebig's cursory approach did not consider the many other essential elements in soil. For optimum growth, plants typically require seventeen or more essential elements. The interrelationship between chemistry and biology is extremely intricate, as Liebig himself began to realize toward the end of his life, when he wrote that he had "sinned against the wisdom of the Creator." Nor did his research consider the fact that farmers were depleting natural storehouses of these elements, leaving the soil bankrupt. Liebig's discovery led to a "just add water" mentality, in which farming was practiced in the manner of someone baking a cake from a box.

Over the year, fertilizer, irrigation, and pesticide became a matching set of technologies with a single goal: to increase production and therefore profit. As tractors got bigger and more efficient, more and more acreage was farmed to pay for them. As acreage increased, more money was tied up in investments such as fertilizer and pesticide, and the farmer grew more dependent on the profit from increased production to service his debt.[2] Agricultural productivity in the century following Liebig's discovery has been awesome, encouraging human population to expand exponentially. Yet many soil scientists and ecologists warn that modern agriculture has been writing checks that the environment can't cash. A lot of our topsoil is depleted of minerals and organic content and virtually devoid of the myriad life forms that exist in healthy soil. (A single gram of good soil can contain as many organisms as there are humans in China.) According to the Nebraska Sustainable Agriculture Society, "In 1950 the world produced 624 million metric tons of grain with 14 million tons of fertilizer—a response ratio of 46. In other words, every ton of fertilizer produced 46 tons of food. By 1985, the response ratio had dropped to 13—a ton of fertilizer produced only 13 tons of food."[3]

The new "industrial agriculture," or agribusiness, came to be dominated by large outside interests, among them petrochemical companies, equipment manufacturers, the grain industry, pharmaceutical giants, and wholesale-food concerns. Today, while a large percentage of the U.S. economy is involved in some fashion in the business of food and fiber, the vast majority of it is now off the farm. Agriculture, moreover, influences or is influenced by the medical industry, transportation systems, energy and water supplies, and the manufacturing sector.

Inputs and Outputs: Toward a Cycle of Quality

There's no question that corporations are in control of American agriculture. The large family farm, 500 acres or so, is still the mainstream operation, but that typical farm's inputs come from the giants. Fifteen companies account for 60 percent of all inputs to farm production, including seed stock, fertilizer, pesticide, animal feed, veterinary drugs and vaccines, genetic breeding stock and hybrids, and building materials and equipment. Agriculture has become more like a factory than a living system of production. With chemicals, mechanical equipment, computers, hybrid seeds, and biotechnology, we can make nature do as we say. Or can we? Alternative farmers question this "technologic," putting their faith in concepts such as intentional diversity, natural fertility and pest control, and multidimensional management. Many of their inputs are local, already a part of the system. As Iowa farmer Ron Rosmann says, "It seems backwards to continually look off the farm for solutions to problems that occur on the farm."

Let's assume we want agriculture to provide us with the following:

Human health
Environmental health

Stability
Resilience
Continuity
Energy savings
Economic viability
Genetic diversity

What inputs will produce these? Biological assets such as:

On-farm energy (human, solar)
Nitrogen from the air
Minerals released from the soil
Manure, cover crops
Crop rotation and diversity
Biological and mechanical pest control
Seed produced on the farm when possible
Seeds developed for specific traits
Timing, precision, vigilance

Many of America's best farmers are learning to add value to their product locally. They use on-farm resources in all senses of the word—by making fruit into jelly or grain into bread, for example, or custom-making farm equipment in their own welding shops. Some farmers supplement their income by planting crops such as amaranth with emerging markets, marketing organic produce, setting up pick and pay operations, and so on. Paul Buxman is a landscape painter, and when his farm's produce is not quite paying the bills, he paints the farm. East Coast grower Ward Sinclair, a retired writer for *The Washington Post*, takes out "subscriptions" for his fruits and vegetables, which he personally delivers. Thus he knows how much to plant and reduces some of his economic risk.

The point is, many farmers are breaking the cycle of dependence on outside sources by discovering one of the most critical inputs of all, resourcefulness. I asked Colorado farmer Jim Anderson, "What's the most efficient, resource-conserving way to grow corn?" "It depends," he said. He would farm differently in a wet spring than in a dry one. Pest populations were unpredictable and influenced his farming techniques, as did residual nutrients in the soil, its organic content, seed variety, price per bushel of crop, projected use of a field in the following year, and many other changing variables. His explanation made me realize more clearly that what comes out depends on what goes in. Good farming requires creativity and flexibility. Farmers who follow conventional prescription methods are trying to reduce uncertainty and simplify complex work. This inclination, while understandable, is simplistic. Alternative agriculture, which uses less chemistry and more biology, requires the farmer to understand, anticipate, and prepare for system disruptions. Colorado vegetable grower Bob Sakata, who farms right in the middle of a hail belt, reduces his risk by farming fields that are strategically scattered up and down Interstate 25. If a few of his fields get hit, others will survive.

Alternative farmers look beyond the obvious to calculate total value, using concepts such as life cycle analysis and total energy use. Richard Cutler, a student at Colorado University, has done follow-up research on embodied energy in agriculture, comparing conventional and alternative energy inputs for machinery manufacture, irrigation, drying harvested corn, fuel, pesticide, and fertilizer. He concluded that on a particular Colorado farm that had made the transition to alternative practices, 21 percent less total energy was used, the equivalent of 53 gallons of crude oil per acre. Alternative farming, valuable for society as a whole, also profits the farmer. Much of the energy consumed in conventional farming takes the form of expensive fertilizer, which isn't needed in alternative farming. Among its many other benefits is less water consumption. Cutler discovered that only a third as much irrigation water was required by alternative methods, because they promote water retention in soil.

What type of farming represents the largest embodied-energy costs? Without a doubt, the meat industry. Many ecologists point to cattle, pig, goat, and sheep farming as history's most environmentally damaging human activity, one that has destroyed whole bioregions. There are many embodied costs, aside from serious damage to soil and native flora. Worldwatch Institute researcher Alan Durning estimates that the average 1-pound feedlot steak costs 5 pounds of grain, 2,500 gallons of water, 1 gallon of gasoline, and about 35 pounds of eroded topsoil. Michael W. Fox and Nancy E. Wiswall figure that the annual cost of the U.S. beef industry approaches $100 billion when all hidden factors are considered.[4]

Ultimately, the price of meat and other food will have to reflect total costs to society. Today, we value natural resources for what they produce, not for what they sustain and support. "The farmer

Table 2

**Annual Hidden Costs of Beef
Consumption in the United States
(millions of dollars)**

Atherosclerosis	$37,000
Colon, breast, and	
prostate cancer	28,000
Osteoporosis	1,000
Salmonella	8
Brucellosis	64
Tuberculosis	4
Federal meat inspection	
program (FSIS, USDA)	392
Soil erosion	6,000
Western grazing lands	
(direct and indirect cost)	480
Water pollution	20,000
Pesticide pollution	839
Transportation injuries	22
Federal beef research funding	
through ARS and CSRS, USDA	50.5
Total	**$94,000**

Source: Michael W. Fox and Nancy E. Wiswall, *The Hidden Costs of Beef* (Washington, D.C., 1989). Humane Society of the United States.

can depreciate equipment and buildings, but nowhere on the standard tax form does it ask for quantification of soil losses," comments Paul Faeth of the World Resources Institute.[5] We won't practice sensible agriculture until tax structures, prices, incentives, and consumer expectation reward it.

Phase I: Efficient, Low-Input Techniques

There's a clearly identifiable pathway that leads from shallow, distracted, brute-force agriculture to intrinsically superior farming. It begins with greater efficiency and precision—getting more service per unit of resource, whether land, water, or nutrient. As with hazardous-waste minimization and energy conservation, the first step is to tune up current practices in order to lessen adverse effects on the environment and society.

How, for example, can we provide soil with just the right amount of nitrogen? If we add more than is needed, it will cause groundwater contamination, acid rain, ozone depletion, urban smog, global warming, and eutrophication of lakes (algal blooms that choke off oxygen supplies). Obviously, it is best to supply nitrogen by efficiently using what is already in manure, sludge, processing waste, and compost. And because the air we breathe is 79 percent nitrogen, we want to tap into that supply.

Until fifty years ago, most of the nitrogen required by the world's biomass, or living matter, came from precipitation and from legumes, whose root-dwelling bacterial colonies pull it out of the air. Now as much nitrogen is coming from fossil fuel–derived fertilizer as from nature. In other words, more of the element is being dumped into the environment than it's used to, exacerbating problems such as acid rain. Today's nitrogen-containing fertilizers, spread as a fine mist, are more prone to distant transport by wind than earlier-generation fertilizers applied in dry form. A Phase I approach would be to apply the fertilizer more efficiently, while a Phase II approach would be to supply it directly with leguminous cover crops and crop rotation, preventing the problem of environmental overload.

Farmer Lewis Ashton in King George County, Virginia, tries to account for every molecule of nutrient, "because I paid for the stuff and I want to keep it here at home."[6] Farming land that has been in his family since 1660, he's careful to avoid runoff into the Potomac River on which his farm fronts. "Some of my neighbors are fishermen," he says, "and if farmers like me pollute the river and the Chesapeake Bay, we'll put them out of business." He stood on the riverbank and proudly held up a species of seaweed that had once been endangered by excessive nutrients from regional farming. "We're glad to see this coming back, because it means our farming is getting better." One of Ashton's many conservation techniques is to apply nitrogen only when it's needed. Corn, for example, needs nitrogen at various times during its growth cycle, but an excessive application early in the season will simply wash away.[7]

For economic as well as environmental reasons, agriculture is moving from imprecise, wasteful methods like spray irrigation and aerial pesticide application to bull's-eye techniques that pay their own way, such as trickle irrigation and spot treatment of pests. The fertilization technique of Colorado vegetable grower Bob Sakata is a perfect example: using a customized drip applicator on his tractor, he spoon-feeds fertilizer within a three-inch radius of his plants, fertilizing them rather than the field and adjacent waterways. These improvements don't require earth-shaking change; they just administer resources more intelligently to create less waste.

The pathway to deeper design is to gain an understanding of systems, allowing us to take advantage of inherent resources. Take, for example, biological control of pests. The solution lies within the system. Without a doubt, pesticide application is a central component of factory farming. At first, pesticides appeared to be miraculously effective in eradicating weeds and insects. They played a key role in the phenomenal post–World War II productivity boom that fed the world's hunger and bolstered the U.S. balance of trade. Consequently, they were seen as the correct moral as well as economic and technological choice. To this day, many farmers and agricultural advisors continue to believe that pesticides are the best way to go. Furthermore, they don't want to risk a year's investment. They feel they are actively combating pests when they spray.

However, many farmers now are equally convinced that pesticide use is not the best practice. Rejecting the "spray and pray" mentality, they are adopting practices that attack the problem in a different way: least-effect, least-cost pest control. They're aware that thirty times as much pesticide is now being sprayed as in 1945, yet the percentage of crops lost to pests has actually gone up because pests are becoming resistant to chemicals. They are aware of the far-flung effects of spraying, such as pesticide residues in Arctic mammals, and of much more immediate effects, such as high rates of cancer among farming populations.

One solution to the problem is natural pest control, a primary tool of integrated pest management (IPM), a technique now in practice throughout the world. IPM helps farmers determine when to spray and when not to spray, based on careful monitoring and computer modeling of pest populations. It minimizes spraying by the calendar, often a waste of time and money because a pest is either not present or is not at a stage of development when it is vulnerable to a given chemical. By knowing the precise habits, life stages, and populations of pests, farmers can use a hierarchy of strategies to control them, not just applied chemicals.

The Campbell's operation in Sinaloa, Mexico, is a good example of IPM. In 1986, that company's entomologists began observing

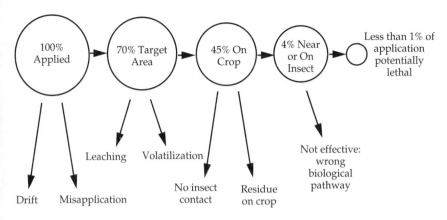

Figure 8
Inefficiency of the aerial application of conventional insecticide.

SOURCE: ENVIRONMENTAL PROTECTION AGENCY.

alarming degrees of pest resistance in their fields and in the fields of contract growers. Explains Campbell's IPM expert Bob Curtis, "In our Mexican operation, we seemed to be fighting an uphill battle. We were using the same techniques that had worked in the past, but pest damage was increasing. Standard practices were beginning to fail. We had a tough year in our tomato fields—25 percent damage from the tomato fruitworm—and we decided to tear our system apart and put it back together more effectively."[8]

On the advice of Campbell's pest-control experts, Mexican growers released natural predators, *Trichogramma* wasps, that brought the fruitworm under control and enabled a 90-percent reduction in pesticide spraying. Results with pinworm, whitefly, and several fungi and viruses were equally impressive. For example, fields were carefully monitored until the pinworm population reached a certain size, at which time pheromone dispensers were placed throughout the fields. Males couldn't mate effectively with females because they couldn't find them—the released pheromones jammed their sexual signals. This strategy cut pinworm pesticide use by 50 percent and saved $470,000 a year in chemicals. The approach with whitefly was different. Experts identified specific hot spots to avoid, such as irrigation canals where virus-carrying seeds were dispersed. Tomatoes weren't planted close by. And fields with a high risk of virus infection were planted only after the whitefly population had dropped below a certain level. By coordinating their planting with natural conditions, growers completely eliminated the need to spray. To prevent fungus disease, Campbell's pest-control advisors monitored air temperature and leaf-surface moisture, which allowed them to predict outbreaks. They then sprayed specific fields with just the right amount of the right pesticide at the right time.

Overall, Campbell's Mexican operation has reduced pesticide usage by 60 percent, an accomplishment closely observed by company management. Tangible results include better fruit, and less culling in processing plants, resulting in more tons per hour. It also gives Campbell's more insurance against a potential market catastrophe, the perception by consumers that its soup is not "good food."

What do Campbell's growers think of the IPM policy? One farmer in Davis, California, has mixed feelings. He feels caught between the processor's grading requirements and IPM directives, which are not mandatory in California: "My per-acre costs for growing tomatoes are about $1,500, and typical pesticide application costs are $150, so if I can be assured by experts of when I should spray and when I can hold off, I'll be glad to listen. But we had a crop last year that got badly hit with tomato fruitworm, and some of the crop didn't make Campbell's processing standards for diced product, since it had too many insect parts by percentage. So we feel like we're being pulled in both directions."[9] He added that contracts are renewed based on performance, and that having a truckload of produce refused at the plant doesn't help in the securing of next year's agreement.

On the learning curve toward pesticide reduction, there will be much uncertainty from growers. IPM sounds good, but when the time for change comes, can they make the leap of faith? Probably not until they have more data and operating experience will more cautious growers be reassured that IPM can work for them.

The campaign against spray and pray reaches beyond corporate boardrooms to the government level in some nations. Denmark, Sweden, the Netherlands, and Canada all have formal programs to cut overall pesticide use by 50 percent. One, instituted by the provincial government of Ontario, Canada, seems especially likely to succeed. The program began more for political than for environmental reasons. Responding to public opinion, the party that won the election in 1987 included in its platform a promise to get farmers to reduce pesticide use by 50 percent.[10] This figure was a combination of science and marketing, based both on the committee findings of experts and on political appeal. Fifty percent had a nice advertising ring to it.

Yet the reasons behind Ontario's campaign were substantive. Because of regulatory costs, small markets, and transportation expenses, Canadian farmers pay a premium for pesticide, and the new administration agreed that one way to overcome the problem was to reduce Ontario's reliance on pesticides. Another consideration was the inevitable rise in the cost of pesticide, since they are derived from fossil fuels, that is, a nonrenewable resource that will ultimately inflate in price. Increasing resistance to pesticides was another consideration. With Canadian regulatory bans extending their reach to a growing number of active ingredients in pesticides, resistance would continue to escalate. And then there was the human dimension. Farmers began worrying about their health, and some feared that their profession, with its pesticide obsession, was no longer revered by the outside world.

The well-funded program ($10 million Canadian dollars for the first five years of a fifteen-year program) includes research on alternatives and mandates licenses for the purchase and use of pesticides. Licenses are only issued after farmers have completed training sessions on pesticides. The program also embraces two research areas that are often neglected in pesticide-reduction strategies: the new generation of lower-volume, lower-impact pesticides, and weed control with biological strategies such as the release of seed-eating larvae. Hundreds of thousands of acres of weed-infested prairie are already being biologically treated in Canada.

Is a 50-percent pesticide reduction possible in the United States? American pesticide expert David Pimental of Cornell University says yes. His research reveals huge opportunities, since nearly three-quarters of the herbicides are applied to just two major crops: corn and soybeans. Twenty-five percent of all insecticides are used on cotton and corn. Of the total estimated 434 million kg of pesticides used in the United States, 69 percent are herbicides, 19 percent insecticides, and 12 percent fungicides. What are some of the highest-return opportunities? Pimental identifies a handful of approaches that could cumulatively reduce chemical use by half. They include planting corn, cotton, and soybeans in appropriate climates where pests have natural predators, the use of pest-resistant seed varieties, crop rotation, and more realistic expectations about a field's appearance.[11] It's not really a question of whether U.S. agriculture can significantly reduce pesticide use, but what psychological and cultural factors will enable it to happen.

Whether or not a 50-percent reduction in pesticide application will be achieved in the United States remains to be seen. Meanwhile, the experiences of enlightened farmers are significant steps.

Letting Go of Pesticides

Paul Buxman, who grows fruit in Dinuba, California, had personal reasons for going cold turkey on pesticide. His son got leukemia, and when he had his well water analyzed, it was found to contain high levels of pesticides. Buxman was determined to grow peaches, plums, and kiwi without relying on chemicals that might further threaten his son's health. And so began a long, arduous process of learning to think like a bug. He carried a Swiss Army knife with a magnifying glass on it. "When you have one of these," he explains, "the whole world opens up to you. Instead of spraying everytime you see a pest, you begin to look for the good bugs, to see if the farm is under biological control. For example, you look for one mite predator for every ten mites, and your work is being done for you."[12]

Buxman makes a distinction between blanket spraying and spot spraying, and doesn't rule out attacking a hot spot if necessary. But he usually doesn't find it necessary. On his farm, there are about twelve different pest insects and about the same number of predators. He had to become familiar with all of them and observe what they were up to. The only other option was to remain ignorant and at the mercy of pesticide salespeople.

Buxman discovered many new allies in his orchard when he stopped spraying. He had never seen a katydid, a pest, on his crops until the year after he switched. But once the bird population recognized the camouflaged pests, they didn't escape the beak. A pair of red-winged blackbirds came from off the farm and started feasting on them. They made such a commotion that other birds caught on—house sparrows, thrushes, robins, and meadowlarks. "It takes nature a while to figure out there's something new in town, so you have to be patient," Buxman says. "You also have to take care of your predators. We didn't have many predators when I was spraying, that's for sure."

Another ally turned out to be the peach twig borer, an uninvited guest from the pistachio trees of Iran.

In its own niche, that bug is probably not a problem, but out of place, it has no enemies, and it was making a mess out of my peaches. After three years, we were losing 20 percent of our crop, and I went out and got some scientific help concerning the habits of the insect. I found out that during one stage of its life, it devours the tips of the twigs, which really isn't a bad thing, because we have to go in otherwise and prune those twigs to keep them from blocking sunlight to the fruit. But at another stage of the life cycle, it starts attacking the peaches. After a very quick yet thorough search, we found a biological pesticide based on a bacteria, Bacillus thuringiensis, that fortunately held the insect's damage to less than 1 percent of the crop. So in effect, we live with that level of damage or less in trade for the pruning the insect does earlier in its life cycle. We've converted an enemy into an ally.[13]

Buxman takes the same approach with the weeds that grow in rows between his trees. Rather than trying to eradicate them, he simply manages them by periodic mowing. They are better suited for the climate than the cover crops sold by the seed companies, he's observed, requiring less water and, when they are mowed, providing material to feed his soil. The weeds have another advantage: they help keep beneficial insects around. These insects are "meat and potatoes" bugs that eat the "vegetarian" pest.

It hasn't been easy convincing neighbors that pests aren't escaping from his relatively small 40-acre orchard. The reason Buxman was able to control pests, some of them said, was that they were keeping surrounding farms free from infestations and giving him free protection. He believes otherwise, and he's got his magnifying glass to prove it. (He can identify 20 different predators and pests.) When he decided to stop spraying, he thought he'd have to sacrifice crop yield and profits, but after a year of adjustment, nature started taking control. Another complaint from neighbors was that his weeds were using up valuable water. Buxman countered that when the weeds decompose and become humus, they absorb and hold water.

There's a special feel to the Buxman ranch that goes beyond the brightly colored wildflowers and the vitality of its owners. The orchard is healthy. It resonates. The birdsongs tell you that, and the dark green foliage, and the juicy, tasty peaches. Paul Buxman believes that finding the proper variety of fruit is central to achieving his essential goals of taste and nutrition—but without healthy soil, not even a good variety will be nutritious. "An orchard is what it eats," he summarizes.

What can be learned from a system such as Paul Buxman's? That knowledge is power. Once he began to understand its biological dynamics, Buxman was willing to get out of the way and let the orchard take care of itself, under his watchful eye. Is his farm earning money? As much or more so than when he was a pesticide addict. His fruit now commands a premium price because it is residue free and high quality. The relatively small operation allows Buxman to hand-pack his peaches and plums in boxes, reducing the bruising that occurs with vats. This gives him a competitive advantage in marketing. But the biggest payoff is in quality of life. "You won't see any skull-and-crossbone signs here warning that pesticides have been sprayed. But you will see brightly colored orioles and tanagers. And you will see a healthy orchard that delivers more than just fruit: our ranch provides clean air and clean water—resources that are getting pretty hard to find."[14]

Phase II: Changing the Shape of Agriculture

Dr. Richard Cruse, an Iowa State University agronomist, likes to hunt pheasants, but they are becoming increasingly hard to find in a landscape dominated by monoculture corn and soybeans. In experiments originally intended to improve wildlife habitat in Iowa's farm fields, Cruse and his colleagues came up with deep-design innovations that reach far beyond pheasants.

Many Iowa farmers already rotate soybeans with corn, helping break pest cycles and providing natural fertility with the nitrogen-fixing soybean crop. Cruse has introduced another method, and it is like adding a third ball into a juggling sequence: strip-intercropping. Intercropping is planting four to six rows of three (or possibly more) crops in an alternating pattern across fields that used to be just for single crops.

The next year, the crops are rotated, so in effect the system adds diversity both temporally and spatially. In the most common scenario, oat strips underseeded with clover (to add nitrogen) are followed by corn, soybeans are followed by oats and clover, and corn is followed by soybeans.

Two young farmers in northeast Iowa pioneered strip intercropping, with assistance from Iowa State University, an association called Practical Farmers of Iowa. Tom Frantzen and Mike Riecherts, who went to high school together years ago, heard about the innovation and it made sense to them conceptually. "When you have a single crop, with all the rows going in one direction, it's going to increase the likelihood of erosion," says Frantzen. "The strips definitely prevent erosion for two reasons: heavy rains soak in quicker rather than running off because the soil is in such great shape, and the cover crops provide a barrier to runoff."[15]

The contrast between Frantzen's strip-planted fields and his neighbor's single-crop fields was striking. In mid-July, the neighbor had just replanted his soybean fields because his first planting had washed away in a heavy rain. Water samples collected immediately after that rain showed cloudy, sediment-laden water running off the neighbor's fields but clear water coming from Frantzen's stripped fields. Bedrock protruded from the neighbor's fields, while Frantzen's were covered with vigorous, multicolored crops: the oats were golden and getting close to harvest, the soybeans were bushy, like small hedges winding on the contour toward the horizon, and the corn shimmered in the sun, shoulder-high. Frantzen's fields were like a well-kept garden that had escaped into the surrounding acres.

Frantzen was quick to explain that while the system looks complicated to plant and manage, it's really no more so than the typical block-planted field. He's been practicing ridge tillage for a number of years. The ridges remain permanently in place, while the heavy wheels of machinery travel in the same tracks (Frantzen calls them highways) year after year, reducing soil compaction in the rest of the field. With ridges to mark the fields, Frantzen plants four rows, skips eight, and plants another four rows of the same crop. Then he goes back and in the skipped rows plants the next crop. By the end, he has three fields of crops woven into a single system. Frantzen quips, "The only problem was I had to slow the combine down to harvest all that extra corn."

In addition to reducing erosion, raising fertility, and providing natural pest control, strip intercropping boosts crop yields. Richard

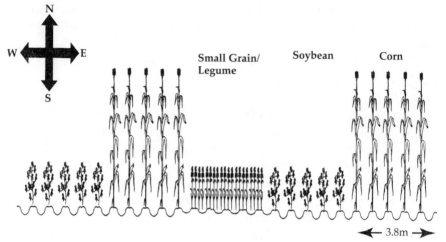

Environmental factors and plant resources altered by the system:

Above Ground
- Surface residue and cover
- Soil erosion control
- Air speed and motion
- Air temperature and humidity
- Light
- Crop-canopy temperature
- Surface soil temperature and moisture
- Weed species, spectrum, and pressure
- Insect population dynamics
- Wildlife
- CO_2 enrichment in crop canopy

Below Ground
- Water storage
- Evapotranspiration
- Nutrient uptake
- Root penetration (time and space)
- Microbial activities
- Soil physical properties
- Nitrogen enrichment
- Soil organic matter content

Figure 9

Strip intercropping: A system that meets many of its own needs.

Cruse stands with Reicherts in front of these rolling acres, exchanging ideas on why the system requires fewer expensive inputs such as fertilizer and pesticide. Reicherts used to spend $70 an acre for fertilizer under the old system, while now he averages only $10. And partly because of his wife's allergies, he has stopped spraying herbicide.

Cruse points out that the corn is not as tall in the sunny outside rows of each strip: "That's good, because it means that more energy is going into the grain rather than for stalk elongation. Those outside rows are getting plenty of sunshine, and corn really benefits from that." A typical field of corn competes against itself, shading individual plants and causing a "race for height" that reduces yield. But with large, open areas and lots of outside rows (because oats and soybeans are shorter crops), corn yields have been exceptional. On fields that typically produce 130 bushels of corn per acre, strip intercropping has yielded up to 200 bushels. Oat yields have in general improved, while soybean production has held steady. The taller corn also provides a windbreak that slows down the transpiration rate from the leaf surfaces of oats and soybeans. "Strip intercropping is a system that works both above and below the soil," Cruse says. "Because the oats and clover are planted earlier in the spring, they don't compete with the other crops or against themselves— they have all the moisture and sunshine they need. Then as temperatures get hotter, they actually benefit from the shading and cooling the corn provides."

Ecologists refer to the edge effect in ecosystems, where populations and species are abundant and diverse. At the edge of an ecosystem, there's a balance between the high productivity and high waste of an immature system on the one hand, and the high "protectivity" and high preservation of mature systems, on the other. Strip intercropping recreates a similar balance by mimicking the edge effect throughout a field.

What are the underground advantages of strip intercropping? For one, the oats and clover leave the soil loose and crumbly with hair roots. This results in millions of channels for water to penetrate, and enables Reicherts and Frantzen to work their land much earlier in the spring. The strips avail themselves of what nature provides free—sun, soil, and water. Strip intercropping is a technique that rewards high levels of management, not high levels of capital. Reicherts points out that the system is really advantageous for the small farmer, who typically has narrower, less expensive equipment. The narrower the strips, the more edges or borders can be created. Reicherts is convinced that high levels of debt hamper creativity. The large companies take away a farmer's flexibility; the lenders want to see conventional farming practiced on the farms of borrowers.

One of the most economical methods adopted by Reicherts and Frantzen is mechanical cultivation instead of herbicides. A single year's worth of pesticide savings enabled each farmer to buy a state-of-the-art cultivator that controls weeds without chemicals. The new cultivators have electronic guidance systems that sense where the rows are and automatically keep the machines on target. Reicherts calculated that he could buy a new cultivator every year and throw it away for what he saves on herbicides.

The basic recipe for strip intercropping has already been established. Now, Cruse and his colleagues are fine-tuning it. They've been looking for an annual clover that can't survive the winter, because conventional perennial varieties that reemerge in the spring rob water from the corn crops. A Middle Eastern variety called berseem clover seems promising. Some farmers are introducing livestock to eat the oats directly. There will be many variations on this theme, such as the substitution of wheat for oats in the rotation. Cruse predicts that when a farmer adapts the system for each specific farm, strip intercropping will save a lot of money and a lot of soil. "The government," he adds, "has tried two basic approaches to prevent soil erosion—the carrot and the stick, or regulations and subsidies. But both approaches cost the taxpayer money. Wouldn't it be better to switch to practices like strip intercropping that prevent erosion by design?"[16]

Perennial Polyculture:
Farming in Nature's Image

I pulled off the dirt road and into the driveway of the Land Institute, an enclave of deep design in Salina, Kansas. Wes Jackson and his colleagues are taking a significant step beyond conventional practices to convert agricultural vision into reality. How, they're asking, can we create agricultural systems that have minimal impact on the environment yet yield total value and satisfaction for society and for the land? Taking a natural ecosystem, the prairie, as a model, they're seeking to invent a higher order of agriculture.

As I walked up to the Institute's office, located in a converted farmhouse, I saw staffers and interns scattered across the farm's 277 acres, performing their slow, steady research. Their aim is to make perennial crops high-yielding, sustainable substitutes for conventional and often destructive annual crops. Someone was tending an experimental plot near the office, and I remarked as I walked by that it looked as if they'd gotten quite a bit of rain the night before. "Three-quarters of an inch," she replied, "and we sure needed it." The prairie smelled fresh. The locusts and crickets, in full chorus, seemed to appreciate the morning humidity.

I was excited to be at the Land Institute, having followed the group's research for ten years or more. In 1978, Wes Jackson had a critical insight: agriculture needs to be as diverse and resilient as nature itself or it will inevitably disrupt nature. With a background in evolutionary biology, Jackson knew that conventional farming mimics an immature, crisis-ridden ecosystem rather than what ecologists call a climax ecosystem. Our major seed and grain crops are mostly annuals, the evolutionary role of which is to colonize bare patches of earth that need to be quickly covered to prevent soil loss. Jackson felt that "formula farming" was an admission that we don't understand specific ecosystems. Because each farm has different climatic, soil, and geological conditions, it needs to be farmed with methods that respond precisely to those characteristics. Jackson's friend and colleague Wendell Berry has consistently pointed out in his writings that a lack of biological understanding is at the core of our unsustainable, ecologically damaging agriculture: "We came with visions of former places but not the sight to see where we are. As we came across the continent, cutting forests and plowing the prairies, we never knew what we were doing because we never knew what we were undoing."[17]

Since 1978, Jackson's vision has developed into the deepest of agricultural designs. His "perennial polyculture" seeks to understand what nature needs and to nurture the successes of evolution. Jackson tells a story of a Sioux Indian standing at the edge of a prairie being plowed up in the last century. "Wrong side up," he is said to have commented. To force a field into ecological crisis is to invite the inevitable: erosion, vulnerability to pests, and the need for heavy inputs of energy to compel crops to grow.

In *Becoming Native to This Place* Jackson writes,

It became clear to me that on sloping ground, regardless of terraces and grass waterways, soil would erode on wheat fields, corn fields, soybean fields, sorghum fields—wherever monocultures were planted. On the other hand, it was also clear that soil would more or less stay put in perennial pastures, in native prairie grassland, and in forests, independent of human action. But there was more, for to those annual monocultures came pesticides, commercial fertilizer, and a need for fossil fuel for traction. The prairie, on the other hand, counted on species diversity and genetic diversity within species to avoid epidemics of insects and pathogens. The prairie maintains its own fertility, runs on sun-light, and actually accumulates ecological capital—accumulates soil. Observing this years ago I formulated a question: Is it possible to build an agriculture based on the prairie as standard or model? I saw a sharp contrast between the major features of the wheat field and the major features of the prairie. . . . Because all of our high-yielding crops are annuals or are treated as such, crucial questions must be answered. Can perennialism and high yield go together? If so, can a polyculture of perennials outyield a mono-culture of perennials? Can such an ecosystem sponsor its own fertility and pest control?[18]

Over the years, Jackson's small research institute has been taking an inventory of potential perennial species to answer such questions. Any flowering plant species from anywhere in the world that was herbaceous (as opposed to woody) and perennial (as opposed to annual), and that could withstand the prairie winter, was planted in a five-meter-long row at the Land Institute. After fifteen years of working with species such as eastern gama grass and wild sorghum, Jackson and his researchers have increased seed yield without sacrificing perennial vigor. The implications of their findings cut against the grain (so to speak) of agricultural history. The reason annuals have been farmed throughout human history is that they germinate quickly, complete their life cycles quickly, and produce large quantities of seeds. In the absence of advanced understanding of ecology, annuals were the most convenient pathway to survival. The strategy of an annual species is to get seeds out into the world, so vital energy is channeled into its reproductive parts. In effect, what Wes Jackson proposes is to create a new kind of agriculture by shifting to less quick-fix perennials that can confer benefits other than just yield.

The Land Institute's ecologist Jon Piper and I walk across the road from the farmhouse into a near-virgin prairie. He explains that what we are seeing is 99 percent perennial plants, in four categories: warm-season grasses, cool-season grasses, legumes that fix nitrogen, and composites such as sunflowers and daisies. "Every year that I come out here," he says, "it's a different mixture of plants, because every year has different climatic and soil variations. You can read the prairie like a history book, if you know the language. The big themes of the prairie are diversity and perenniality. Regardless

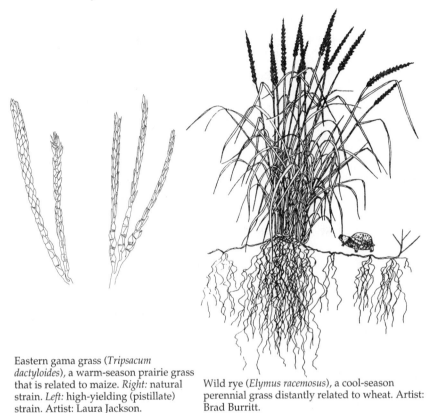

Eastern gama grass (*Tripsacum dactyloides*), a warm-season prairie grass that is related to maize. *Right:* natural strain. *Left:* high-yielding (pistillate) strain. Artist: Laura Jackson.

Wild rye (*Elymus racemosus*), a cool-season perennial grass distantly related to wheat. Artist: Brad Burritt.

Figure 10

Examples of potential perennial seed crops.

Source: Courtesy of The Land Institute, Salina, Kansas.

of the weather and the precipitation, some species will thrive here, while others will temporarily decline, hanging in there until conditions meet their requirements."[19] A prairie system meets its needs by storing a diverse set of solutions upon which to draw. In drought years, the deeply rooted perennials go down for moisture and nutrients, some with taproots and some with massive systems of hair roots. If wildfire or grazing animals take their toll on the surface, the prairie resorts to its underground stored reserves and becomes even more vigorous. The prairie is far more than a sea of grass; it is a system that responds to a cycle of grazing-fire-drought-temperature extremes with organic soil buildup–species diversity–perenniality.

What are the potential pest-control benefits of polyculture? "The largest percentage of pesticides used are herbicides to control weeds," Piper tells me. "Perennials provide continuous ground cover to suppress weed germination, and their overlapping growth patterns use soil nutrients and sunlight to block weed development." Their roots also inhibit weed growth like natural herbicides. Moreover, the diversity of a polyculture reduces the flourishing growth of host plants that pests thrive on. A polyculture's chemical interactions mask enticing odors and jam the signals of pests. As a result of all this, polycultures are more stable systems. They can harbor beneficial insects as well as populations of neutral insects that serve as alternate food for beneficial insects whose primary food supply, pests, has temporarily run out.

The Land Institute uses the term "overyielding" to describe the concept that the whole is greater than the sum of its parts. The experimental species Illinois bundleflower has been proven to yield better when interplanted with wild senna than when planted by itself. Eastern gama grass planted with mammoth wild rye has shown similar results. While total yields of such alternative crops have not yet approached the benchmark 1,800 pounds per acre that low-input wheat achieves, results have been good enough to make Jackson, Piper, and their colleagues optimistic. Illinois bundleflower, with a nutritional profile equivalent to soybeans, routinely yields 1,200 to 1,500 pounds per acre.

As we stand next to a field of experimental plots, Piper explains his latest experiment with obvious excitement. He has combined four basic native species in various patterns and is "letting the community assemble as it will," under the assumption that strengths will self-select. Piper's approach reflects a concept that is beginning to affect design in many different fields, chaos theory, which looks beyond traditional cause-and-effect relationships. He compares agricultural natural selections to two actors with similar levels of talent. "Why does one of them become a star, while the other continues to drive a taxi? There are unpredictable events that jump into the scenario to affect the outcome—variables that are beyond deductive reasoning." In agriculture, for example, no species can be considered in isolation from its biological and cultural context, which is shaped by ever-changing and unpredictable forces.

If biotechnology (the engineered manipulation of genes) offered a quicker pathway toward some of Piper's goals, would he practice it? "Our overall goal is to maintain diversity, and we won't violate that principle," he answers. "If biotechnology could give us a perennial crop whose seeds didn't 'shatter' [disperse too soon for effective harvesting], we might be interested. But a quick-fix like the nitrogen-fixing corn that supplies some of its own fertility is suspect because it's still an annual monoculture that lacks wide-based diversity."[20]

Piper and I head back toward the institute's office to get glasses of cold water. We meet Wes Jackson by the refrigerator and go into his office. He explains that his vision is based on ignorance rather than the rational "certainties" of the past few centuries. "Most scientific research is function-based, looking at individual variables and trying to maximize them. What we do is come at it from a different angle, to see the larger patterns and context of agriculture." Jackson is interested in combining science and sociology to produce not only sustainable agriculture but also a sustainable culture. "If we use this fossil fuel slack time to create an agriculture that's as permanent and resilient as a prairie or other climax ecosystem," he says, "we'll be building a very useful bridge to the future."[21]

Is polyculture a viable design alternative in ecosystems other than prairies? Jack Ewel and his associates at the University of Florida have demonstrated that it can work as well in tropical and subtropical ecosystems. Working in the rain forests of Costa Rica, the Ewel team substituted analog species for indigenous ones, concluding that if the system is mimicked precisely enough, it can continue to function perpetually. According to Piper, experiments are also under way that mimic temperate forests and other ecosystems.

I thank Wes Jackson and Jon Piper and drive away from the Land Institute realizing once again that design informed by the requirements of nature is what our battered environment really needs. The deep design of sustainable agriculture is not really about what we don't do wrong—that's Phase I—but about what we do right.

Chapter 6

A Near-Perfect World, If You're a Wheel

Designing Communities That Work

American cities and communities are environmentally costly and spiritually numbing because of a deadly trio of poor design: the transportation infrastructure, resource consumption by buildings, and the obliteration of open land and habitat. There is a strong analogy between the word sprawl as it relates to communities and scrawl as it relates to the scribbles of a preliterate child. The patterns we've created in our communities are immature and lack meaning. That's what this chapter is about: designing patterns right so that resources flow smoothly through our human habitat. Good community planning follows the pathway toward deep design, integrating highly efficient pieces to meet the needs of both culture and nature. When a community works, it is flexible, diverse, renewable, biologically aware. When a community works, it incorporates the criteria of deep design.

What are some Phase I steps toward sustainable communities? First, individual buildings, parks, theaters, and streets can be better designed. New buildings can realistically achieve a cost-effective 75-percent reduction in total energy use, a 65-percent reduction in the use of electricity, and a 50-percent reduction in water consumption. They can be built with materials that are 50-percent recycled. A building can and should be targeted to last a hundred years rather than the typical forty years.[1] Similar targets can be set and achieved in transportation. Through effective public goal setting, for example, design upgrades in public transit and "access by proximity," a community can consciously reduce vehicle miles traveled and increase the number of passengers per vehicle. And the public works departments can set such goals as using more recycled asphalt and tires for roadbuilding and reducing leaks in natural-gas lines as well as water and sewage lines. Town councils can actively research and implement programs for the collection of municipal compost and other progressive initiatives.

These are efficiency tune-ups. In Phase II of community design, the pieces are fit together as an integral system that provides many of its own needs by optimizing natural rhythms and minimizing wasted effort. Many communities of today require complex engineered solutions to overcome disjointed patterns. The very shape of American cities and towns often inhibits flow rather than enhancing it, causing pollution and stress. Traffic flow is awkward, and services are scattered and often accessible only by car. Neighborhoods where one could once walk to shops, parks, and offices have been replaced by mile after mile of homogenized streets, garages, and houses, isolated by zoning law from fundamental services and needs. Streets have become barriers, delineators of separation rather than avenues of access. A person whose backyard adjoins a shopping mall may have to drive a mile to get there. The flow of water, waste, and energy is also crudely inefficient in the typical American community, requiring layer upon layer of redundant infrastructure to overcome the shapeless chaos. In principle, cities should be tools to minimize travel and maximize information exchange. In reality, they are becoming congested machines that convert resources into pollution.

It hasn't occurred to many of us in recent decades that the elements of a community need to be consciously connected and integrated. In the words of innovative planner and futurist Peter Calthorpe, "Architects, planners, landscape architects, traffic engineers, civil engineers, biologists, developers, environmentalists, bankers and neighborhood groups too often seek to optimize only a segment, an issue, or an individual system. This divides a region into dysfunctional pieces."[2] Calthorpe thinks at the regional level, integrating community design with attributes such as climate, topography, and existing transportation systems. However, he regrets that our best design and engineering efforts are being overshadowed by the needs of a single entity, the car.

Keeping Cars Happy

By creating convenience for our cars, we make life miserable for ourselves. The conventional "curb radius" that permits easy turning for cars doubles the distance that pedestrians must walk (or run) to get across streets. The retail parking lot is designed for convenience, but we often walk a quarter of a mile through paved car territory to get to and from the store. Parking lots raise summer temperatures and create conduits for floodwater. Indoor parking lots concentrate carbon monoxide and other pollutants. We think of our own car requiring a single parking space, but when our share of community parking is calculated, the car requires something more like eight spaces. So institutionalized has parking become that most building codes require new office buildings to provide parking space for employees. Many elements of deep design have actually been declared illegal. To build a neighborhood around the needs of people and environment, an innovative developer must seek variances and exemptions in zoning and coding regulations.

If the car demands speed and space,

> *the wants of a transit system are quite different. Its fundamental desire is for more riders. This calls for high-density land uses (housing at ten units per acre at a minimum), dedicated right-of-ways (for easy movement), infrequent station stops (one-mile minimum), frequent arrivals and mixed-use destinations. Its destinations also need to be walkable so that riders are not stranded when they arrive.*
>
> *Pedestrians want close destinations: shops, schools, services, and recreation. They want direct links to these destinations free of cul-de-sacs, parking lots, or massive intersections. They want safe, interesting and comfortable streets to walk on: tree-shaded, with houses and shops fronting directly on them for interest and security. They want detail and human scale in the edges and places of a community. And they want narrow streets lined with entries and porches leading to local shops, schools, and parks, not curving streets lined with garage doors leading to six-lane arterials.*[3]

Pedestrian-friendly communities not only feel good, they are economically viable. We pay good money to visit places like Alexandria, Virginia, and Annapolis, Maryland, just to experience the quaintness. Property in towns like Seaside, Florida, recently designed from scratch to please the pedestrian perspective, is selling at rates 600 percent above conventional nearby real estate, which shows how rare it is. The typical modern American city, "violated by urban renewal, suburban flight, parking structures, and freeway interventions," satisfies neither pedestrian, car, nor transit. Peter Calthorpe's aim is to forge a new synthesis of the three variables.

The shape of our towns has disturbing social implications, especially for the young and the elderly. When children can't walk anywhere, they typically become television addicts. As for the elderly, when their licenses are revoked because of failing eyesight, they become stranded. Even those quite capable of walking are discouraged because there are few services within walking distance. Moreover, there's a dramatic mismatch between what Americans designed in the post–World War II era and our current needs. We're not the Cleavers or the Nelsons anymore. More than a quarter of all Americans live alone. Of the approximately 17 million new households formed during the 1980s, only 27 percent consisted of married couples with or without children. People over the age of 65 will make up 23 percent of all new households. The traditional three-bedroom, detached home is becoming less and less relevant.[4]

The Ahwahnee Principles

Today's demographics point to a huge opportunity to incrementally reshape our communities. Land, energy, and resources should be used more efficiently, traffic should be reduced, homes should be more affordable, children and the elderly should have more access, and working people should not be burdened with long commutes. Calthorpe and some of his colleagues have come up with a set of design imperatives for creating the post-suburban metropolis. They are called the Awahnee principles because they were formulated at the Awahnee Lodge in Yosemite National Park:

• All planning should be in the form of complete and integrated communities containing housing, shops, workplaces, schools, parks, and civic facilities essential to the daily life of the residents;

- Communities should be designed so that housing, jobs, shops, and other buildings/activities are within easy walking distance of each other;
- As many activities as possible should be located within easy walking distance of transit stops;
- A community should contain a diversity of housing types to enable citizens of different ages and from a wide range of economic levels and socio-economic backgrounds to live there;
- Businesses within the community should provide a range of job types for the community's residents;
- The location and character of the community should be consistent with a larger transit network;
- The community should have a center that combines commercial, civic, cultural, and recreational uses;
- The community should have ample open space in the form of squares, greens, and parks, whose frequent use is encouraged through placement and design;
- Public spaces should be designed to draw people at all hours of the day and night;
- Each community or cluster of communities should have a well-defined edge, such as agricultural greenbelts or wildlife corridors, permanently protected from development; and
- Streets, pedestrian paths, and bike paths should contribute to a system of fully connected and interesting routes to all destinations. They should be small and spatially defined by buildings, trees, and lighting to encourage pedestrian and bicycle use and discourage high-speed traffic.[5]

To Calthorpe and his colleagues, pedestrians give meaning to a place and make it livable. Without them, "an area's focus can be easily lost. Commerce and civic uses are easily decentralized into distant chain store destinations and government centers, and a community's common ground—its parks, sidewalks, squares, and plazas—become nothing more than obstructions to the car."[6]

What would the environmental benefits be if the Awahnee principles were followed, that is, if the geometry of human activity were readjusted to emphasize pedestrians, bikes, higher density but more open space, town centers, decentralized energy and water treatment, and so forth? The following benefits and many more:

- Fewer materials would be required to perform comparable levels of service, because pipes, wires, and streets would service more people per unit of material;
- Services such as police and fire protection and sanitation would be delivered more cost effectively;
- Less energy would be used, both for direct use as well as the exportation of waste;
- The habitat of living things and the support-system benefits they provide would not be threatened; and
- Life would be more satisfying and productive, less stressful, and less expensive.

Is it possible to create new communities from scratch that better fit the environment while meeting human needs more effectively? Is it possible to reshape existing cities, towns, and communities so they work better? The answer is yes to both questions, but such change won't happen on its own. First, it has to be imagined; then the right design seeds have to be planted. We have to ask, What do we want? What works best in the world's best-loved places?

Many of today's best architects and planners believe that we've designed ourselves into a blind alley. Our built environment is the skeletal framework of our culture, and it is their conviction that some of the major bones are broken. Fortunately, people like John Clark, Michael and Judy Corbett, and Tom Gougeon are earnestly trying to reset them.

Haymount: More Than a Field of Dreams

For the past five or six years, developer John Clark has been asking himself and many others, What makes a community great? He is steadily converting a dream into reality by designing a new kind of development that blends traditional and high-technology features into a community that works. After spending eighteen years in the trenches as a banker and assembly-line developer, Clark is committed to something far beyond the conventional. His community, which will take fifteen years to build after construction starts in 1995, is a deep-design blend of the distant past and the near future.

Haymount will be a community in Caroline County, Virginia,

about an hour from Washington, D.C., and twenty minutes from Fredericksburg, where the visionary becomes pragmatic. This walkable, mixed-use town will have a beautiful setting of woods, wetlands, open meadow, and river. Located within ten minutes of a light-rail commuter stop, it will include an organic farm and farmer's market, parks, fourteen churches, and a college, all stated in the architectural language of the region, mid-Atlantic colonial, and adapted to solar energy. "It is as inappropriate to build a civic building colonial style in Los Angeles as it is to build terra-cotta architecture in Caroline County," Clark remarks.

Clark's underlying theme is just that, appropriateness. Haymount is a contract between people and their environment, which requires a thorough understanding of the needs of each. Before Clark's design team could know how to develop Haymount, they had to know and understand the land around it.

I walked and drove around the site with Clark and his attorney and co-designer Dan Slone, by fields of winter wheat and hay, along the winding Rappahannock River, a watershed that parallels the Potomac, past the site of a burned-down plantation house on which trees had reclaimed old tobacco fields, under the wings of red-tailed hawks and bald eagles and the shady branches of tulip and oak trees. One part of the property rises 270 feet above the river. It was easy to imagine colonial commerce on the river 250 years ago.

Clark's overall philosophy for developing Haymount is that it will be restorative rather than merely sustainable. In other words, he wants to make the community more ecologically viable than it was when he started. There are 302 species of animals at Haymount, and Clark wants their numbers to increase. He plans to plant an additional 50,000 trees and shrubs on the property, in addition to preserving much of the vigorous forest that's already there.

Clark is respectful of Haymount's heritage as well as its ecology. As part of an inventory of Haymount's resources, an in-depth archeological study was performed that uncovered 17,000 artifacts dating back 7,000 years. "They were hunting and fishing at Haymount at least 2,500 years before they started pushing rocks around at Stonehenge," says Clark in his typically colorful way. "This is good evidence that people have always found Haymount to be a good place to work, play, and raise families." We walk to the site of a burned-down house built in 1650. "Abrams Moon established a tobacco plantation here," Clark tells me. "You can still see some of the furrows. Another house was built and sold to the Turners in the 1820s, but it burned down too. Right at the threshold of the house, we found the key to the front door in the dirt." One of Clark's development proffers to the county will be a public museum that documents Haymount's heritage. "The museum will cover prehistoric times, the 1600s when John Smith stood on the site, and the Civil War period, when Stonewall Jackson defended Fredericksburg from an encampment nearby."

The community will integrate 4,000 living units with 500,000 square feet of commercial and light industrial space and 250,000 square feet of retail. Clark has platted five "villages" on the property, each of which is functional—a college, a farmer's market, a river park, a commercial center, and a school. Bicycling will be encouraged as transportation between villages; every new house comes with two new bikes. The most desirable land from an ecological perspective, including bald-eagle habitat, will be left undeveloped.

Clark will incorporate the best qualities of traditional towns like Alexandria, Virginia, which is laid out on an access-enhancing grid. Time-tested architectural proportions will result in a comfortable, human-scale environment. But Haymount will also break new ground with "biotechnical" innovations such as wetlands wastewater treatment. A state-of-the-art energy code for buildings is being developed by Clark's design team, and he is also evaluating the inclusion of alternative energy systems such as photovoltaics and fuel cells. Careful consideration is being given to the life cycle materials that go into buildings, roads, and other features. In keeping with the style of regional architecture, there will be many bricks used at Haymount. Local brick suppliers have already approached him, and although Clark is interested in their product, he's asking questions such as, Where do they mine the materials that go into their bricks? "It's not enough to be a local supplier," he says, "although that's a good start. I asked them how they fire their kiln. How do they ship their bricks? How do they mine the materials that go into the bricks? That's the way we change society—one well-designed brick at a time."

How did Haymount get started? "Back in the 1970s, I read a book called *Limits to Growth,* and its message really sank in," explains Clark. "I knew I had to do something constructive in two areas: population and energy. But I wasn't sure where to begin. I became involved in the construction of energy-efficient homes, but they were still just part of the problem, really, because their context was sprawl. Individually, they used less energy per square foot, but collectively, they were still part of the disease. I was killing society with my developments." And so Clark began scrutinizing the ideas of the world's best town builders. He had heard about places like Seaside, Florida, where good design enables people to live an un-hurried lifestyle, interact with their neighbors, and walk to the bakery.

I was itching to try out a blend of the best ideas I'd come across, in-cluding a few of my own. So I linked up with a real-estate broker/whitewater canoe-outfitter who showed me a nice-looking 1,000 acre property, all zoned and platted for large lot sprawl. I just couldn't build another development like all the rest, con-verting land into car food. The property is not near mass transit, it's not hooked up with anything, it's just another piece of the problem. I launched into a long, enthusiastic speech telling them about Duany's ideas, and about things we could do environmen-tally, for the first time ever, with the right piece of land. Besides, with the price of that 1,000-acre parcel, I'd have to live to be about 800 to make any money on the deal. The broker said he knew about another piece of land that was further out than the other piece, and therefore more affordable. We knew light rail was coming down from D.C., and that was a real plus for the property even before we saw it. It was strategically connected to both urban and rural amenities, including a front-row seat on the Rappahannock River. The seller had developers give him every song and dance a man could hear, but when I started talking, I could tell he was listening. As it turned out, he not only sold me the property, but he changed his plans to move and stayed on as a partner because he liked the idea so much.[7]

By no means has the evolution of Haymount been as effortless as that auspicious beginning might suggest. Clark and his partners have endured three lawsuits from neighbors, nature groups, and others whose view of Haymount is expressed in the slogan, Right plan, wrong place. Clark and his investors have thus far paid more than $600,000 in legal fees to defend their idea. The major objections are that the property is located on a pristine river and that its devel-opment will bring people to a rural part of the county. Clark has re-peatedly and patiently countered that the land will be developed in any case—it's currently zoned for 160 "farmettes"—and that his plan will make far better use of the land. Opponents have tried all the arguments they could think of to block Haymount, for example, maintaining that Clark's plan to donate land to fourteen interested churches was a violation of the separation of church and state. One neighboring farmer even argued that when he sprayed pesticides aerially they drifted onto the property that will become Haymount, and therefore that the future development would be unfit for human habitation.

Throughout all this, Clark and his partners have remained level-headed and noncombative, knowing that their idea was environmentally, socially, and financially sound. Instead of creating more sprawl on chunks of land too small to farm and too large to mow, they would be creating a dynamic community that left more than half the land undisturbed. In fact, Michael Finchum, the county director of planning and community development, is considering applying some of Haymount's design standards elsewhere in his jurisdiction. Finchum is intimately familiar with the design features of Haymount, because getting the required amendments to the land-use plan took about thirty months.

Throughout five long years of planning, it was Clark's own personality that kept the project from being derailed: a combination of boyish innocence, the patience and diplomacy to work with even his most vocal opponents, a boundless curiosity about social and environmental needs, and an ability to adapt and synthesize a wide array of concepts.

In the process, he crossed uncharted legal and regulatory territory to create a new kind of comprehensive plan. When they were explaining their vision to county planners, Clark and his attorney partner Dan Slone asked a key question about the zoning that had been approved before Haymount came along: Where would people do their shopping? What kind of environmental impact would the travel have? Though somewhat remote, Haymount will offer the commercial enterprises its residents need. Already, Clark has recruited a collection of small businesses. The plan is to provide many local jobs, eliminating a lot of commuting.

John Clark, Dan Slone, and I sit around a huge, elaborate model of what Haymount will look like. The model, meticulously constructed by a graduate architecture student from the University of Virginia, is located in the sturdy old barn that Clark has converted into Haymount's office. He explains that a good many Caroline County residents have sat here, too—planning commissioners, environmentalists, and citizens. Clark's open-door policy has been effective. "What's really helped convince people that Haymount will be a great place to live," he says, "is getting an eagle's-eye look at it, from the model."[8]

Clark's finger hovers over the model as he explains some of the features that Haymount will include. "One of the key features is that of the entire three miles of waterfront, only 15 percent will be touched by development, and that will be limited-access park." County residents will be given public access to the river for boating, the only such access in all of Caroline County's 526 square miles. However, because bald-eagle habitat is nearby, there will be restrictions on the number of boats that can use the river. When the eagles are nesting, the dock will be closed.

Concern for the natural environment is also expressed in Haymount's aikido-engineered approach to water supply. There were three options for providing Haymount's potable water. Clark's team ruled out deep wells because they would deplete the aquifer, a water supply for farmers. Drawing water directly from the river would have caused erosion and disruption of aquatic life. So they settled on a third system: getting water from shallow vertical wells that would be recharged with horizontal wells drilled under the riverbed.

Storm water will be managed where it falls, rather than channeled away, with the help of such features as constructed wetlands and roads paved with porous material. The wastewater-treatment system will combine conventional and state-of-the-art methods to keep the Rappahannock pristine. A batch reactor will manage the effluent load to prevent the discharge of raw sewage. Sewage will flow through a series of constructed wetlands, where it will gradually purify. Reed beds will protect wildlife from fecal material. At the end, an ozone treatment system, instead of chlorine, will disinfect the purified water.

How did the design team incorporate all their different concerns into Haymount's developing plan? A wildlife consultant and a forester analyzed the plant and animal species, all 302 of them, and laid out the wildlife corridors. This information was loaded into a software program called CAD (computer-assisted design), along with data on the site's geography, topography, ecology, arche-

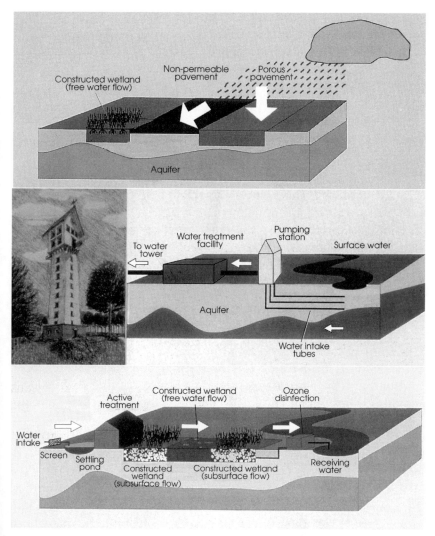

Figure 11

The water cycle of Haymount: (*top*) storm water management; (*middle*) gallery intake system; (*bottom*) wastewater treatment.

ology and hydrology. Then they examined the projected "built environment" and how its services—potable water, storm water, wastewater—would flow through the site. They also considered larger factors such as the migration of wildlife through the site and the preservation of the so-called viewshed—what neighbors would see when they looked at Haymount and beyond. Clark explains, "All of this information was in layers in AUTOCAD before the architects arrived. We knew what the land was, and what its strengths and vulnerabilities were, before we started planning things like treatment of wastes and placement of roads and buildings. The way it happens currently, the traffic guy does a design that's either accepted or rejected, then the archeologist, then the wetlands or wildlife guy, and on and on. But it's all the same issue, and it doesn't need to go through seven expensive, time-consuming iterations."[9]

Clark is adamant that Haymount be diverse, both culturally and economically. The best way to achieve diversity, he maintains, is to provide affordable housing of all types. Haymount will include townhouses, duplexes, apartments, carriage houses, and "granny flats" on alleyways, in addition to more opulent housing.

The two men know what sort of businesses they would like to see first at Haymount. A microbrewery will serve to attract visitors, and a thirty-room bed-and-breakfast will put them up. They also want to see a country-style general store that would meet many of the needs of construction workers, visitors, and early residents. The design team has analyzed a hundred small businesses that towns typically need, from a bicycle shop through banks, hardware stores, and barbers. By word of mouth as well as a mailing to 25,000 regional businesses, Haymount's commercial properties are already being spoken for.

Clark and Slone consider public buildings to be a critical framework around which to organize communities—town halls, libraries, and schools to which children can walk, overcoming the disconnectedness that plagues so many of our communities. Churches are a key integrating feature at Haymount also. Clark comments, "Like other aspects of development, churches have been zoned out of our neighborhoods. We have reintegrated them as places not only of worship but for day care, elderly care, and displaying civic art." He and Slone invited the leaders of fifty-five religious denominations to dinner at the barn, offering free land to interested churches. "In our discussion that night," Slone says, "we started developing the idea of terminating vistas, in other words, siting the churches in prominent places so they could be organizing features of the community."[10]

Clearly, they've done many things right by looking at Haymount as a living system. If that design ethic carries forward into the day-to-day life of Haymount, the community will be the kind of place residents will work to preserve and protect.

Village Homes: The Redistribution of Value

Village Homes, a unique subdivision in Davis, California, is like a reversible jacket with the more attractive side turned in toward the village. Developers Michael and Judy Corbett intentionally turned conventional community design inside out to favor people rather than cars.

In this popular eighteen-year-old community, houses front on bike paths and open space rather than on streets. Homeowners have cars, but they are parked in the back, with access to narrow, tree-shaded streets. Because cars are forbidden in the inner sanctum of open space at Village Homes, my first impression as I walk through the 70-acre, 270-house community is how quiet everything is. All I hear is birds in fruit trees, kids playing at the day-care center, and the sound of bike tires on wooden bridges that cross creeks and swales designed for natural drainage. The mail carrier is making his rounds on the pathway, a woman is busily at work in the large community garden, and an elderly couple is walking through. According to resident Virginia Thigpen, people from neighboring subdivisions enjoy walking through Village Homes because it's so quiet and lushly landscaped.

Village Homes has been incredibly successful by many different measures, among them, security, value per square foot, and energy and water conservation. The crime rate is only one-tenth that of the surrounding town of Davis. That didn't happen by accident. One of the most important design principles employed by the Corbetts was "eyes on the commons," which means the houses are arranged so residents can easily see what's going on and can protect each other.

Thigpen was the first resident of Village Homes back in 1976. She's watched the community grow from its early, unlandscaped days into maturity as a shady, quiet neighborhood with an "edible landscape." On any day of the year, she tells me, residents can pick fresh fruit—citrus, almonds, apricots, cherries, peaches, pears, persimmons, plums, and other crops. They just have to go to the common area and help themselves. The idea of incorporating horticulture as a central theme in the community was at first overruled by local bureaucrats on the grounds that it would be unsanitary. But the Corbetts overcame this and many other obstacles to their dream with persistent and exhaustive letters to government officials. They found responsive ears in Davis's forward-looking city council, which overturned decisions made in the planning, zoning, and building-code departments.

The Corbetts were equally adamant about de-emphasizing cars. They wanted narrow roads going through their subdivision to prevent vehicles from racing through the neighborhood and keep development costs down. But building codes wouldn't permit the narrow width. Rather than give up, as most developers would, they asked, Why? Officials replied that roads needed to be accessible for two side-by-side fire trucks with their doors open. The Corbett's design solution was innovative: they retained right-of-way on the narrow streets with formal easements, so that in case two firetrucks ever needed to get past each other, they could do it by driving over roadside flower gardens. For their trouble, the developers introduced many benefits to the community besides reduced noise, less crime, and more social contact. The streets, ten to fifteen feet narrower than conventional streets, cost 20 percent less to construct and will save on repaving costs. They are shaded and cooled more easily, lowering ambient temperatures by ten to fifteen degrees and thus lessening dependence on air-conditioning. In place of roads, Village Homes has lavishly landscaped pedestrian and bicycle paths connected to those of Davis. Thigpen recalls, "To create the paths, Michael walked ahead of a tractor dragging his foot and marking the locations." This was one of many unconventional touches that give the community a people-friendly feel, the feel of being designed rather than engineered.

Michael Corbett left architecture school before completing his last year because he "was a radical and always getting into arguments with the faculty over ecological issues and design."[11] This strong sense of mission came in handy in the creation of Village Homes. He visited many lenders before landing capital for the project. The Davis Planning Department, the Davis Public Works Department, and the Federal Housing Administration (FHA) were all very cool on his ideas as well. "FHA's greatest resistance was to agricultural uses in a residential area, narrow streets, and a natural drainage system," recalls Corbett, "but they were also wary of a place that looked different, that integrated housing types, that mixed rentals with houses, and that included on-site commercial enterprises owned by the community."[12]

The architecture in the community is indeed diverse, ranging from neo-Mexican (simple stucco with red-tile roofs) to California modern and even a few earth-sheltered houses. Though relatively modest, these homes carry price tags that reflect their true value. Initially, they cost the same as homes in adjoining neighborhoods, but the success of Village Homes has driven values up to $11 per square foot more than comparable homes nearby. In 1991, it took an average of 133 days to sell a home in Davis, while in Village Homes houses sold in 55 days.

Another design feature that adds value to Village Homes is natural drainage. Typically, water that falls on a subdivision is flushed off-site to avoid flooding. Michael Corbett used aikido engineering to retain storm water on-site. The land on which Village Homes sits was once a tomato field, and the soil was sandy and had excellent drainage. Corbett took advantage of that asset, designing in swales, or surface indentations to capture and hold the rain. During a storm, water flows through property, soaking into the ground rather than being piped away, treated, and returned for irrigation. "Virtually all the rain that falls on these 70 acres stays here to recharge groundwater supplies and irrigate our crops," he says. Thigpen recalls one very rainy winter when Village Homes actually handled excess water that the Davis storm-water system couldn't deal with. With the $800 per household the Corbetts saved by designing natural drainage into Village Homes, they were able to finance the planting of orchards and community garden spaces. These common areas in turn produce supplemental income for some of the residents in the form of flowers, fruit, nuts, and vegetables.

The significance of Village Homes as a model for future design is that it creates a sense of community among people, and between people and their environment. When people are dissatisfied, they tend to neglect their surroundings. When they are satisfied, their surroundings tend to flourish. "You'll come home from work, and there'll be a flag posted on one of the common areas, which means that someone is hosting a pot-luck picnic." Thigpen says, "That evening, a hundred or more adults and children will have a wonderful time eating, playing ball, and just being a community together."[13]

What if every neighborhood had a vacant lot that could be used as a commons? What if slightly higher-density zoning was approved to enable neighborhoods to have such a commons without losing tax-based value? What if we turned our reversible jackets inside out, allowing our houses to face open green space rather than asphalt speedways? What if we began to disassemble those cities and suburbs that are not meeting our needs and reassemble them into something more relevant, and satisfying?

Deep Designing a Cast-Off Airport

Denver's old Stapleton Airport is uniquely positioned to be something far beyond the ordinary. After a citywide referendum approved the construction of a new Denver airport in 1989, a consortium of Colorado businesses and foundations got together to create a nonprofit organization, the Stapleton Redevelopment Foundation, whose purpose is to articulate a vision for the recently vacated airport. The site, seven square miles, is roughly the size of Manhattan. The foundation's "Stapleton Tomorrow" vision is "to be responsive to community needs, future-oriented, resource-sensitive and economically viable." As the foundation's CEO, Tom Gougeon, puts it, "One of our biggest challenges is to get beyond short-term market forces that favor subdividing this huge piece of real estate into warehouses, factories, and suburban sprawl."[14]

In other words, the mission is to create total value by design rather than fragmented value by default—an integrated, sustainable community, not land development that fills in vacant space. The foundation hopes to create 20,000 jobs and attract 30,000 residents. If redevelopment proceeds according to the foundation's vision, more than a third of the property will be parks and open space. A series of urban centers or villages will provide a mix of employment, housing, recreation, services, and access to this open space and to public transportation.

We've already looked at Wal-Mart's Eco-Mart in Lawrence, Kansas, which incorporates "adaptive reuse so that the next generation can use the building as offices or apartments." At Stapleton, the vision is even broader. The intent is to recycle a chunk of regional infrastructure that's been one of the world's busiest airports for sixty-five years. As Gougeon puts it,

We're living off World War II infrastructure now that was designed to meet the goals of that era, but we need new infrastructure that begins with different assumptions. For example, we don't

want isolated, walled communities that make driving inevitable, but rather integrated living/working/recreational communities that make sense socially and environmentally. We don't want huge pipes that channel water off-site, especially in an arid region; we want to think of water as a system, and optimize its use. Whether it falls from the sky or is gray-water effluent from domestic or industrial uses, we want to be able to efficiently use it on-site. We don't want a landscape that paves over nature; we want to live and work and play within nature. We don't want to get so hooked into central utility systems for power, water, and waste that we are unable to use rapidly evolving innovations in the future, but rather we want an infrastructure that's flexible enough to co-evolve with innovation.[15]

Instead of conventional, one-dimensional targets for development, "property sold" and "tax base created," the foundation's targets are jobs per resident population per acre, open space per resident, walking distance to public transportation (ideally, less than a quarter mile), and fewest materials used per service. When the thousand acres of runway are excavated at Stapleton, the plan is to use on-site materials in roads, buildings, and other infrastructure.

How will goals such as conservation of resources be achieved? Gougeon talks about creating self-enforcing mechanisms. For example, to encourage the efficient use of water, water fees should be a little higher than normal and more responsive to daily peaks. By giving residents and industrial occupants better signals about the real value of water, they'll come up with the best innovations to save both water and money, such as low-use plumbing fixtures, on-site water reclamation, and efficient irrigation systems. Gougeon doesn't want to specify particular technologies, he wants to inspire new thinking about how to avoid cost, adverse effects, and unforeseen liability.

Terry Minger of the Center for Resource Management, who has helped with the Stapleton Tomorrow project comments, "When you start with objectives like mixed uses rather than monoculture, you're steering the design process in a completely new direction. At Stapleton, the opportunities are very ripe, because the property is publicly owned and is large enough to stimulate bigger-picture thinking. It's exciting to propose that the old zoning and planning rules be challenged here, and I hope Denver's political leaders will seize this opportunity."[16]

Redevelopment at Stapleton is a dance of opposites. There's a dynamic tension between the potential of using existing infrastructure such as pipes and wiring and creating new infrastructure that favors fiber optics, natural drainage, and decentralized energy technologies such as photovoltaics. While people like Tom Gougeon build conceptual Noah's arks designed to get us through inevitable changes, too many developers still cling to the familiarity and convenience of the speedboat. The question is, Can the speedboat survive the flood of problems we're going to have if we stick with the status quo?

Flowing in the Right Direction: The Deep Design of Wastewater Treatment

In converting communities into integrated social ecosystems, we have to create closed loops for the material and energy that move through them. One critical flow is water, the sleeping giant of environmental crises. We should be handling water as a single-cycle system, capable of purification if properly designed. Our current way of dealing with wastewater devalues a precious resource by diverting it to major waterways. We spend billions on concrete, excavation, chemicals, mechanical equipment, and energy to channel a vital resource away from our communities, creating mountains of toxic sludge that we pay taxes to dispose of. We fail to value the nutrients and the water that transports them as vital pieces of our cultural/ecological jigsaw puzzle.

Susan Peterson of Ecological Engineering Associates in Massachusetts is trying to market an alternative pathway to "the Big Pipe." With her colleague, ecologist John Todd, she envisions greenhouses filled with flowers rather than rivers filled with ammonia, chlorine residuals, and sludgeworms. The current system, she says, directs water to only one place, and that place is the wrong place. Wastewater should be treated locally so that it can be recycled in the community. The water can go back into the ground close to where it originated, the nutrients can be used for growing plants, and the solids can be used as fertilizer. Leaking sewage pipes are just one symptom that the Big Pipe has to go: "People are often surprised to discover that most sewage pipes leak in the opposite direction than they fear. They leak in, sometimes doubling the flow to treatment plants. Instead of overloading the treatment plant, forcing operators to flush it into our rivers, storm water should flow or be pumped to swales, bogs, fens, deciduous or subtropical swamps, grassy wetlands and dells, where it can be filtered and treated by soils, roots, stems and leaves and their associated microorganisms."[17]

In an era of increasing water scarcity, our whole design orientation is backwards. Treatment plants are engineered to serve high-volume, low-wasteload flow when they should be designed to handle low-volume, high-wasteload flow. Rather than retaining waste long enough to let microbes work effectively, plants resort instead to energy-intensive aeration and chemical techniques.

Peterson explains how we became locked into the current technology: "The large systems were built because the federal government, attacking symptoms rather than root causes, paid for 90 percent of the design, engineering, collection pipes, treatment plants, and discharge pipes for decentralized systems." Peterson is aware that economic inertia keeps communities on this conventional pathway. Her company offers an alternative, "living machines." These waste-treating greenhouse ecosystems represent design at its deepest level. Because they don't consume a lot of energy or chemicals, and don't require a costly infrastructure, treatment is more efficient and less expensive overall. Peterson and her colleague John Todd, who developed the technology in the late 1970s, refer to it as solar aquatics.

Todd adapted the solar aquatic concept from a village in Indonesia where animal and human waste drain through a series of ponds to raise fish. Functioning like one of nature's most prolific designs, the marsh or wetland, solar aquatics converts nutrients into plants, fish, mollusks and other species with a small amount of residual sludge. A guiding principle is diversity. A living machine has enough natural variety and resilience to be able to deal with any pollutant stream, including those that contain toxins such as heavy metals. Instead of reacting generically to the challenge of wastewater treatment, solar aquatics asks, What does this particular waste stream need to become fresh water again? Todd considers which plant species are best suited for the job, their growth rate, inflow/outflow volume, bed gradient, and many other variables, and tunes up the system.

Solar Aquatics at Jim Davis's PAWS

The cartoon character Garfield has become an institution, and so has his creator's home and office. Jim Davis lives north of Muncie, Indiana, in the middle of cornfields that are seven feet tall in late August when I visit the PAWS, Inc., solar-aquatic facility. Located not far from the main building where the Davis family lives and fifty or so employees work, the greenhouse facility looks from the outside like a typical farm nursery. But I wouldn't have traveled a thousand miles if it were. My mission is to see firsthand how one of John Todd's prototypes is performing.

The PAWS facility is essentially a greenhouse holding six 700-gallon fiberglass tanks, a basin that simulates a lagoon, and a soil-filled planting area that simulates a marsh. Carefully chosen species, from bacteria and duckweed to fish and roses, inhabit each part of the facility, converting the PAWS waste stream to 99 percent clean water as it flows through the system. Russ Vernon, the horticulturalist who runs the plant, explains to me how the innovative treatment system came into being:

> I overheard Jim Davis and his business manager talking about the hassles of getting a septic installed to treat a 1,500 gallon-a-day flow. A neighbor had given me a Harrowsmith magazine that had an article on birds, and it also happened to have an article about John Todd's solar aquatic designs. So I quietly slipped the magazine onto Jim's desk, opened to the wastewater article. Within a week or so, he had invited John Todd to come visit PAWS. We worked with Todd's Ocean Arks Institute and Michael Ogden's Southwest Wetlands Group to size the facility, consult with the state, and put together an equipment list.
>
> The Indiana Department of Environmental Management had a few concerns at first, but luckily, there are some young people in that office who were receptive to new ideas. They also knew that Jim had money and could replace or upgrade the system if it didn't perform right. So PAWS became the first permitted plant of its type in the country, and you can bet they were watching the system's performance."[18]

There are many small communities in Indiana that discharge their waste into a field-tile system because they can't afford a conventional plant. Federal dollars have dried up for treatment plants, leaving states and municipalities to fund their own systems. Consequently, there is ample opportunity in Indiana—and elsewhere in the country—for solar aquatics to gain a foothold. Vernon estimates that a plant the size of PAWS's costs only three-fifths as much as a similarly sized conventional plant to build, and about two-fifths as much to operate. One of the things Vernon is proudest of is helping stimulate the Indiana Department of Environmental Management to publish a set of guidelines for alternative wastewater systems.

Vernon personally keeps track of his system's dissolved oxygen and pH levels, which are consistently better than the standards. He hires a "circuit rider" to do monthly analyses of other indicators, biochemical oxygen demand, suspended solids, and ammonia. Pointing proudly to an extensive collection of monthly graphs, he says, "Even in January, our coldest month, the system achieved about a 98-percent removal efficiency on each of the three indicators." These are pretty high grades for a technology that's still on the learning curve. If it continues to prove successful, with a little more operating experience, solar aquatics will begin to find niches in communities that have reached their maximum flow capacities in existing plants. "Towns that have heard of this kind of alternative will start building them for a new subdivision, office park, or industrial park," Vernon predicts.

Cost and improved treatment aren't the only advantages of facilities like the one at PAWS. Aesthetics is an added benefit.

The PAWS facility is rich with the fragrance of roses and angel trumpets. Because most of Indiana's native plants go dormant in the winter, Vernon looked around for tropical plants that would bloom year-round. In addition to roses and angel trumpets, he's got elephant ear, wild aster, hibiscus, caladium, variegated orchard grass, wild iris, smartweed, and other species growing in the marsh. Together, they "polish" the water before it's discharged in purified form into the field tile system.

Upstream from the small wetlands/marsh is a lagoon that's 4 feet wide, 20 feet long, and 2.5 feet deep. The lagoon holds 5,000 gallons of water and has subsurface irrigation hose through which air is pumped. Vernon reaches into the water and pulls a snail off the wall. "I used native snails I found in local ponds," he tells me, "and the bluegill fish we stocked in the tanks love to eat them." The lagoon and the six fiberglass tanks also contain populations of koi, goldfish, mosquito fish, and algae eaters. But the system's real

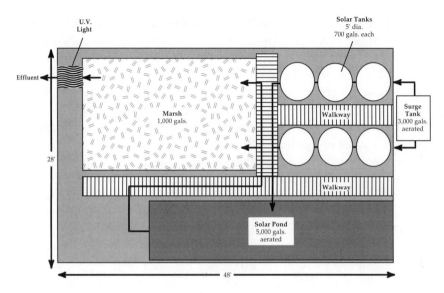

Figure 12

PAWS, Inc.'s solar-aquatics sewage treatment facility in Muncie, Indiana.

workhorse species are water hyacinths and duckweed growing in the fiberglass tanks. In the summer, when the system is most prolific, Vernon harvests hyacinth foliage for compost every two weeks. In the winter, when the sun is low in the sky and productivity declines, he harvests the leaves every month and a half.

Vernon needed no extraordinary training to operate the plant. A horticulturist with a straightforward wastewater certification, he believes that the facility could be run by any observant operator. About the only ingredients he adds are a little baking soda to adjust the pH, about half a cup a day, and an occasional sprinkling of grease-eating and nitrifying bacteria to recharge the system. Most of the solid waste decomposes on plant roots colonized by bacteria. Slight electrical charges on the root hairs attract opposing charges of suspended solids, binding the pollutant particles to them. "There's really not much sludge left over after the ecosystem has used it. It's really just dark water, but I don't want to overload the marsh system, so we pull it off for irrigation water."

Vernon and I walk up to a large garden of vegetables and flowers, next to which is a huge compost pile. "You've seen the whole cycle now," he says. "These are the final products, and I guess it's fitting that many of these vegetables, fruits, and flowers go back into the same building their nutrients originally came from."[19] We cross the road to the PAWS building so I can get Jim Davis's autograph for my kids. Davis tells me about some of the other projects happening at PAWS, such as wetlands recreation and the restoration of farm fields to woodland. Davis and Vernon are not engineers by trade, but their conviction about nature's capabilities and needs is a model for conventional engineers and designers.

Toward a New Community Norm

In fifty years, we could be living in lush green communities where social and environmental needs are met simultaneously, by design. Is this a pipe dream? No. Alternative energy and manufacturing, resource-recycling systems like solar aquatics and neighborhood composting could be commonplace by then. By asking the simple question, What do we really need? we will have discarded many of our misguided assumptions and the designed infrastructure that shadows them. A new community norm based on deep design criteria will be established.

One illustration of community deep design is called cohousing, in which residents play an active role designing their own neighborhoods and homes. Typically, facilities such as a community dining area, gardens, and workshops are designed into the community to enhance social interaction. Cars do not dominate, and the community becomes a pedestrian village. I'm currently involved in the design of such a community in Golden, Colorado. One of the village's best features is that people will be able to walk to stores and restaurants and, without battling cars, bike to stretches of publicly owned open space.

Our community is a deep design because it began with the question, What exactly do we want? We knew we wanted to create a friendly neighborhood, and we agreed that the three items of highest priority were quality construction, energy efficiency, and affordability. After putting together the site plan based on the most popular (and affordable) features, we began to outline what we each wanted for our homes. Four months away from beginning construction, we're anticipating that the common effort that has gone into it will result in a community that satisfies many needs.

The Greening of Harlem

In Harlem, New York, another group of residents is at work on the redesign of an existing community. Bernadette Kosar, an employee with the City of New York Parks and Recreation Department, targets both social and environmental needs in her thriving Greening of Harlem project. Kosar used to be a gardener for one of the parks:

> *I had a group of teenagers following me around. I don't think they ever saw a woman pushing a garden cart with a rake and a hoe and loppers, and . . . being raised the way I was, I decided that they couldn't just watch me work, they had to help me work. So I gave them tools, and to my ever-loving surprise they were quite good at it and they kept coming back day after day. I found the funding and got them hired on to help me work in the park, and then I realized that if they could do the work, they could do it in parks and vacant lots in their own neighborhoods, and that's how Greening of Harlem got started.*[20]

Five years later, the group has reclaimed a handful of major parks, including the historic Marcus Garvey Park, and constructed about twenty neighborhood gardens. The project has attracted the participation of the elderly as well as the children, schools, hospitals, and energetic nonprofit groups all over the community. With the momentum of the project riding a crest, she continues to ask the right questions: "Why can't we take the vacant lots that we're turning into gardens and playgrounds and make them a source of jobs as well? I can see us growing everything from food to herbs, everything from dyes to potpourris and tomato preserves."

Kosar's vision gives meaning and purpose to all generations in Harlem. She believes that nature and people are one. "Nature doesn't make people wild, it doesn't make people uncivilized, but I think concrete, asphalt, and steel does. It makes people hard, it makes people cold, it makes people inhuman. We have to figure a way to bring nature back to our cities," she says.

These are more than the experiments of a handful of sentimental visionaries. They are the first bold steps down a pathway that leads to a new kind of community.

Chapter 7

Design Criteria That Work

How Should We Think about Design?

There are two distinct phases on the pathway to deep design. Phase I is about improving the quality and performance of our current designs so they deliver more service per resource unit and per "unit of stress." Each car should use the least possible amount of gasoline per vehicle mile traveled; each consumer product should emit the lowest possible level of given toxins; each board-foot of lumber should be precisely sawed to minimize waste; and each industrial process should generate the least possible amount of hazardous waste. In Phase II, things begin to look and feel radically different. For example, Phase II agriculture is less reliant on hazardous chemicals to control pests and more attuned to natural cycles. Basic needs are met more directly in Phase II. For example, communities meet social needs by offering more options and reducing the need for travel as well as the compulsion to consume.

But how do we get ourselves on the pathway to Phase II? With what criteria should we set our course? That's what this chapter is about—how to get started down the right pathway. The conception and development of Wal-Mart's experimental store Eco-Mart in Lawrence, Kansas, is presented here as an illustration. While Eco-Mart incorporates aspects of Phase II design such as sustainable forestry, it is still very much a Phase I effort that makes incremental changes in conventional design. Nevertheless, the Eco-Mart effort may have huge implications for the way America thinks about the environment. In terms of overall results, pushing a commercial monolith like Wal-Mart even an inch may be as productive as moving a hundred smaller ventures a mile. The importance of Eco-Mart is that it helps teach us how to think about and move toward deep design. Additionally, en route to Phase II, Eco-Mart helps institutionalize Phase I, making recycling and green consumer products a little more acceptable to America's mainstream.

In my research for this chapter, I kept being reminded of the negative impact Wal-Mart had on the economies of hundreds of small towns. Wal-Mart stores promote urban sprawl, and their buying power effectively shuts down the stores that used to line the Main Streets of America. While such criticism is relevant to the concerns of deep design, it overlooks the benefits of getting started on the path to Phase II. And it overlooks the possibility of redirecting the momentum of the huge Wal-Mart enterprise. Though not perfect, Eco-Mart is a good beginning.

Criticism of the Eco-Mart concept is reminiscent of comments made concerning the partnership formed between McDonald's and the Environmental Defense Fund to study the environmental implications of McDonald's packaging such as the styrofoam clamshell. Some environmentalists criticized the effort because it was a compromise struck within the corporate structure. The purists seemed to overlook the ground-breaking implications of this partnership, which sparked a lot of innovative thought about life cycles. To get McDonald's thinking about such matters was to budge a very large boulder indeed.

Nothing comes from nothing. We need to proceed from where we are. Phase I design efforts such as McDonald's and Eco-Mart blaze the trail for more comprehensive designs in the future.

Deep-Design Criteria: Where the Pathways Begin

In 1990, Terry Minger and Meredith Miller of the Center for Resource Management (CRM) in Denver proposed the idea to Wal-Mart's environmental board of building a prototype "environmentally conscious" store. The board, founded in 1989 by Sam Walton and chaired until 1992 by Hillary Rodham Clinton, unanimously endorsed the idea. Soon it became CRM's "mission impossible" to implement an exciting but still fuzzy concept.

Minger recalls, "The environmental committee had been very active and gotten some tangible results. But it became obvious to us that activities like nationwide recycling and waste audits at Wal-Mart headquarters were only part of it. If they wanted to really make a difference they had to change the way the store itself was put together. They had to take a hard look at the materials and design of the retail building as well as the products that flowed through it."[1] The company motto, The Best Possible Product at the Best Possible Price, needed to become The Best Possible Store at the Best Possible Price. Adhering to the highly successful Wal-Mart formula, how could the board move one step closer to a sustainable retail operation? Wal-Mart was opening three stores every week. Wal-Mart management wanted to see which environmental innovations were winners, and then educate their customers with in-store learning materials that told the story of Eco-Mart's design. And more than the building's design would be environmentally friendly; management also wanted the store to market green products.

As the idea evolved, the advisory board began to regard their prototype store as a discrete part of the Wal-Mart enterprise, an educational tool. The board knew that energy efficiency was a good investment, and they suspected that from a marketing perspective, a green image would also translate into profits. "In 1989," explained Wal-Mart president Bill Fields, the chain began "receiving letters and requests from our customers indicating environmental concerns and asking us to take action. The Eco-Mart concept gave us an opportunity to work with our vendors to produce environmentally improved products; to act as environmental educators; to create new markets for recycled goods, and be a good neighbor in the communities."[2] The educational benefits of a store where millions of people would shop every day intrigued Meredith Miller:

We realized that if we could envision, design, and construct a new kind of store, we could help change the way we Americans think about the environment. The Wal-Mart store could become a model for others to follow, reported in both technical and mainstream media.

The leverage that Wal-Mart can exert on both its customers and its suppliers is staggering. For example, if Wal-Mart requests green products from their vendors, they'll get them. Really, it's models like these that move the whole society toward a new environmental norm.[3]

The first hurdle the design team faced was the question, What does green mean? Progressive? Functional? Sensitive? Attractive? Exciting? Natural? The team began to assemble the environmental and social criteria for developing what would later be known as Eco-Mart. Many of the concepts that emerged were deep-design criteria that could be applied just as easily to the design of a package or an appliance. The board began with big-picture concepts such as ecological wisdom, respect for diversity, and selection of appropriate technologies. They then compiled a slightly more specific list of criteria that related to the construction and operation of a building.

DESIGN CONCEPTS

- *Ecological Wisdom* Live within the ecological and resource limits of the planet. Apply technological knowledge to the challenge of an energy-efficient economy. Build a better relationship between urban and rural America. Guarantee the rights of non-human species. Promote and respect self-regulating natural systems.
- *Respect for Diversity* Honor cultural, ethnic, racial, sexual, religious, and spiritual diversity of all beings within the context of individual responsibility. Respect and maintain biodiversity, or a diversity of living species.
- *Global Responsibility* Maintain awareness of the impacts of our actions on global, ecological, economic, and social systems.
- *Focus on the Future* Help institutions and individuals think in terms of the long-range future, not just short-term selfish interests. Make quality of life, rather than merely open-ended economic growth, the focus of future thinking.
- *Inter-relatedness, Interdependence, and Natural Process* Learn these lessons from the ecosystems we are a part of.
- *Soft-Energy Production Alternatives* Work with the cycles of the sun, water, wind, and geothermal energy rather than depleting finite resources that can be more effectively used elsewhere.
- *Select Appropriate Technologies, Regenerative Agriculture, and Minimal-Impact Waste Strategies for Radiation By-products and Unrecy-*

clable Wastes Use the right tool for the right job. Less waste means less cleanup, less conflict, and fewer costs.

- *Trace the Origins and Future Destination of Each Store Component/System* Don't let actions taken in the present leave a gaping hole in the future.
- *Incorporate Biology and Physics into Designs*

DESIGN CRITERIA

- Use design solutions that accomplish three or four things at once. For example, plants conserve water, reduce erosion, soak up greenhouse-forming carbon dioxide, and have a cooling effect on urban landscape all at the same time.
- Account for costs with the full lifetime of the product in mind. What environmental costs are not accounted for, we'll pay for in taxes, poor health, or a deteriorating quality of life.
- Design for the future. Think about future use, reuse, or disposal requirements of a given material when designing it. In the area of disposal, design for natural processes like decomposition and nutrient cycles.
- When designing, think about whether the user will be able to understand the result, maintain it, and feel satisfied with it.
- Design to increase, rather than limit, people's options.
- Design to enhance users' self-reliance and self-worth, rather than creating dependency and insecurity.
- Design to take maximum advantage of existing infrastructure and recyclable resources.
- Design to enhance creative thinking.
- Design to accommodate household hazardous-waste products.
- Design to allow point-of-sale recovery of packaging materials.
- Design with consideration for the specific site—existing ecosystems, location relative to transportation systems, proximity to community environmental infrastructure, etc.
- Design to enhance the educational possibilities of the store.
- Design using systems and materials that are flexible enough to accommodate improvements and retrofits.
- Design to avoid groundwater and surface contamination.
- Minimize the use of off-site electrical energy for heating and cooling, with efficient design, load reduction, and on-site production of energy.

- Reduce "embodied energy" costs, or life-cycle costs of materials and systems, including extraction, manufacturing, shipping, and disposal costs.
- Compensate for negative impacts created by the store by developing off-setting positive systems.
- Limit painted surfaces as well as surfaces requiring adhesives, carpet, or solvent-based maintenance with floor wax, polish, cleaners, etc.
- Minimize construction waste by finding recycling markets.
- Develop vendor partnerships to ensure the ecological manufacture/supply of packaging, building materials, and store merchandise.
- Increase daylighting systems and reduce electrical lighting requirements.
- Minimize transportation-associated energy use and pollution (both customer and operations).
- Reduce impervious surfaces that also retain heat. Reuse heat where possible, and use alternative surfaces for parking, roof surfaces, etc.
- Landscape using native species, xeriscaping, and low-maintenance species.
- Create opportunities for energy savings through passive design such as building volume, geometry, footprint, etc.

The Design Team Gets Under Way

Soon the advisory board began to zero in on what Eco-Mart should be. They agreed that the new store should serve as a model for future Wal-Marts, and that the environmentally friendly characteristics of the store should be highly visible. At the same time, the store had to be familiar looking and unintimidating to Wal-Mart customers. Wal-Mart president Bill Fields wanted to send the message that these customers could have the same services but delivered in a way that met the needs of a mutual customer—the environment. The project, moreover, had to be cost effective as well as designed and operational within a year.

Specifically, the board defined their goals for the store as low energy use, minimal waste production, sustainable development, and recycling. These would be met by employing recycled building materials, energy-efficient architectural design, low-input land-scaping, and integrated solid-waste management.

The interdisciplinary team that CRM and BSW, Wal-Mart's primary architectural firm, pulled together for the initial phase of design included several consultants whose environmentally conscious approaches to design are internationally known: Amory Lovins, physicist and systems designer; William McDonough, architect and eco-philosopher; and Hal Levin, building ecologist. Although these three experts were not able to attend all the design sessions, their influence was felt throughout the process. Because they are holistic thinkers, the design focused inevitably on the notion of designing a society.

In its first design "charettes" (brainstorm sessions), the team immediately raised the question, What will the store be when its Wal-Mart lifetime is over? Typically, a Wal-Mart store is either replaced or expanded within eight years. Why not design it for "adaptive reuse"—in McDonough's words—and avoid the unsustainable practice of disposable architecture? It was decided that the wall's concrete blocks, for example, would be spaced in a way that would allow the installation of windows later on. Ceiling height would permit the subsequent addition of a second story. The building might one day be converted to apartments. The entire life cycle of the building was considered, from origins to end uses. If concrete block was to be used, where would the gravel come from? Wal-Mart wouldn't want headlines to read, "Wal-Mart Destroys Fish Creek to Mine Gravel for 'Green Store.'"

In an early design session, McDonough suggested that the group carefully examine the life cycles of all materials and products used in the store. He cited aluminum as an example of how conventional materials may have more of an impact than is commonly perceived. "If somebody asks if aluminum is a good or bad building material, the answer has to be, 'It depends.' Does it come from bauxite mined in a Jamaican rainforest? Is coal used to power the smelting process? If so, is it a high-sulfur coal that was shipped all the way across the continent, creating pollution in several different ways? The energy requirements for making this kind of aluminum are significantly more than for recycled aluminum originally made in Canada using hydropower—they're two entirely different materials in terms of environmental impact."[4]

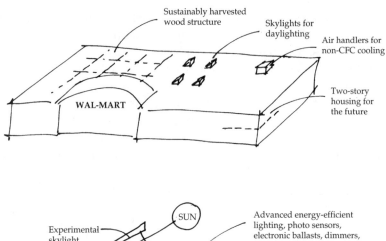

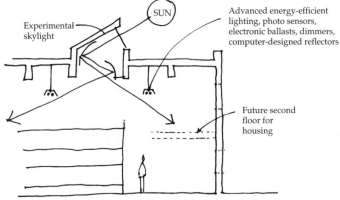

Figure 13

Sketches of the Eco-Mart by William McDonough illustrate the major environmental advances incorporated in the store's design. They include a roof made with sustainably harvested domestic timber; an HVAC system that operates without the use of CFCs; and a building that is designed to be easily converted to housing.

SOURCE: *Interiors*, MARCH 1993.

Designers like McDonough go out of their way to specify "made from recycled materials" partly because of the inherent energy benefits: it takes about 6 percent as much energy to produce aluminum from scrap as it does to make it from ore.

This concept of "embodied energy" was at the center of the design team's decision to recommend wood rather than steel in the store's huge roof. They balanced many variables to reach that decision, including the amount of energy that goes *into* each type of material in its manufacture. A steel and glass building might use 300,000 Btus per square foot, while a concrete block building might provide the same structure for 200,000 Btus per square foot. That difference would mean that the equivalent of 10,000 fewer barrels of oil were used to construct the concrete building.

CHOOSING THE RIGHT MATERIAL

- Choose materials/systems that help create markets for recycled products.
- Choose materials/systems purchased, manufactured, or processed locally.
- Choose materials that are durable and appropriate for recycling/reuse.
- Minimize solvent-based architectural coatings.
- Minimize formaldehyde-producing pressed wood products.
- Seek sustainably harvested wood.
- Try to limit the number of different materials in a single product.
- Pursue the lowest possible weight in materials.
- Try to avoid using scarce materials.
- Try to avoid using composite materials, complex alloys, or laminates.
- Use materials that don't require excessive maintenance.

Although many of Wal-Mart's California stores have wooden roofs, because it is a least-cost, locally available material, standard practice in stores throughout the country is to use steel. When the group was deciding which material to use for roof decking, they had to take the Kansas snow load into consideration as well as the availability of materials. Wood still emerged as the preferred material. The decision was also partly based on the principle that the lowest-energy pathway should be chosen if it was comparable in cost and performance. The design team planned to convey this and other such messages in several different ways: with a special in-store learning center for the children, with active community outreach by a green coordinator, or environmental liaison, and through the media.

Once the decision for wood had been made, based on economics, thermodynamics (embodied energy), and educational value, team members proposed an innovative notion: that the lumber specified for the project be certified "sustainably harvested."

In Search of Sustainable Forestry

Within recent history, more than a third of the earth's forest cover has been removed to make room for crops, pasture, and cities. People have regarded timber as something that has more value dead than alive: something that should be either destroyed or diced up and sold. The fact is, wood is advantageous both dead and alive, a point the Eco-Mart design team was eager to make. Not only were the beams in the store useful for support, they also once helped sustain habitat in Oregon and Virginia. They were part of living systems that absorbed and stored carbon dioxide, prevented erosion, and provided shade. Their value stretched back to a time before Eco-Mart customers were even born.

Every year, new Wal-Mart stores demand twenty square miles of forest. The design team saw an opportunity here to support sustainable forestry. They approached a company called the Forest Partnership, which searched the entire country to find opportunities to harvest and certify "good wood" for the Eco-Mart project. The company discovered that the Virginia estates of Presidents Zachary Taylor and James Madison both needed careful thinning. A third tract near Eugene, Oregon, was also a prime candidate for certification. According to the company's founder, Richard Miller, "All harvests had to conform to the Forest's Partnership's guidelines, which reduce or eliminate the following: clearcutting, high-grading [removing the best trees], cutting old-growth timber, conversion of forests to plantations, use of pesticides and herbicides, and other techniques that negatively affect the soil, water, and wildlife."[5] In part, the message behind Eco-Mart's sustainably harvested beams is that environmental damage has been prevented by design.

It is also notable that fewer trees were used to provide the same or better service. When the Eco-Mart design team opted for innovative I-joists (from Trus Joist Macmillan) in the ceiling rather than conventional glue-laminated beams, they saved 30 percent of the overall wood stock required for the 122,000-square-foot store. Glue-laminated beams often require long, continuous slabs, which tend to come from old-growth forests. By choosing I-joists, the team was doing its part to preserve endangered old-growth ecosystems.[6]

Another innovation the Eco-Mart project helped nurture is a designer data base, the Forest Resource Information System (FORIS). An outgrowth of the "certified sustainable" industry, this tool will help architects, interior designers, furniture makers, industrial designers, and others use the right wood for the right reasons. The data base is an electronic encyclopedia of wood that includes scientific, aesthetic, and engineering information. According to Berne Broudy, FORIS project coordinator, "Wood users are often reluctant to use alternative tree species because of a lack of information about their properties and characteristics. Although there are about 90,000 different species of timber in the world, only 3,000 are used commercially."[7] She added that ignorance results in many species being unsought and undervalued, while commonly known species are becoming depleted.

Rather than pursuing the single goal of high immediate yield, sustainable forestry balances multiple goals. Instead of withdrawing from the public bank account, the sustainable forester is making a deposit. Sustainable forestry is a good analogy for where our whole culture needs to be going. As a discipline, it asks, What do we want? What do we value? The answers go beyond profit and hardwood floors to include vigorous ecosystems with abundant wildlife and clean rivers, a stable climate, and the precise wood for the job.

The Ecology of Design

Energy can be saved and comfort enhanced by integrating high-performance technologies in a system. The best building design is an orchestrated symphony, not a dissonance of clashing solos. This became clear at an early Eco-Mart session that took place at the Rocky Mountain Institute (RMI) in Snowmass, Colorado.

RMI's director of research, Amory Lovins, gave the Eco-Mart design team a tour of RMI. High-efficiency lighting, a solar atrium, high-performance glazings, thermal mass, and insulation are integrated to provide comfort (and bananas) at an altitude of 7,000 feet, where in winter temperatures can drop to –47°F. Steve Brown of BSW, was impressed. "We had a chance to see what natural daylighting and 'superwindows' could do in combination. Some of the products Amory was referring to were not even on the market yet, but his thinking about what buildings can be forced us to stretch our own thinking."[8]

RMI is a model of integrated systems. Fifty tons of oak beams and 40-centimeter stone-and-foam walls provide mass to store the solar energy that streams through the atrium into the "jungle." Even in 0° weather, the 4,000-square-foot building requires no heating system—or rather, the building is the heating system. RMI is so efficient that it produces rather than consumes heat energy, the equivalent of one barrel of oil a day. At the Eco-Mart meeting hosted by RMI, the design team sat next to an indoor waterfall. As sunlight streamed into the building and the waterfall trickled in the background, Lovins introduced his design approach, "elimination parametrics:"

> *You begin with people and work out. You ask yourself, What are they going to be doing? You then proceed to provide their needs as efficiently and elegantly as possible. You look at lowering the wattage per square foot while still supplying optimum light levels, lowering the "plug load" by making things like computers and appliances more efficient, upgrading motor systems to operate more effectively, and so on. All this lowers the internal heat gain. You also look at external heat gain—at features like superwindows, shading, landscaping, and lot reflectivity. The fact is, people want qualities like coolness and lack of glare—they really don't care if some high-tech/high-maintenance device supplies them or not.*
>
> *For example, if given the choice, they'd opt for light that contains the full spectrum of wavelengths, like natural sunlight. And it so happens that the new windows, operating with electronic dimmers, can provide that natural lighting while radically cutting back the electricity bill.[9]*

The fact that glazing can be "tuned" for specific applications means that designers can make the most of natural light without having energy-guzzling air conditioners work overtime. Additionally, the high-efficiency lights that are rapidly becoming the norm emit far less heat, pushing dinosaur HVAC (heating/ventilation/air-conditioning) systems closer to extinction. Making them much smaller or eliminating them altogether would fulfill one of Lovins's primary challenges: to identify and install technologies that "cost the same or less, yet work the same or better." [10] Although high-tech windows would at first glance seem prohibitively expensive, they are in fact a great bargain when whole-systems costs are considered, because they permit the downsizing of HVAC systems. Good design can supply elegantly what even highly automated technology supplies rather primitively. RMI saved more by eliminating the need for a furnace and ductwork than it paid extra for superwindows, superinsulation, and heat exchangers. When engineering rules of thumb are challenged and mechanical equipment is downsized, benefits such as the following cascade throughout the system:

- More usable space (the space next to fan rooms and chillers is now very quiet);
- Less metal and labor (using small, round ducts instead of large, rectangular ones);
- Savings of $80 a square foot on the skin of the building (plenum height reduced by 6 to 8 inches because of smaller ductwork);
- Less structure to hold up;
- Less electricity to supply, therefore fewer wires; and
- Less complicated and expensive control systems.

As Lovins made clear to the group, relying on standard practices can only result in standard flaws. He challenged them to move beyond conventional thinking: "We can't do it by the book, because we're all writing the book."[11]

Comfort Here Without Pollution There

As the design began to take shape, the team decided exactly what kind of HVAC equipment they wanted to specify for Eco-Mart: a highly efficient unit sized to meet the exact needs of the store, without any CFCs. There weren't any CFC-free units available. So they decided to have one custom-made but they couldn't get it.

At a 1930 meeting of the American Chemical Society, Dr. Thomas Midgely inhaled a beakerful of CFC gas and then extinguished a candle by exhaling the gas, demonstrating that the new creation was not only nontoxic but also nonflammable. The compound, commonly known as Freon, seemed like the perfect designer chemical. Soon it revolutionized the technology of refrigeration and air conditioning. Over forty years later, in 1972, several scientists wanted to exploit the chemical stability of CFCs to trace global wind patterns. When they researched the life cycle of CFCs, they discovered the compound is so stable that many molecules of it eventually reach the stratosphere, where solar energy causes the chlorine atoms to break free. In turn, chlorine atoms pull apart adjacent ozone molecules, puncturing holes in the ozone layer, which shields life on earth from ultraviolet radiation.[12] (One of the scientists was asked how the wind-pattern project was going. He replied, "The work is going very well, but we could be looking at the end of life on earth.")[13]

Although CFCs are being phased out, a perfect alternative has not yet emerged. The Eco-Mart designers looked at various alternatives and ranked them according to their "ozone-depletion potential." In the end, they chose R134a, which still emits CFC but is the best alternative around. The substitute will reduce Eco-Mart's responsibility for ozone-layer destruction. Meanwhile, the HVAC system is designed to substitute a superior replacement compound when it becomes available.

The Eco-Mart team kept coming back to a basic ground rule: to design an integrated building, they could not look at any components in isolation. As they focused on the design requirements for the HVAC system, the team spelled out goals in addition to the elimination of CFCs:

- Reducing carbon-dioxide emissions;
- Meeting or exceeding nonregulatory standards (ASHRAE) for indoor air quality;
- Achieving energy efficiency;
- Providing comfort; and
- Experimenting with ice storage to permit the use of off-peak electricity.

They agreed that preference should be given when possible to locally available materials. This made the cellulose insulation they specified even more attractive, because it came from Lawrence, Kansas, where it was manufactured from recycled newsprint. The design team calculated that a ceiling insulation standard of R-30 was necessary to balance the building's various features, including an array of high-tech skylights and the advanced air-conditioning unit.

The issue of insulation represented a web of possibilities: How to provide R-30 in order to minimize heat loss/gain, in turn helping downsize the HVAC system and optimizing lighting coming through the skylights, in turn minimizing the need for electric lighting, in turn reducing the need for heat (because lights give off heat) and insulation?

Early on, the decision was made to meet the newest and most stringent standards for air-exchange rate (ASHRAE). The design challenge was how to supply 30,000 cubic feet per minute of air economically and effectively, so that air would neither be stagnant nor blow forcibly on customers. The designers opted for thermal storage, in which ice would be made during inexpensive, off-peak hours to cool the store the next day. This meant that they would be working with lower supply-air temperatures than typical systems have. On hot, muggy days in the middle of summer, when relative humidity in Lawrence was 60 percent or higher, the huge ice cube would supply 37° of coolness. The team knew that there is an inverse relationship between coolness and humidity: cooler air is dryer. They couldn't just use a regular diffuser to deliver cold air, because if the air wasn't mixed right it would fall to the floor "like a waterfall," commented Gary Rose, an engineer who worked on the customized design. "We opted for a special slotted diffuser that enabled us to use the cold air from the ice-storage unit and still get a good air mix."[14]

The system as installed was state of the art, customized by Engineered Air Company of Salt Lake City. But in buildings as in nature, unforeseen events can sometimes disrupt the whole system. A forest ecosystem, designed for a certain range of temperature, certain soil conditions, even an occasional fire, would have trouble withstanding the impact from a meteorite or a zealous bulldozer. The events that occurred following the opening of Eco-Mart were not that radical, but they did test the flexibility of the HVAC system.

There were record hot temperatures in Lawrence during the summer of the store's opening year. Moreover, Wal-Mart invited McDonald's to set up shop inside. This added heat to the store that the mechanical engineers hadn't anticipated. More heat came from the lighting system, which was remaining on longer than expected. It took a while to get the high-efficiency fluorescent lights, designed to dim automatically as natural light from the skylights increased, synchronized. And then there was the fact that the store was popular right from the start—an engineering problem because customers flocked in, opening more doors and letting in more heat than anticipated. Store operating hours were extended, which decreased the amount of time available to make the ice to cool the building the next day.

Like an ecosystem, the store had to adjust. "If we'd had just one or two changes, the system could have handled it," engineer Art Shelton pointed out.[15] "But it was necessary to add capacity with all the converging factors." After these adjustments, the system began to perform the way the engineers hoped. In addition to achieving the right temperature and air flow, Shelton knew they'd been successful because the building felt right.

Pushing the Spec Boundaries

Eco-Mart's designers wanted the store to blend into its surroundings, both natural and social. The Lawrence office of Landplan Engineering, familiar with the site, was given the opportunity to integrate the parking lot, signs, and landscaping into the overall plan.

Landplan was told by Wal-Mart that the store needed to face Main Street, have direct contact with Iowa Street, and be recognizable as part of the Wal-Mart chain. The company was still able to introduce several key innovations, including the incorporation of 15 percent more recycled asphalt content than had ever been used in a parking lot—50 percent in all. The material had to be specially tested before county and state officials would approve it. The asphalt, recycled from local highway and street projects, also contained waste fly ash from a Topeka power plant. Recycled materials were likewise incorporated in parking lot signs and picnic tables. The project required so much recycled plastic that several companies' inventories were depleted. There was a bowling alley on the site of the new store, and much of that building was recycled as well: the maple floor was used in a bowling alley elsewhere, and the big steel trusses and wood from walls and ceiling were recycled in construction projects, most of them local.

Another innovation the Eco-Mart team availed itself of was "gray water," or wastewater from fixtures other than toilets. At first, Douglas County Health Department and the Kansas Department of Health and Environment were adamantly opposed. There was a "nuisance" stipulation in local codes that said that plumbing installations could not smell, and officials cited this regulation. But Landplan was persistent. In an exhaustive series of meetings, they presented officials with documentation on similar systems in Arkansas, Oregon, Montana, and Alaska. The State of Kansas is fairly conservative, but the company finally persuaded officials that the gray-water system would be orderless and would significantly conserve resources, and they approved it.

Rainfall in Lawrence averages 30 inches per year, an estimated 16 million gallons of water on the store site. Inside the building another quarter million gallons of gray water would be generated annually from sinks and other fixtures. In a conventional design, all that water would be permitted to leave the site, exporting with it nutrients, sediment, and metals to be flushed into receiving streams and rivers, where they could damage aquatic habitat. Then a similar amount of water would have to be purchased from the city to irrigate the landscape. Eco-Mart designers closed the loop, creating an on-site hydrological cycle that will not only save a lot of money but also minimize downstream water effects. According to C. L. Maurer of Landplan, "The single factor that finally seemed to sell county and state officials on gray water was our willingness to use it for subsurface irrigation, rather than spraying it in the air for surface irrigation, as the well-documented system in Arkansas does."[16] Landplan agreed to use the gray water for ornamental plants only, no edible crops. The company also volunteered to perform quarterly samplings on water quality. In the first year of operation, the system's effluent has been close to drinking-water quality. The 2,000-gallon, gravel-lined pit that delivers the clean water has sand in it and perforated pipes to draw off effluent for irrigation. About every five years, it will have to be reverse flushed with high-pressure jets of water, and ultimately the sand will have to be replaced. But by that time, it will have gotten double duty out of millions of gallons of water, eliminating the need to purchase a similar amount of potable water.

Preserving the Prairie

The buffalo have long since vanished from the land of which Eco-Mart is located. But the Eco-Mart landscape includes plant species that were there when the prairie was buffalo pasture. Indigenous trees, shrubs, and turf provide natural habitat for red-winged blackbirds, doves, and many other species. Before any plants were introduced, the landscape team had to reroute a 16-inch natural-gas line that fed Topeka 20 miles away. In the words of Maurer, "If that high-pressure line went up, the whole town of Lawrence would have gone with it."[17]

When the landscape design was completed, it included low-maintenance plant species such as daylilies and buffalo grass that can thrive without a lot of water. Maurer estimates that the buffalo grass lawns, which require only 0.5 inch of water a week as opposed to 1.5 inches for conventional fescue, will save 3 to 4 million gallons of water a month during the summer months. Buffalo grass can also do without a lot of fertilizer and pesticide; in fact, this kind of turf can't tolerate such pampering. The lawn will not remain green as long as fescue or bluegrass; rather, it will fade to a brown that is more natural to the prairie.

One of the most innovative, low-impact techniques in the project was the preservation of trees already on site. A huge vehicle with a tree spade attachment arrived one morning and, in a single eight-hour day, carefully transplanted more than fifty trees to strategic new locations in the landscape. The tree spade has steel cones that scoop 6-foot-diameter root balls. One by one, honey locust, hackberry, eastern redbud, Siberian elm, and other trees were salvaged, with just a single tree lost in the process. At $200 to $300 for comparable nursery-bought trees, the landscape team covered the cost of the spade and crew and still saved thousands of dollars.

The team also had to do some emergency transplanting of drought-tolerant shrubs such as sages when driving rain unexpectedly arrived and pelted the construction site. The shrubs were temporarily removed to the protection of nurseries. Laura Bevilacqua, Eco-Mart's construction coordinator, commented, "It rained from the day we started. We had to make accommodations for the weather in landscaping, in drying the soil, in materials delivery, and in construction itself. We put up huge tents and used portable heaters to finish the project, but we came in just about on schedule."[18]

One feature the landscape team was unable to get approved was porous pavers, for which there was a local supplier. Unlike monolithic asphalt barriers, porous pavers, some of which resemble concrete blocks placed on their sides, permit rain to be absorbed in grass-covered soil. The feature might have reduced heat gain around the building as well as increased water retention, but local permitters would not deviate from standard practice, citing concerns about structural integrity. About $300,000 was paid for asphalt, twice as much as would have been spent for porous pavers. But as Maurer points out, "We made a dent in their thinking, and maybe a similar project in the future will incorporate this technique." According to Denver landscape architect Bill Wenk, federal regulations on stormwater are indeed steadily moving toward design solutions such as porous pavers and swales, that is, basins and trenches that capture and utilize rainwater on site. He attributes this change in orientation to the cost of expensive infrastructure that exports a valuable resource. Why pay to channel water away, and then pay again to pump it back?

Another innovative aspect in the landscape is the Wal-Mart sign. Though it looks and functions like a typical sign, it has photovoltaic cells that convert sunlight directly into electricity and store it in batteries for nighttime use. Solar cells draw on a renewable energy source that pays for itself, not only because sunlight is free but also because the cells bring down infrastructure costs such as trenching, wiring, and repaving. With its solar cells, the store is delivering a message for the future: photovoltaics, by saving on infrastructure and electricity costs, could some day reduce the need for huge, polluting power plants.

According to Meredith Miller, "A kilowatt-hour of electricity generated from fossil fuel puts a pound of carbon dioxide into the air, potentially compounding the global warming problem. Wal-Mart's sign, though just a tiny contribution, can reduce the amount of carbon dioxide by 12,000 pounds over its projected lifetime. More importantly, it can help educate the general public and Wal-Mart management that this technology is already economically viable under certain conditions."[19]

Letting Natural Light In

Meredith Miller and I took a tour through the Eco-Mart store whose design she had spent so many hours helping coordinate. As we walked through the huge sunlit foyer, she was aware of features the general shopper would miss. For example, a typical shopper wouldn't see that the entryway carpet was made out of recycled tires, or that the furniture in the environmental-education room was made out of recycled plastic. The typical shopper wouldn't have a clue how many hours of meetings, telephone calls, cost evaluations, and life-cycle analyses had gone into the decision to use sustainably harvested wood beams. Much of the environmental value of the store was invisibly incorporated in building materials and design features.

However, one thing did jump out at me: the way it felt as I walked into the store. Most discount stores have an uncomfortably confining, fluorescent-light feeling. My instinct is to do my shopping as quickly as possible and get out. The Eco-Mart didn't make me feel that way, and looking up at the ceiling I realized why: the skylights. These provide natural lighting for what Wal-Mart calls its "soft" merchandise, such as clothes and linens. The impression was blues, greens, and whites, which are highlighted by natural light. Under the fluorescents in the other side of the store, reds and yellows jumped out at me.

While there are no definitive data as yet comparing sales at Eco-Mart versus similar merchandise in other Wal-Mart stores, anecdotal evidence indicates that the natural daylight is extremely popular, both with shoppers and employees. Indeed, research at Rensselaer Polytechnic Institute and elsewhere has demonstrated the marketing advantages of natural lighting. "We wanted the skylights to provide a sense of well-being," said Bill McDonough. "And we wanted light with a high 'color-rendition index' because people feel better and look healthier—you can see the blood in a person's skin, for example."[20] This is a new direction in the design of lighting, that productivity and profit are affected by quality of light.

The design team's pioneering system combined natural daylight and dimmable, high-efficiency fluorescents. This looked effective on paper, but it proved challenging to implement. Until their dimming control system was debugged, the fluorescent lights had a habit of turning off even when natural light levels were low, causing some shoppers to wonder if the store was closing early.

Lighting is one area in which the Eco-Mart project has been a driving force for innovation. Andersen, the nation's leading window supplier, customized the skylight prototype for Eco-Mart's specific needs. The window manufacturer had to determine the most cost-effective skylight-to-roof ratio. Too much daylight would result in excessive heat gain, putting an energy load on the cooling system. Too little daylight would not cut back on electrical lighting requirements. Andersen's innovation, which makes use of mirrors and tiny lenses to refract and distribute light, delivers 50 percent more light than conventional skylights, with half the aperture.

With a typical flat window, the amount of light entering a building depends on the angle of incidence. When perpendicular to the window's surface, solar rays penetrate effectively; otherwise they bounce off. Andersen's domed light-house design permits more sun to penetrate throughout the day than conventional designs. A result of rigorous computer analyses and enlightened understanding of the properties of light and materials, the prototype is being considered for use in other Wal-Mart stores. The underlying message is that designers and engineers can simultaneously reduce energy consumption and its sweeping impact and enhance quality of life. Andersen engineers calculate that over a seven-year period (the typical lifespan of a Wal-Mart store), Eco-Mart's skylights will prevent 5 million cubic feet of carbon dioxide from being dumped into the atmosphere by power plants.

The Baby's First Steps

As Miller and I continued our tour, Eco-Mart's green coordinator Patty Perez met us in the environmental-education room. "It's booked half a year in advance," she told us. "Community groups, teachers, and small businesses all regard our facility as a resource. The community comes here to have meetings, recycle, and shop for environmentally conscious products, so we see our role as facilitators in the process of environmental education."[21] The town's teachers seem to be the store's biggest ally. Perez told us about one particular class at Hillcrest Elementary School that received a $5,000 grant from Wal-Mart to set up an outdoor classroom with things such as planters, a grape arbor, and butterfly-hatching equipment. A videotape playing in the education room told the story of the design and construction of Eco-Mart. Much of the furniture in the room is made of recycled material, and the walls are covered with photographic murals of such scenes as a redwood forest, and a bird's nest woven with bits of yarn and other naturally recycled materials. "Teachers bring their classes to this store and the kids walk away with a new understanding of environmental problems and solutions," Perez said. "They go home and teach their parents environmental awareness."[22]

We left the education room and walked up and down the aisles. While in general they resembled the familiar Wal-Mart's, hundreds of items carried green flags as a mark of environmentally friendly design. A fishing rod from Zebco was one. Rather than being packaged in plastic, the rod was simply mounted on recyclable cardboard. "Packaging is supposed to help sell products," Perez pointed out, "but we've observed that sometimes minimal packaging sells pretty well, too." She took the fishing rod off the shelf. "If people can get the merchandise in their hands, they may be more interested in buying it." Another green-flagged product was a line of recycled paint from America's Choice. The price of a typical gallon of paint is $8.97 per gallon, but Eco-Mart sells this quality-controlled recycled paint for $5.00 for two gallons. We passed Natural Choice cotton socks with no dyes or chemicals, biodegradable fishbait from Newell, and Spic and Span in a 100-percent recycled plastic container.

Many of these products were actually altered to meet Wal-Mart's newly defined goals. In the early stages of the Eco-Mart design, Bill Fields, then Wal-Mart's vice president, sent a letter to the chain's many vendors and suppliers. "As merchandisers and manufacturers," it said, "we have helped create a demand for convenience that has in turn created many of today's environmental problems. As suppliers meeting this demand, we have a responsibility to help rectify problems resulting from our actions."[23] After describing the Eco-Mart concept, Fields requested products that could be displayed with no packaging, recycled products and packaging, and products that were more environmentally efficient. Companies such as Procter and Gamble, Helene Curtis, Clorox, and Colgate Palmolive began responding to cues that Eco-Mart would be a showcase, and that successful green products and packaging would later be marketed in other Wal-Mart stores. Improved designs started appearing on Eco-Mart's shelves.

Our tour continued on to Eco-Mart's recycling center, staffed by physically and emotionally disadvantaged Lawrence residents from the Community Living Opportunities program. The center, popular with locals, recycles 220 tons of materials per month.

Recycling is not a new concept for Wal-Mart. There are about 1,700 bins in place at more than 1,000 stores across the country that have already recycled 40,000 tons of newsprint, 750 tons of aluminum, 2,300 tons of plastic bottles, 170 tons of tin, and 30 tons of glass. Some of the recycled material is remanufactured into products subsequently sold in Wal-Mart stores. Examples of such closed-loop efforts include:

- Stretch wrap and plastic bags collected from customers and recycled by Poly America into a plastic sheeting sold in Wal-Mart hardware departments (over 1 million pounds were recycled in 1991);
- New batteries recycled by Wal-Mart and then sold in its stores; and
- America's Choice recycled oil, found on Wal-Mart shelves, a significant portion of which comes from oil recycled at Wal-Mart Auto Centers.

Eco-Mart has developed some strong partnerships in recycling. The City of Lawrence's recycling coordinator, Patricia Morvain, told me that Eco-Mart's comprehensive facility—it recycles nineteen different types of material—enhances the local government's recycling program. Lawrence will avoid hundreds of thousands of dollars in costs by not having to pick up the trash that Eco-Mart is recycling. The savings enabled the city to start a household hazardous-waste program. Morvain noted that there has been widespread use of the Eco-Mart recycling facility. "It's not just Lawrence that's using the drop-off facility, it's really the whole region. I know a woman from Garden City, about 300 miles away, who brings her daughter to school here at Kansas University and drops off all her cans, bottles, and newspapers every time she comes."[24]

Is Eco-Mart a Deep Design?

What began in the boardroom as a loose collection of good intentions, a green store, ultimately evolved into a thriving operation. But the significance of Eco-Mart extends beyond documented reductions in the consumption of energy, water, and toxic materials, and beyond increases in recycling. The project is an educational statement as well as a testing ground for innovations. The important point is that the store helps change the way people think.

Eco-Mart asks questions that are relevant not just in architecture and retail but throughout the economy: Where do things come from, and where do they go? The significance of Eco-Mart is not so much the building as the new kind of culture it proposes and encourages. CRM's Terry Minger believes that "what Wal-Mart attempted to do with the Eco-Mart store is the single most exciting approach to environmental problem-solving in American business today. The market has arrived, asking for these products and innovations, and Eco-Mart supplies them. When the decision is made to move forward in design, not just sideways, the only way the innovations will be available is if they've been field-tested, as at the Eco-Mart."[25]

The field tests are promising. Three additional green Wal-Marts are being built in 1995, one in southern California, one in Moore, Oklahoma, and one in Harrison, Arkansas. The California store will incorporate a second-generation skylight prototype as well as a large array of photovoltaic cells to reduce dependence on electric utilities. The photovoltaic project is being undertaken through a partnership with Southern California Edison, the region's utility company.

As Wal-Mart management is aware, moving from green to deep design requires a continuing effort to respond to local needs. The discount giant may have to change some of its habits by locating in downtown areas with culture-sensitive architecture, buying more materials and products from local vendors, and most important, focusing on products incorporating qualities such as durability and repairability, even if that leads to higher prices. The chain will also have to address the problem of its power to hurt local merchants by underselling them. Numerous critics maintain that Wal-Mart's price-slashing muscle has encouraged the disintegration of local communities. One recycling expert has suggested that the corporation could "become a buying club, a friendly wholesaler which buys en masse and sells to local retailers who form the backbone of rural communities."[26] If the overall direction of our society is toward reducing consumption without reducing quality of life, then high-volume, low-priced retail may have to be transformed into medium-volume, medium-priced, but best-quality merchandise.

Chapter 8

Design for Environment

Making It Better

Over the past ten millennia, humans have been busy discovering and inventing things. In the process, we got way ahead of ourselves. We became increasingly disconnected from nature as we began to sell pieces of it. We outpaced our support systems, like the mouse in the cartoon who sawed off the tree limb he was perched on. We've always been creators and designers, but only in recent history have we focused this aptitude on producing surpluses and manipulating whole ecosystems. When things were still made for the family and the town, design was a function of need; it usually reflected a social ethic and often an environmental one. But as humans continued to put wheels and gears on their inventions, technology began to dominate and define culture, and ethics became an afterthought.

Large-scale manipulation began with irrigation, road building, and metals smelting. Centralized government was a half-step behind, responding to the need to administer and control expanding technology. Today, in nearly every human activity, our behavior is defined by the capabilities and limitations of technology. Farm fields are square and tomatoes hard skinned to accommodate machinery, houses are located and built to meet the needs of the car, schedules are arranged around favorite television shows, cities are megasized to manipulate resource flows. We've synchronized our cultural metabolism to match the capabilities of technology.

165

One of these capabilities is to deliver comparative indestructibility in products like plastics, preservatives, and long-life pesticides. The thread of indestructibility and its by-product, toxicity, has been woven throughout human culture, putting us at odds with nature rather than in synch with it. Once we have a device or process in place and it seems to be working, economic inertia sets in. Our inventory of designs and technologies begins to resemble the electrical equipment in an old house—you start with the basic service and add extension cords, even if they're unsafe.

The dominant theme of our era is that we have bent ourselves out of shape to accommodate each new technological innovation. Our ingenuity may be impressive, but the overall result often limits rather than expands our options. Deep design bucks this trend by demanding more flexibility and human participation in the creation and use of designs. We need to do less than we are technologically capable of doing, and we need to demand that design and biology remain linked. Having legs, we want to walk; having fingers, we want to help plants grow. Being human, we want more than speed and indestructibility.

If the tension between the industrial revolution's supply side and human nature's demand side is resolved, we may suddenly change the way we view the world. Instead of asking meekly, What are our choices? we may learn to reassert our innate sense of craftsmanship and say out loud, This is what we want: designs and devices that are nontoxic, easy to understand, manufactured using renewable energy, capable of decomposing or being recycled, easy to repair or modify—economical in every sense of the word. Instead of adapting to the supply side's obsession with what comes out, we'll insist on higher quality in what goes in. Why is it that gardens with indigenous plant species don't require a lot of maintenance? The answer is simple: the right ingredients have gone in.

This chapter discusses the best way to make a computer. More important, though, it is about the way things in general are made. It introduces the bigger, more pressing questions: What's the best way to make anything? What are the best things to be making?

Such are the questions being asked by AT&T's Brad Allenby, who calls his vision of twenty-first-century manufacturing "design for environment."

The DfE approach was a natural extension of the AT&T Design for X program. Such production cycle goals as design for manufacturing and design for testing were deepened to include DfE goals like design for recycling and design for disassembly. A new approach called green-product realization was developed to put product development into a system context. For example, to make product recycling cost effective, a product must be designed for recyclability, which in turn means that an infrastructure must be created to recycle the used products.[1] AT&T management is carefully watching Germany's so-called take-back legislation, which requires manufacturers to recycle used products. With indications that other European countries and Japan may adopt similar regulations, AT&T is trying to safeguard its international markets.

Although the first phase of take-back legislation deals only with packaging, the next will include durable products such as electronic components. Take-back legislation can potentially move industrial design many steps down the pathway toward deep design because it forces industrial designers to use life cycle analysis. Products have to be easy to convert back into raw materials, and their components have to be nontoxic to avoid worker exposure. Take-back laws could also help drive a stake into the heart of planned obsolescence, because increased product life will be more cost effective than constant collection and recycling.

There are many other motivations for DfE, illustrated by Brad Allenby's investigations into substitutes for toxic lead solder in computers. After looking methodically at indium and bismuth alloys as possible substitutes, Allenby was surprised by the results of his research, which suggested that the substitutes might not be environmentally preferable. While standard industrial evaluations don't consider environmental effects until the manufacturing or consumer stage, Allenby's evaluation considered the stage preceding product manufacture. Research established the fact that indium and bismuth ores exist only in very low concentrations, and moreover, that world reserves are scarce. Therefore extraction would be energy intensive and environmentally damaging.

A similar thought process can and should be applied in the manufacture of anything. To make aluminum from virgin ore (bauxite) requires temperatures near 3,000 degrees Fahrenheit, while making aluminum from recycled scrap requires only 1,200 degrees Fahrenheit, saving up to 90 percent of energy consumption. Consider, for a moment, another industrial pathway, food packaging. We can't always buy fresh food from local sources to eliminate packaging altogether, but we can change the way packaging

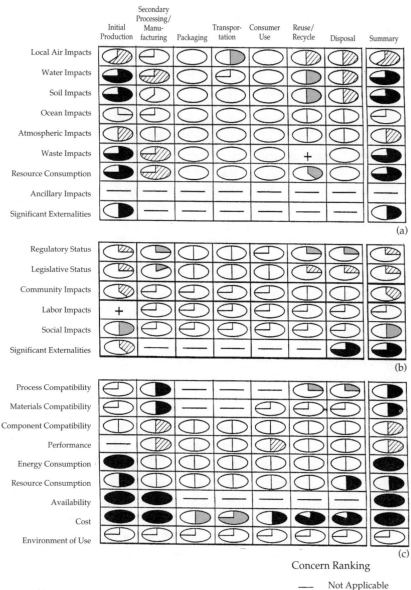

Figure 14

The life cycles evaluation of (a) environmental,
(b) social, and (c) industrial implications of indium
as a solder.

SOURCE: BRADEN R. ALLENBY, "DESIGN FOR ENVI-
RONMENT, IMPLEMENTING INDUSTRIAL ECOLOGY,"
PH.D. DISSERTATION, RUTGERS, 1992.

Concern Ranking

— Not Applicable

+, ++ Positive

◯ No Concern

◓ Minor Concern

◕ Moderate Concern

● Significant Concern

is made. Packages with composite layers are especially impressive from an engineering standpoint. But from a deep-design perspective, they are questionable—they're difficult if not impossible to recycle and made from nonrenewable resources.

Composed of nine different layers, the state-of-the-art snack food bag is only 0.002 inches thick. Which layers are designed for the environment? None. Yet because composite packaging requires less material and offers the advantage of preserving contents against spoilage, many companies who are genuinely trying to be "green" justify its use. Ben and Jerry's is one. The ice cream company was looking for an alternative to the cardboard box that packaged their Peace Pop because they had received negative customer feedback on it. Their progressive management wanted to do the right thing environmentally. They were investigating a plastic-aluminum laminate, and the Center for Resource Management, where I worked at the time, was asked by Ben and Jerry's to brainstorm about the alternatives. It seemed like a tailor-made

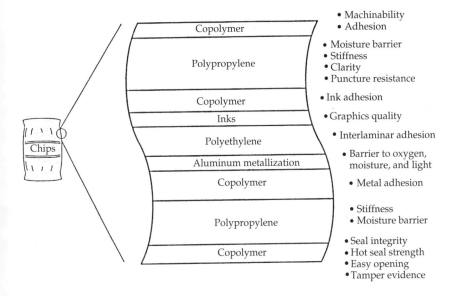

Figure 15

Cross section of a snack chip bag, illustrating the complexity of modern packaging.

Source: Council on Plastics and Packaging in the Environment.

opportunity to create packaging that would have a loftier end than simply to occupy landfill space.

The packaging, we decided, should deliver an implicit message about the environment. Like Ben and Jerry's other packaging, it might include printed information about where the ingredients came from and comment on their quality. Maybe there was even a way to let consumers cast a vote with the packaging. Should it carry a business reply form with prepaid postage? Obviously, that would raise the price per unit considerably, and the company had said that the cost margin per package was narrow. The total price of the ice cream bar had to be competitive with its chief rival, Häagen-Daz.

Maybe, we thought, the packaging should be something that could be recycled as a child's building material or piece of a puzzle. Certainly, it should embody the best characteristics of natural packages such as the pea pod. As we continued to brainstorm, we went back to a few of the essential themes of deep design: What's the purpose? Who's going to use this product? Where do the materials come from? Where are they going?

The deepest design we could imagine resulted in a package that was either a compost-seeking missile or a peanut shell. That is, ideally, the package would be either biodegradable or made directly from nature's own packaging, like the eggshells, peanut shells, cocoa and vanilla bean hulls, and corn husks that were by-products of the Peace Pop's manufacture. Why not repackage the product using those by-products, already proven to be good packaging? We even considered having the package be "hyperdegradable," incorporating certain herbs or enzymes that would help get a compost pile working.

The same day, in connection with another project, I had talked to a chemist about nutrient cycles at the planetary scale. He summarized the way America currently meets its nutritional needs: a large percentage of our nutrients originate in the heartland, are shipped to the coastal population centers, and discharged into the oceans. He had a point. We knew that nutrients have to be designed back into the system. But what were the economics of setting up a new production process to make packaging out of by-products? We called up a U.S. Department of Agriculture lab researching biodegradable plastics. The director informed us that he was looking for a partnership in the private sector to test a new kind of plastic made of cornstarch. It would have engineering properties similar to the nine-layer snack food bag, but would be biodegradable, and edible.

Hypothetically, the package would coat the ice cream bar like another layer of chocolate and then be enclosed in ordinary paper. The paper wrapping would not have benefits such as moisture control, but because of the cornstarch coating, a high-tech wrapping would be unnecessary. All the paper wrapping would have to do is inform the consumer that he or she was about to eat a deep design.

We reported back to Ben and Jerry's, suggesting that one option was to form a public-private partnership with USDA to try out the innovative packaging, partly at government expense. Five or six months later, I held the design the company had chosen: a package that eliminated the cardboard box, but was still a Phase I effort. Made from polyester, polyethylene, and ionomer plastics, the package announced that 165 tons of solid waste would not go into the landfills because of the change. Ben and Jerry's is modifying its artwork to reduce the package by another quarter of an inch on both sides, which will save materials and also restrict the pop's movement in distribution. After conducting shipping tests, the company decided they didn't need a pillow pack design—the ice cream bar was not as fragile as they had thought.

The Deep Design/Craft Connection

Technology and science have followed parallel but separate paths throughout history. One discipline is about making a functional device, the other about how and why it works. Until today, engineers were not required to know or care about the environmental implications of their projects—their assignment was simply to make them work. The prototype piston engine was invented by tinkering engineers without the benefit of the science of thermodynamics. Together, the two disciplines soon produced a device so powerful that billions were mass-produced in a single generation. In countless cases, technical ability has preceded scientific understanding. Well into the twentieth century, tinkerers seemed to have a better intuitive understanding of the properties of materials than theoretical scientists.

Convergence of science and technology is what deep design is all about, that is, mixing the right ingredients by design rather than serendipity. Deep design allies the scientist with the designer. It also, as we have seen, allies itself with society. When the three variables, science, technology, and culture, come into balance, the visionary will become pragmatic: we'll know what we want and need, we'll know what nature needs, and we'll be capable of designing for those needs. This new approach radically differs from the dominant industrial paradigm in which the invisible hand of the market rules, and consequences are assumed to be minimal until a crisis occurs—an ethically passive, quantity-driven, biologically insensitive way of conducting business. The new paradigm is just the opposite: actively in search of quality, biologically aware, and socially informed.

How will the world of manufacturing change with the rise of the new paradigm? It will become more responsive and more responsible. Instead of the prevailing attitude, Here's what you can have, industry will increasingly say, Tell us what you want.

Manufacturers will think about product assembly differently. They used to focus on ease of assembly; they didn't worry about disassembly because products weren't recycled. Product safety was compromised. Because many of a device's components wouldn't come into contact with people, it didn't matter from a liability standpoint if those components were made with toxic ingredients. And because few manufacturers took durability into consideration, structural excellence was not a priority.

Manufacturers will also acquire more materials regionally, reducing travel, enhancing local economies, strengthening social connections. An idealized, sustainable future will have less corporate anonymity, less centralization of production, and more accountability. Even in Western economies this is a good strategy, for many of the activities toward which we need to move, such as recycling, sustainable farming, and restoration/preservation of habitat, are labor intensive.

A recent shift in the economy of northern Italy illustrates that this concept is more than just a hypothesis. In the past twenty years, Italy's Emilia-Romagna district has implemented many decentralized "flexible manufacturing networks," with the following results: 20,000 new manufacturing jobs; wage rates 175 percent above the Italian average; and second in per-capita income among Italy's twenty-one regions in 1985 (up from seventeenth in 1970). How were these results achieved? By changing the shape of manufacturing. The region now has more than 325,000 small firms, including 90,000 in manufacturing. Ninety percent of these firms employ fewer than twenty-two people each, while manufacturing firms employ just five workers each. Each tiny company has the support of a huge pool of highly trained artisans and employs the latest technology in the production of shoes, agricultural equipment, motorcycles, medical equipment, and clothing.

This model of industrial ecology has been actively promoted by trade associations that provide such services as assistance in payroll, billing, inventory control, accounting, law, and insurance. An industrial extension network, similar to America's agricultural extension, keeps the companies competitive. The goal is quality work that is less wasteful and more responsive. Similar networks, or industrial ecosystems, are being formed in the New Hampshire electronics and Ohio cabinetmaking industries. As explained by Sebastano Brusco of the Italian University of Modena, "By using the foresight and imagination of so many artisans, the productive structure is able to offer an extraordinary variety of products which cleverly interpret the needs of consumers and shifts in their tastes."[2]

In the corporate as well as the manufacturing world, the goals of renewability, reversibility, equity, resilience, proximity, and precision are actively being sought by forward-looking companies that want to avoid the tangled web of lawsuits, consumer boycotts, and recalls that can ensnare firms with a business-as-usual attitude. When industrial ecology begins to be more widely accepted, corporations will begin to fulfill their primary mission: to provide service.

The Conquest of Space and Time

If technology is imagined in the shape of a pyramid, surely the CD ROM–equipped computer is perched on the apex. Had automobile technology advanced as quickly as computer technology, a Maserati would cost something like two dollars and get two million miles to the gallon. Computers have become the fastest growing and one of the largest industries in the manufacturing sector, representing 11 percent of America's GNP.

Deep design is directly implicated in the computer's phenomenal leap forward. The ability to model and modify designs, from molecules to shopping malls, eliminates much of the waste and imprecision that have shadowed our products until now. Architects can walk through the virtual reality of efficient buildings-to-be, and chemists can survey the far side of imaginary molecules to come up with designs that meet our needs. Computer capabilities like Geographical Information Systems (GIS) enable the most appropriate use of resources by, for example, minimizing waste. Because of their precision and incredible speed, computers can catch and correct a mistake before it escalates. But the computer is just a vehicle waiting to be driven somewhere. The device itself is useless without the interpretation, foresight, and wisdom of the human mind.

The deep design of a computer involves much more than knowledgeable assembly. To steer the computer in the right direction, we first have to know where we're going, and why. There is a glaring downside to the pace that computers make possible: computer-controlled machines are churning through resources faster than nature can regenerate them. What remains to be seen is whether the computer will end up contributing to environmental demise or enhancing human creativity in response to the environment. Design within this industry has developed so quickly that we need to catch our breath and look at how we might direct the computer's potential in the most beneficial ways.

The evolution of computers actually began centuries ago when mathematicians developed an equation to reduce the time it took to perform mathematical calculations. During World War II, interest in a device that would quickly perform calculations intensified. The result was an electronic computer, the ENIAC, introduced in 1946.[3] With electronic tubes for data storage, the ENIAC could perform mathematical equations thousands of times faster than the old mechanical methods. While the ENIAC sped up the calculation process, its 18,000 vacuum tubes took up 3,000 cubic feet of space, and consumed 140 kilowatts of energy. Furthermore, the ENIAC could only work when fully powered. If it lost its electrical source or was shut off, it would not retain any memory of the data stored in it.

The next stage in design was to make the computer smaller and more efficient. Structural design became the focus of efforts for the next twenty years. At each step the computer became smaller and more efficient. It also became more versatile: in addition to functioning as a calculator, it became an efficient tool for information flow. Inevitably, the market for computers grew, in turn driving continual improvements in design. Capacity and speed became the primary design criteria in the race for primacy within the industry.

A major breakthrough in computer design was development of semiconductors, that is, crystalline materials such as selenium, germanium, or silicon that conduct electrical current in ways that can be controlled. Found naturally in the earth's mineral deposits, they can be "grown" and purified in laboratories for circuitry use. Engineers found that semiconductor crystals could be used to make transistors or diodes. This reduced the size and augmented the capacity of the computer in the late 1950s and early 1960s. The silicon transistor prevailed until the development of the integrated circuit, (IC), a silicon chip that could house several transistors and had connections to get current from one circuit to another. This greatly increased the reliability of data storage and transfer, and reduced size.[4] With the IC, a computer could do five million additions per second, a hundred times faster than the old vacuum tube. In the late twentieth century, more data can be held in 0.25-square-inch chip than could be held in the entire ENIAC of mid-century.[5] With this development the computer industry has skyrocketed into prominence, making computer design, manufacture, and use as big a business as the American automobile industry. Today computers are a major influence on the world economy and on the culture of the global village.

In retrospect, it is clear that the search for speed generated improvements in computer size, capacity, and availability. Last year's model became obsolete long before it wore out. Consumer demand for features that expanded information storage and usefulness spurred improvements. The result is that computers have done more than any other technology in the history of humankind to conquer space and time.

Pollution Prevention in the Computer Industry

A Carnegie Mellon University study estimates that over 150 million personal computers and workstations will have been sent to landfills by the year 2005. Metals such as lead and chromium leach off printed circuit boards and slowly contaminate groundwater. The plastics that go into making computers do not break down in landfills for hundreds of years. Processes used to manufacture semiconductors generate a tremendous variety and amount of liquid and gaseous waste.

Recycling computers is a partial solution. Initial efforts were directed at recovering precious metals in printed circuit boards. However, over time it was discovered that other components can be economically separated and resold, resulting in less "throughput" of materials. This business is growing across the United States, with corporations like IBM now offering to take back computers for re-cycling.[6] Major obstacles still have to be overcome, though. Sorting and separating is labor intensive, transportation is expensive, and the market for components made of recycled material is smaller than the infrastructure for collecting and reformulating them.

Slowly, an approach called pollution prevention and waste min-imization filtered through the computer industry. This approach targets the beginning of the manufacturing process, before regula-tory controls are required. Engineers anticipate by-products before they are generated. For example, at Hewlett Packard, printed circuit boards used to be cleaned after soldering to remove contaminants and improve performance. The process involved 1-1-1 trichloroeth-ane, a hazardous waste and ozone depleter. A careful examination of that process resulted in the complete elimination of the solvent.

How did it happen? In 1989, Hewlett Packard's chief executive officer committed the corporation to cooperation with the Montreal Protocol, which called for a gradual elimination of ozone-depleting substances. Hewlett Packard executives launched a project to elim-inate CFCs in the circuit-board cleaning process. The project that began in Hewlett's corporate offices in Palo Alto, California, soon involved a research team of engineers and technicians from various Hewlett Packard facilities. According to Kevin Allen, process engi-neering manager at the company's Fort Collins, Colorado, plant, printed circuit boards were immersed in a "freon wash," that is, a tankful of 1-1-1 trichloroethane. A fine mist of the chemical was sprayed just above the liquid to assist the cleaning. Afterward, the boards moved to the assembly department.[7]

The corporate research team began by compiling a list of alter-natives to 1-1-1 trichloroethane. They looked at competitors working on similar projects to see the options being considered. They found common alternatives to be aqueous cleaners (including soap and water) and hydrocarbon solvents, among others. Another possibility that occurred to the team was simply not to clean the board at all. This led to an investigation that challenged some as-sumptions about so-called dirty circuit boards. The company dis-covered that performance was not as significant an issue as appear-ance, because most of the dirt particles were too small to interfere with performance. Because this option would generate no waste, it seemed to be the ideal pollution prevention solution.

Ultimately, the Palo Alto team narrowed their alternatives

down to aqueous and no-clean. Each company plant was approached and given a choice. Engineers in the Fort Collins facility decided to pursue the no-clean alternative, not only because the aqueous process was costly, but because no-clean would incur fewer environmental costs. But the project required a major change in board processing. Moreover, capital equipment investment costs were high, greater than $1 million per plant. According to Allen, "We established that a material, solder paste, had to be changed, that the printed circuit board had to be redesigned, and that a different oven-baking process would have to be used. These changes made the initial conversion an expensive proposition."[8]

Because the redesigned board would look different, customers were consulted. The Fort Collins plant's primary customer was a Hewlett Packard final-assembly facility in New Hampshire. Advance information about the changes was sent out to that manufacturing plant and its sales organizations so that they could prepare for the changes. Questions arose about the quality of the newly designed board, but once information about test results was reviewed, most objections disappeared. The slightly dirty boards performed well. In 1993, the no-clean process was implemented at the Fort Collins plant, and at other Hewlett Packard plants worldwide.

The project was expensive, costing several million dollars for development and implementation. However, in the future, expenses could be more than recouped from a reduction in waste disposal and from manufacturing improvements. The project was successful, meeting its goal of eliminating class I CFCs during production. As Allen points out, the project brought several other benefits as well: there is no problem with hazardous-waste disposal, plants require less production space, and Hewlett Packard's public image has benefited.

Letting Computers Get Some Sleep

In the search for environmental return on investment, the area of energy consumption is extremely promising. Electricity production generates sulfur dioxide and nitrogen oxide (acid-rain precursors) and consumes natural resources such as water. Normally, cost-conscious companies try to reduce energy by looking at computer manufacturing. How can the production process be altered so that less energy is used? Common solutions are reducing temperature in ovens, cutting fan horsepower, and changing energy sources. Recent analysis by the EPA, however, found more energy being consumed by computers in use than by those in manufacture. In fact, computer operation accounts for 5 percent of annual commercial electricity consumption in the United States, with the number estimated to grow to 10 percent by the year 2000.

The EPA's Energy Star program gives industry an opportunity to reduce consumption significantly and at minimal cost. The program is a partnership between the EPA and industry to develop personal computers that will "sleep," or power down, when not in use. Over 90 percent of America's leading suppliers of computers and components, led by charter partners Apple, Compaq, Digital Equipment Corporation, Hewlett Packard, IBM, NCR, Smith Corona, and Zenith Data Systems, have joined the program and pledged to include power-management features in their products.

Studies show that the personal computer, when left on twenty-four hours a day, can consume up to 1,314 kilowatt-hours (kwh) per year, the equivalent of leaving a 150-watt-light bulb on for an entire year. With special components to power down when not in use, a computer's energy consumption could be reduced to as little as 25 kwh per year. Intel has programmed such capability into several microprocessor chips to save battery power in laptop computers. The company has also indicated that it intends to build this capability into all future SL (power management) chips.[9] Given that Intel chips are the building blocks of 80 percent of the world's personal computers, this commitment is significant.

IBM has introduced power-down features into its PS1 personal computer and a number of energy-saving features into its PS2E computer. In terms of the total environmental cost of manufacture, these products are not completely green designs, but they represent a step in the right direction.

Some firms have participated in the Energy Star program by adding screen savers to their software that automatically blank a display screen when it is on but not in use. Added expense is no more than thirty dollars, a small investment that pays great dividends and that can be absorbed into the cost of the personal computer through volume and competition. It is also good public relations for manufacturers, which can have Energy Star logos displayed in their promotional materials.

Energy Star is a rare opportunity for the EPA to work in cooperation with industry and make a significant dent in pollution. According to Catherine Zoi of the EPA's Office of Air and Radiation, it is estimated that "by the year 2000, EPA Energy Star computers and other campaigns to promote energy-efficient computer equipment will lead to savings of 25 billion kwh of electricity annually, reduced from a current estimated consumption of 70 billion kwh per year. These savings will prevent carbon-dioxide emissions of 20 million tons, the equivalent to the carbon dioxide emissions of 5 million automobiles. Reduced, too, will be emissions of 140,000 tons of sulfur dioxide and 75,000 tons of nitrogen oxides, the two pollutants most responsible for acid rain."[10]

Why should the computer industry support Energy Star so strongly? First, significant energy reduction can be achieved with a small investment. Second, it encourages a shift in attitude away from command and control legislation as the only way to reduce pollution effectively. If this trend continues, industry may gain more freedom to reduce pollution on its own, rather than shouldering the economic burden of regulations.

Dfe in Computer Workstations

Waste minimization and energy efficiency are significant steps toward the deep design of computers. A little further down the pathway is comprehensive analysis of how computers are made.

In 1992, the electronics and computer industry, in conjunction with the Microelectronics and Computer Technology Corporation (MCC) and the U.S. Department of Energy, decided to use Dfe in an analysis of computer-workstation designs. Though not exhaustive, the results of their study, published in March 1993, suggest design principles that could lead to industrywide improvements in the workstation.

The workstation analysis included more than a hundred participants from over forty organizations, including industry, National Laboratories, the Department of Energy, and the EPA. Seven task forces looked at various segments of the computer workstation to come up with ideas on how to incorporate cost-competitive environmental design into workstations.

MCC, with guidance from Greg Pitts, director of environmental programs, coordinated the analysis of data collected during the study. Their approach was pragmatic: because the first priority was global competitiveness, not all of the ideas they considered would have the lowest environmental impact. One of the first issues the leaders of the study faced was the complexity of computer manufacturing. To begin with, there are approximately seven hundred different materials and chemicals used in the manufacture of computer equipment, and more than half are hazardous, including CFCs, hydrochloric acid, lead, and polymers. The steps required in manufacturing are also complex. Making the wafer for a semiconductor alone can involve as many as four hundred interdependent tasks. Then there are the countless choices of material and process that could be used in the manufacture of a computer workstation. For example, a number of metals could replace chromium, and for each option an array of issues must be examined, among them, quality, extraction, function, longevity, and recyclability. The job of finding alternatives can be so daunting that substitute chemicals are often employed before their properties are fully understood. The new chemical may be just as bad for the environment as the hazardous material it replaces. Take, for example, solvent substitutes for cleaners and degreasers that contain CFCs. The replacements emit volatile organic compounds that promote smog.

Is there a net improvement? Probably not.

The study team used a hypothetical computer workstation, each component of which was reviewed not only for environmental impact but also for issues relating to manufacture, use, and disposal. Each task force analyzed one of the following: chemicals and materials, semiconductor devices, semiconductor packaging, printed wiring boards and computer assemblies, displays, computer systems, and education and training. They were told to consider not only materials but also energy consumed, waste generated, regulatory burden, recyclability, disposal, and costs associated with each of these. The idea was to look at the workstation from cradle to grave and find design alternatives that best balanced cost with environmental impact.

As the study team knew, design investigation can be expensive and resource intensive. A tremendous amount of information is needed for design engineers to make environmentally sound decisions, and in many cases, because of the computer industry's fast growth, fierce competition, and the cost of development, it isn't available. The study noted two possible ways to address this problem. First, industry might focus design effort on new developments rather than on overhauling existing processes. Second, industry/government research coalitions might share data on DfE research.

Chemicals were closely considered in the study. Participants felt that design goals should look first at reducing the toxicity of materials that are used both in the computer and during its manufacture.

With respect to toxins and what to reduce, replace, or recycle, the advisory committee recommended use of a technique called process hazards review, which produces charts of chemicals used in various production stages. It looked at semiconductor manufacturing and concluded that air pollution and waste-related environmental effects from chemicals such as hydrochloric, sulfuric, phosphoric, and hydrofluoric acid were substantial. They recommended further study of recycling process waste, for example, by purifying and reusing acids and recirculating emissions. However, they also noted the need for larger technological change in manufacturing. The computer industry will have to continue to move away from end-of-pipe solutions and look more seriously at reduction in and substitution for materials.

Computer Materials: Closing the Loop

With the emergence of computers as the fastest-growing industry in the world, recycling must be a serious and integral part of design solutions. Pete Schneider, corporate vice president of development and environmental affairs for IBM, maintains that "a number of our plants are looking at metals recovery and reuse in old computers. One of our U.S. facilities is regrinding computer keyboards and using the material to make new ones. A joint venture in England between IBM, Hydro Goodrich, and the Mann Organization is also utilizing old computer housings and keyboards to manufacture keyboards."[11] Studies have shown that reuse of wastewater in semiconductor manufacturing processes can reduce consumption by 300 gallons a minute. If true, reuse could save a manufacturer 36 million gallons of fresh water a year and tens of thousands of dollars. Metals in wastewater are being recovered with ionization treatment and by separation from printed circuit boards, after which they are remelted.

In the case of the display terminal, remanufacturing also offers opportunity for a more closed-loop system. Companies like Video

Display Corporation can refurbish 200,000 display terminals a year, saving a lot of landfill space.[12] However, a complete display-recovery program isn't likely soon because the major components, glass, lead, and plastic, are sealed inside the terminal. Digital Equipment Corporation has made progress in overcoming this obstacle. In partnership with Envirocycle and Corning Asahi, it has implemented a program addressing the problems of economic recycling and a market for recycled materials. Digital Equipment gets terminals returned to it when their useful life is over, while Envirocycle disassembles them to recover metals and other elements. Glass monitors are crushed and sent to Corning Asahi, where the new glass is produced. The result has been an economic gain for Digital: it is realizing a 45-percent savings in disposal costs, and meanwhile sending less waste to landfills.[13]

The problem of recycling goes beyond display terminals to the entire life cycle of computer manufacturing. It's difficult to sort and separate computers and their components for reuse. Collection methods are labor intensive and expensive for a product sold worldwide. Getting old computer components to a central location is cumbersome enough; once separated, the various parts must be transported again to manufacturing plants for reprocessing.

What about the quality of products manufactured with recycled materials? This is a big issue. Markets are limited because of a perception that such materials are expensive and substandard. Industrial capacity for remanufacturing can also be a concern if there is not enough of a market for recycled products.

However, there are solutions to each of these problems, and they are already being addressed. Researchers in the computer-workstation study recommended that workstations be designed for easier disassembly and segregation of components for recycling. This could be achieved by using more common metals, standardized plastic polymers, and fewer components. Both industry and government are looking for ways to generate markets for recycled products. Recycling centers are being established to recover the more common or valuable components in computers. The State of California is offering economic incentives in the form of zoning, financial backing, and low-interest loans for recyclers to locate their facilities near urban areas, where waste can become raw material. In addition, chemicals and materials used in manufacturing are being scrutinized for their recycling potential.

Changing the Rules

How will the government be involved in the greening of the computer industry? Environmental regulations pose burdens on the computer industry, and further regulatory pressure, continuing the command and control mentality fostered by the environmental movement of the 1960s, is expected. In a 1990 report, the Congressional Office of Technology Assessment noted, "Although there are many environmental and economic benefits to waste reduction, over 99 percent of federal and state environmental spending is devoted to controlling pollution after waste is generated."[14] End-of-pipe solutions are not the only problems. Such legislation as the Clean Air Act, Resource Conservation and Recovery Act, Clean Water Act, Storm Water Act, and Oil Pollution Act have spawned inconsistent regulations. Overlapping requirements, duplication of effort, and demanding reporting requirements force industry to waste billions of dollars annually.

Fortunately, some progress is being made in this arena. Recent legislative action has encouraged or required pollution prevention to be a part of industry environmental-management programs. Voluntary programs such as Energy Star and Green Lights are paving the way for cooperative joint efforts between government and industry. In some European countries, government is playing a lead role in forcing industry to eliminate or restrict use of certain known hazardous materials or chemicals, eradicating problems at the source, not sticking Band-Aids on existing problems. The 800,000 tons of electronic waste generated every year in Germany was part of the impetus for that country's take-back legislation.

Another critical issue is research and development of technologies that can improve American computer competitiveness while allowing for more environmentally sound design. Dominique Cartron, environmental research analyst for MCC, notes that cooperative efforts between industry and government are prevalent in both Europe and Japan. They provide financial incentives for technological innovation as well as the coordination of technology data bases. "They have better industry alliances to compete internationally and comply with regulations," according to Cartron. The same spirit of cooperation does not exist in the United States. Again, this is changing. Though the computer-workstation study was difficult to set up in the United States because of a climate of suspicion between industry and government, relations between the two sectors have improved since the study was completed.

In 1993, members of the Society of Environmental Toxicology and Chemistry (SETAC) led an effort to develop a code of practice for life-cycle-analysis practitioners. This culminated in a draft statement of guidelines for life-cycle analysis. In May of the same year, a group of U.S. government officials, consultants, environmentalists, and industry representatives met with members of the European Community to unveil the guidelines. Meanwhile, the EPA is focusing more on financial support for the electronics industry in pollution-prevention programs, with $20 million recently set aside for environmental research specifically in this field.

Changes are occurring in the computer industry largely for economic reasons. Hewlett Packard's innovations were undertaken to enhance the company's public relations image and profit margin. The industry-government coalition Energy Star was a low-cost opportunity to reduce energy consumption and pollution. The computer-workstation study considered pollution prevention from two angles, competitiveness and cost savings. Each group realized that it was in their best interest to be a good environmental steward by designing to avoid the problem.

The computer workstation study pointed to some of the glaring issues and difficult obstacles that must be overcome before DfE becomes the norm in industry. Defining what the product is or will be, doing a flow chart of all existing and potential inputs, throughputs, and outputs, is a good beginning. From there, each component should be considered separately and from different perspectives, including environmental, economic, technological, and cultural.

The computer represents on the one hand a problem—a product that uses an incredible array of materials, and that enables an unprecedented industrial metabolism—and on the other a potential solution—a tool for understanding the processes of ecological balance and the consequences of our actions. In the design of computers, applied information can accomplish reductions in the use of hazardous chemicals and energy consumption, and enable the recycling of materials—Phase I kinds of efforts. But the deep design of computers—Phase II—involves much more. It requires cultural maturity, that is, the willingness not only to make the machine better but also the society in which it must fit.

Chapter 9

The Evolution of Design Species
Toward a Best-Case Scenario of Diversity, Conservation, and Caretaking

Deep design is in many cases simple design, but there's often a complex thought process to arrive at simplicity. You would probably agree with me that we all have a lot of work to do. We're lucky it's rewarding work. If we make the right design decisions and integrate them in just the right way, we may achieve a sustainable society in which nature and human culture coexist peacefully. If we don't—the consequences are too depressing to contemplate. Why waste our time? The point is that we have a crisis situation, but we also have solutions ready to be deployed. The building is burning, but we have a safe place to jump. A pretty solid picture is emerging of which pathways to take toward sustainability and which to avoid. It's reassuring to realize that we can be the architects of our own destiny.

Our future can be significantly cleaner and saner if we abandon our leaky ship and climb on an ark headed for survival. Obviously, we can't take all our "stuff" with us. We'll need to jettison all but the tools that are essential, not for biological survival alone, but for cultural prosperity as well. Our choices have to be based on a new goal, sustainability, and not on profit by pillage. Today's economy rewards those whose income is drawn from the supply side (land, oil, transportation, and consumer, entertainment, and industrial products), while the rest of us are in effect slaves of that economy,

	Change Course	Accelerate Change	
Educate	Earth and life sciences Biochemistry, Biophysics Systems thinking Life Cycle approach Environmental ethic	Computer modeling Computer graphics Multidisciplinary approach Electronic networking Support academic champions	Knowledge & Attitudes
Demonstrate	Pollution prevention Design for environment Resource efficiency Cost–risk–benefit analysis Life cycle assessment	Benchmarking Alliance building Supply chain management Multidisciplinary teams Total-performance accounting Economic incentive systems Stakeholder management	Skills & Behavior

Eco-Efficient Production
(Survival and Development Values)

	Change Course	Accelerate Change	
Educate	Health and safety Nutrition Intergenerational ethics	Information networks Prioritized risk assessment Women's rights Carrying-capacity indicators	Knowledge & Attitudes
Demonstrate	Conservation Resource recovery Pollution prevention Full-cost pricing	Population stabilization Consensus building Action networks Economic-well-being indicators	Skills & Behavior

Eco-Sufficient Consumption
(Quality-of-Life Values)

Figure 16

The pathways toward sustainability.

SOURCE: CARL HENN, 1994.

forced to earn more money to finance increased supply. In the meantime, the environment has been turned into a battlefield, with society trapped in the middle of the shelling.

Turning It Around: Assuming a Best-Case Scenario

Deep designers resist many of the industrial guidelines of twentieth-century engineering. They know that if they follow the specs as currently written, it will result in inefficiency, isolation, planned obsolescence, lack of quality, environmental decay, and social chaos. If they comply with the regulations currently in place, it will produce the worst culture the law will allow. Deep designers believe it is well worth the effort to shoot for something more inspired.

One standard operating procedure that shortchanges our best design capabilities is the chronic assumption of a worst-case scenario. Instead of redundancy that serves as protective packaging against liability, we need to integrate diversity and flexibility into our designs. For example, a conventional architectural firm will invariably specify enough parking spaces at a shopping mall to ensure parking capacity at Christmas, the busiest time of the year. Similarly, a conventional engineering firm will specify enough air-conditioning capacity to prevent occupants from even noticing the hottest day of the year. Deep designers begin with a more inspired assumption: that designs can be made reasonably fail-safe if they incorporate diversity, flexibility, and biological compatibility, eliminating the need for overengineering. They ask commonsense questions concerning the service and the function of their designs. Instead of specifying a monstrously expensive commercial air-conditioning system, sized for the worst-case scenario, why not design a system that works perfectly 360 days a year? The Phase I approach is to design a building that meets many of its own needs with solar energy, source control of indoor pollutants, natural ventilation, high-performance insulation and glazing, and lights that emit little heat. The Phase II approach simply specifies that employees work at home when the outside temperature exceeds 105°. Instead of a snow day, let the design assume an occasional heat day. And why not provide the shopping mall with shuttle-bus service from the stadium parking lot during the Christmas season? Why not give the customer a little more credit for understanding that on a global scale, flexible strategies based on real circumstances rather than engineering spec books can ultimately save trillions of dollars while improving the quality of our lives?

The supply side's laissez-faire attitude is, Don't question the authority of the marketplace. The truth is, many people are questioning it. They are setting conventional wisdom aside and striving for something more elegant, more comprehensive than standard operating procedures. If, for example, well-designed communities provide access by proximity, the need for cars will diminish. We may opt as a culture to restructure our zoning and tear down inappropriately sited infrastructure, reclaiming paved-over fertile soil and integrating agriculture into our cities and communities.

If commercial transportation and packaging are treated as two parts of the same system, both industries will become more efficient. If more purchasing is done on a regional scale, it will further reduce the need both for packaging and transportation. Regional systems have important spin-offs; local purchasing helps assure accountability and quality.

If the quality of manufactured goods improves as a result of deep design, we may find ourselves buying fewer but better things, which will require less money in the long run. And we may find ourselves with more leisure time by a different route than expected: not by virtue of a hundred thousand labor-saving devices, but by a way of life that doesn't require them.

Regulation will play a major role in encouraging the move away from standard operating procedures and toward multiple-purpose designs. But we must be careful in the writing of our regulations. Do they attach too much weight to waste reduction and too little to creating innovative pathways? Instead of focusing on what we don't want, shouldn't we be moving toward what we do want?

Consider the example of smoking. Acknowledging that smoking is one of the deadliest health risks there is, an individual may decide to cut down on the number of cigarettes smoked each day. That doesn't mean that the smoker has chosen the pathway toward health. It simply means that the smoker is potentially less unhealthy. The pathway toward health would be to substitute exercise, nutritious food, stimulating work, satisfying relationships, and creative recreation for tobacco. It's not what that person doesn't do that's important, but rather what the person does do.

Cutting down on smoking might be compared to the Phase I de-

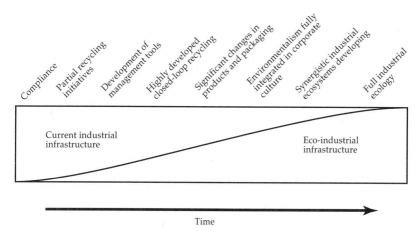

Figure 17
The emergence of an eco-industrial infrastructure.

sign strategy referred to as waste minimization by environmental managers. Certainly, it is critical that waste be reduced, but we can't stop there. Waste minimization doesn't address issues that are more complex: Should the product be made at all? Is it manufactured in a closed system that recycles materials? Does it enrich society and help maintain the viability of ecosystems? A Phase II approach deeper than waste minimization is resource optimization, the strategy that meets targeted social and environmental needs precisely, delivering more value per resource—per watt, per gallon, per acre—rather than simply less waste per widget. A good example of resource optimization is natural pest control. Farmers who practice it don't merely reduce the amount of pesticide, they change pathways. Natural pest control is not a passive strategy but an active one, requiring profound knowledge about climate, soil, hydrology, predator chains, and other systems.

The most comprehensive effort of deep design is the methodical selection and substitution of entire systems of production. As we make technical and cultural substitutions (such as were made in the replacement of the horse by the car, or natural fabrics by synthetic), we have to ensure that replacements are qualitatively equivalent or better. We need a more formal structure for technology assessment and the licensing of industry, but until that happens, it will be up to the invisible hand of the market to assist in the enlightening of design and industry. It's encouraging to know that we are now developing the tools to evaluate innovations based on environmental and human need rather than just on style and technological capability. As co-designers of culture, we don't have to perceive ourselves as adrift in an ocean of uncertainty.

A striking example of qualitative change at the national scale is occurring at U.S. federal facilities, recently cited by the Energy Policy Act of 1992 as prime targets for efficiency upgrades. According to efficiency liaison David Horne, there are 500,000 federal facilities and 9 million federal housing units. The energy legislation sets aside close to $200 million for these buildings to install efficient technologies and also stipulates that some of the energy savings may be kept by utilities via rate increases. Both the supply-siders and the demand-siders are winners. As a result, there's an Oklahoma land rush to upgrade lighting, air-conditioning, windows, appliances, and other end-use fixtures. Horne points out that the potential savings and employment opportunities are so huge they "begin to replace a sizable chunk of the military economy that has recently been phased out."[1] Traditionally, military research has spun off technologies as by-products of national security; the federal research on efficient technologies will redistribute weight to another, deeper aspect of security: the continued viability of resources and ecosystems. Money that has been spent to build military hardware is now being spent on technology that will help prevent resource-related war in the future.

A similar shift is gradually taking place in the national war on pollution. By some estimates, the United States has spent $1 trillion on environmental protection since 1970, and it is quickly approaching $200 billion in annual expenditures for pollution abatement and control. Some of those costs are being alchemized into profit by preventive designs in renewable energy, clean production, sustainable agriculture, closed-loop industry, and so on. As we move toward a best-case scenario, what we do right may ultimately be far more important than what we don't do wrong.

Neither A nor B

Sometimes we don't give ourselves a large enough menu of design choices. There is no correct answer to the familiar supermarket choice, Paper or plastic? because neither material is durable enough for continued reuse. The sugar industry poses another no-win choice, as demonstrated by comprehensive life-cycle analyses comparing the environmental and social effects of sugar beets and sugarcane. The sugar-beet crop, grown in temperate states like Minnesota, North Dakota, Michigan, and Colorado, is more likely to be rotated with other crops. Rotation promotes healthy soil and natural pest resistance, so that the sugar beet is less dependent on chemicals than is the subtropical sugarcane, which typically gets pampered with such inputs. Each crop is well utilized, being converted into sugar, molasses, and fuel-producing bagasse (sugarcane), and sugar, molasses, and livestock feed (beets). However, sugarcane production is typically preceded by the burning of plants, a practice that creates air and water pollution.

In a way, limiting our choice to these two crops is like asking if we want to be robbed or beaten. Sugar commands an almost unchallenged market niche, but that niche is based on social custom, not biology or health. We're consuming a lot of resources in each sugar cube to gratify our taste buds. The ecologically correct answer may be to choose neither A nor B, nor even C, artificial sweeteners. As the health food industry has successfully demonstrated, nature already provides an abundance of sugar molecules that don't bury taste. A person who prefers fresh-squeezed fruit juice is well aware that doing without the eight tablespoons of refined sugar (or its artificial equivalent) in a 12-ounce can of soda is not a deprivation but an escape.

If sugar were gradually phased out as one of the world's most lucrative crops, our health would improve because nutritional value per calorie of food would increase significantly. The postcolonial economies of many sugar-producing countries might also benefit considerably: instead of exporting sugar to earn money to import food, they could grow food. However, there may be no net benefit environmentally if the declining sugar industry were replaced by an industry with an equally poor life-cycle report card, such as the tourist industry that has loaded Hawaii with wall-to-wall condos.

Let's look at another American staple: the hamburger. A hamburger made of organic, range-fed beef takes fewer steps to produce and requires fewer off-farm inputs. Keeping cattle off chemicals and drugs and on the range instead of in the feedlot cuts costs. The resulting manure can be used as valuable fertilizer instead of being

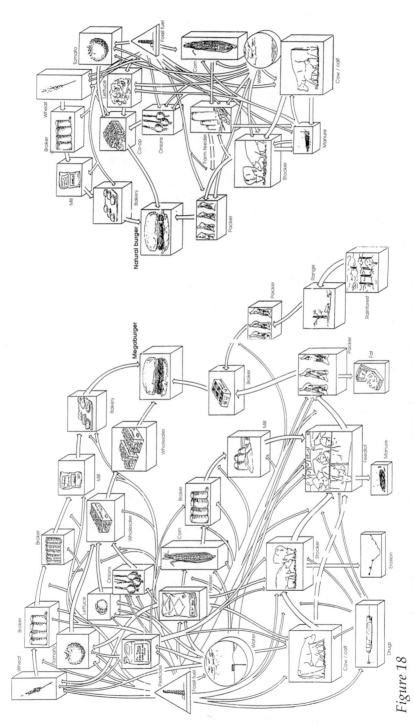

Figure 18

A tale of two burgers: (*left*) conventionally produced; (*right*) organically produced.

SOURCE: ROCKY MOUNTAIN INSTITUTE'S AGRICULTURE PROGRAM.

disposed of as costly waste. Also, by controlling the product from calving to cooking, a rancher can cut out numerous middlemen and increase profits dramatically. The conventional system relies on chemical fertilizers to grow cattle feed and on synthetic growth hormones and antibiotics to make the cattle grow faster—all costly inputs fraught with undesirable side effects. The beef changes ownership several times and is processed by different businesses, each contributing to the cumulative inefficiencies.

By the same logic, if a packaging manufacturer used fewer acids and caustic materials in an industrial process, it would result in less hazardous waste. But it wouldn't address the more essential questions: Do we need that packaging at all? Is its primary function preservation and protection of the product, or merely advertising and commercial appeal? The fundamental question has yet to be seriously debated in America's mainstream: Do we want to promote an economy based on total sales or total value? Although it sounds farfetched, perhaps in the distant future advertising will be taxed to reduce rather than to increase overall sales. Already there are restrictions on tobacco and alcohol advertising—that much we've agreed on.

Choosing one design option over another is not a simple task. It requires consensus on what type of design is beneficial. Designs that reduce damage are a first step. Ultimately, however, it will take more than waste minimization and efficiency upgrades to prevent environmental and social disintegration. We'll need to follow design pathways that meet basic needs with alternative forms of wealth and value: biological and cultural.

Cooperative Caretaking

Fundamentally, deep design is about taking care of things. Many environmental problems can't be effectively controlled; they have to be prevented by whole-systems understanding and caretaking. Wes Jackson gets to the roots of this in *Becoming Native to This Place*. "It was said of my father that no matter what he did, things turned out right. . . . He would lean on his scoop shovel for a half hour or more to watch his hogs eat the soaked oats or boiled potatoes or whatever he had raised. As much as it was due to the times, his good fortune was due to a combination of joy, sympathy, art, and love rolled into one and tuned to the demands of his place."[2]

What Jackson is talking about is craft, connection, and a deep-seated sense of caring, qualities that are free yet carry great value. These values make life worth living. I relate to the feelings Jackson's father experienced because I remember making compost one evening as July darkness fell over the foothills of Colorado. I was harvesting cartloads of tall, native grass before it went to seed—it didn't matter that it was raining outside and that I could barely even see my hands. That passion was worth much more than money.

Michael Heller runs a demonstration farm near the Chesapeake Bay, which is threatened by eroding farm soil and its chemical additives. He told me a story that summarizes what it means to be a caretaker of the environment:

> We took twenty-four farmers out into the bay so they could better understand the relationship of their work to the work of the watermen. One of the watermen, whose skipjack we were on, told us he didn't use depth sounders, loran, or other such navigational devices because when you rely on high-tech equipment, you lose a sense of the currents and you don't need to know the landmarks or read the water. One of the farmers got excited by this comment, because he said he felt the same way about farming: When a farmer becomes dependent on chemicals, it's like baking a cake from a box—he doesn't need to know his soils, or how his land drains, or what crops have been grown on a given field for the last ten years. It takes away the satisfaction of farming.[3]

Whether we're talking about fishing, farming, manufacturing, energy production, or any other activity, it's becoming obvious that we cannot and will not protect our environment until we are sufficiently connected to it and to our work to want to read the currents.

One reason so many people spend their careers "sleepworking" is that the workplace fails to inspire enthusiasm, craftsmanship, and the quest for innovation. Take the difference between the Japanese and American concept of total quality. In America, quality is almost a random offshoot of profit; in Japan, profit is an offshoot of quality. Quality can't be thumbtacked onto a design, a process, or an attitude; it has to be part of the genetic makeup.

One night at a party, I was explaining to a historian of Eastern culture what I meant by aikido engineering. He said, "That reminds me of the Tao approach to mountain climbing. Instead of conquering the mountain with high-tech ropes and gadgets, they study it, read the signature of its natural switchbacks and ledges, and get to the top of the mountain by becoming one with it." Do our designs and technologies strive to become one with nature? Not often enough. I'm not making an antitechnology pitch here, but rather a pragmatic pitch for appropriate technologies that precisely meet our needs and nature's. We don't want technologies that resemble the out-of-control marching broomsticks in *The Sorcerer's Apprentice,* and we don't want technologies that are so complex they destroy the meaning in our lives. Nor, as Paul Hawken points out, do we want technologies whose sole mission is to replace people—not in a world that will add 2 billion job seekers over the next ten years.[4]

Many of us would agree that convenience food isn't satisfying. Boxed food provides a quick but unhealthy meal. One reason it can't satisfy us is that its speed is imposed on us by a culture that wants resources immediately converted into profit. The implicit message is, You don't even have to use your brain or your hands to prepare the food in this box. You can make it and eat it in less than two minutes. Most of the deep designers I've talked with challenge this industrialized attitude, in effect asking, Why would we even want to make and eat a meal in 120 seconds? Instead, let's collectively change the circumstances that require us to be in a hurry. Let's put services and destinations closer together, by design; let's work more at home; let's fund better transit systems. Let's agree to slow the pace of our world so we have time to live our lives rather than hurry through them. They ask incredulously, Why wouldn't we want designs that allow us to make creative use of our brains and hands? We are programmed as a species to use them.

Deep design strategies improve systems by lowering overall costs and giving more satisfaction, yet they don't necessarily increase the GNP. They deliver value by a different route, with a different implicit message: It's not only how much wealth we generate in dollars that matters, but also how smoothly life flows. Our new design goals are more focused on intangibles and less obsessed with unqualified expansion of the economy. We want less maintenance, more time, more flexibility, more safety and security. We want satisfaction, not just gratification by continual reassurance and commercial replenishment.

The Time Is at Hand

How do we turn the 400-year inertia of the industrial revolution around? The way ocean liners are turned around, by many small, calculated adjustments.

Twenty-five years ago, the covers of alternative magazines like *Co-Evolution Quarterly* pictured a future complete with wind generators, organic gardens, and smiling pedestrians. At the time, these visions were dismissed by the American mainstream as the unrealistic dreams of a wild and woolly counterculture. But they're beginning to make a little more sense now. What was not anticipated twenty-five years ago were the jack-out of-the-box energy crises of the 1970s, the exponentially rapid environmental decline of the 1980s, and by the 1990s, the unchallenged dominance of large-scale industry, with its compulsive, culturally destructive supply-side mission.

From the crises of these past three decades has sprung unlimited opportunity. Many of the deep designs mentioned in this book were inspired by the energy shortages of the 1970s, when John Clark began to dream about communities like Haymount, when the printing industry began to look for nonpetroleum ink, and when research on alternative energy such as wind power began to be funded in a significant way. Environmental crises such as leaking landfills deepened understanding of the life-cycle consequences of poor design, and resulted in research on alternatives such as John Frost's pathway for nylon synthesis. Crisis is the seedbed of innovation. Hurricanes in Florida, floods in Missouri, earthquakes in California—these tragedies have to be seized as opportunities for enlightened design. Arguably, the biggest design opportunity in history may involve the pathways taken by developing nations in the twenty-first century. The designs and patterns created and chosen by the world's less affluent populations will largely determine whether the human race continues to be obsessed with material wealth, for the benefits of deep design are magnified in such cultures. A 10kw wind turbine, which would supply one American home with electric heat, is currently pumping drinking water for a village of four thousand in Morocco. In the Yucatán, Mexico's first wind farm was part of an energy strategy to avoid paying $3.2 million for an electric power line. It is critical that developing countries assess their abundant supplies of biological and cultural wealth and opt for high-quality, high-performance design to preserve that wealth, rather than perpetuating and solidifying the obsolete patterns of the industrial revolution.

It has been suggested that from here on out, in a world so starved for new ideas and approaches, the visionaries will be the most practical thinkers of all. While it may be true that there are distinct limits to what the earth's ecosystems can sustain, there are, fortunately, no recognized limits to the capabilities of the human mind. It doesn't take a visionary to see that our world is dysfunctional. Most people know. Economic indicators tell us, No sweat, there's continued abundance ahead—but our senses and instruments tell us that topsoil is disappearing, that global yields of fossil fuels, fish, minerals, and forest products are declining, that the pace of life is becoming too fast to be biologically regenerative. It's time to trust our instinct.

The deep design of culture will require more participation than we've seen in the latter part of this century. It will require cultural alertness and a sense of purpose, not catatonic passivity. In the near future, we'll need less television and more inquisitive, spirited backyard conversation. Less virtual reality and more reality. Less design from the profit-hungry supply side and more design from the quality-seeking demand side. Can we do it? Yes.

Notes

Chapter 1

1. William McDonough, "Building to Save the Earth," a symposium held at Ball State University, Muncie, Indiana, September 11 and 12, 1992.
2. United States Environmental Protection Agency's Science Advisory Board, *Future Risk: Research Strategies for the 1990's*, 1988.
3. Wendell Berry, "What Are Communities For?" *Audubon Magazine*, March/April 1993, p. 104.
4. Paul Hawken, *Ecology of Commerce: A Declaration of Sustainability*, HarperCollins, New York, 1993, p. 177.
5. Personal conversation with Joe Abe, U.S. Environmental Protection Agency, February 10, 1994.
6. Jerry Mander, *In the Absence of the Sacred: The Failure of Technology and the Survival of the Indian Nations*, Sierra Club Books, San Francisco, 1991, p. 43.
7. Donella Meadows, Dennis Meadows, and Jorgen Randers, *Beyond the Limits: Confronting Global Collapse, Envisioning a Sustainable Future*, Chelsea Green Publishing, Mills, Vermont, 1992.
8. Joel Makower, *The E Factor: The Bottom-Line Approach to Environmentally Responsible Business*, New York Times Books, N.Y., 1993.

Chapter 2

1. U.S. Office of Technology Assessment, *Green Products by Design: Choices for a Cleaner Environment*, U.S. Government Printing Office, Washington, D.C., October 1992, pp. 6-7.

2. Personal conversation with Randy Croxton, AIA, September, 1992.
3. Gyorgy Doczi, *The Power of Limits: Proportional Harmonies in Nature, Art and Architecture*, Shambala, Boston and London, 1985, p. 127.
4. Michael Rothschild, *BIONOMICS: The Inevitability of Capitalism*, Henry Holt and Company, New York, 1990.
5. Ibid.
6. Donella Meadows, Dennis Meadows, and Jorgen Randers, *Beyond the Limits: Confronting Global Collapse, Envisioning a Sustainable Future*, Chelsea Green Publishing, Mills, Vermont, 1992.
7. Jerry Mander, *In the Absence of the Sacred: The Failure of Technology and the Survival of the Indian Nations*, Sierra Club Books, San Francisco, 1991, p. 249.
8. Ibid.
9. Personal conversation with Robert Socolow, December, 1993.
10. Taichi Sakaiya, *Knowledge-Value: Or the History of the Future*, Kodansha International, New York, 1992.
11. Jesse Ausubel and Hedy E. Sladovich, editors, *Technology and Environment*, National Academy Press, Washington, D.C., 1989.
12. Robert Herman, Siamak A. Ardekani, and Jesse Ausubel, "Dematerialization," from *Technology and Environment*, National Academy Press, Washington, D.C., 1989.
13. Eric Larson, Marc Ross, and Robert Williams, "Beyond the Age of Materials," *Scientific American*, June 1986.
14. Wendell Berry, "What Are Communities For?" *Audubon Magazine*, March/April 1993.
15. Donella Meadows, Dennis Meadows, and Jorgen Randers, *Beyond the Limits: Confronting Global Collapse, Envisioning a Sustainable Future*, Chelsea Green Publishing, Mills, Vermont, 1992.
16. Rafael Aguayo, *Dr Deming: The American Who Taught the Japanese About Quality*, A Fireside Book, Simon And Shuster, New York, 1990, p. 126, 127.
17. Ibid.
18. Ernest Callenbach et al., *EcoManagement: The Elmwood Guide to Ecological Auditing and Sustainable Business*, Berrett-Koehler Publishers, Inc., San Francisco, 1993.
19. Ibid.
20. Jim Jubak and Marie D'Amico, "Mighty MITI," *The Amicus Journal*, Summer 1993, p. 39.
21. Ibid.
22. Taichi Sakaiya, *Knowledge-Value: Or the History of the Future*, Kodansha International, New York, 1992.
23. Ted Trainer, *Abandon Affluence!* Zed Books, London, 1985, pp. 248-279.
24. Genichi Taguchi and Don Clausing, "Robust Quality," *Harvard Business Journal*, January 1, 1990, p. 65.
25. Allan Hunt Badiner, "Natural Capital," *Yoga Journal*, September/October 1994, p. 64.
26. Allen Hammond, "Putting the Right Gene in the System: How Technology Changes," paper presented at *Toward 2000* symposium, Annapolis, Maryland, June 13-15, 1994.

27. Personal conversation with Jim Lenhart, inventor, January, 1994.
28. Personal conversation with Sally Gurley, September, 1994.
29. Ibid.
30. Personal conversation with Dennis Sohocki, March, 1995.
31. Tom Chappell, *The Soul of a Business: Managing for Profit and the Common Good*, Bantam Books, New York, 1993.
32. Ibid.
33. Ibid.

Chapter 3

1. David Morris and Irshad Ahmed, "Carbohydrates and Pollution Prevention: Making Chemicals and Industrial Materials from Plant Matter," *Pollution Prevention Review*, Autumn, 1993.
2. Paul Hawken and William McDonough, "Seven Steps to Doing Good Business," *Inc. Magazine*, November, 1993, p. 81.
3. "Science and the Citizen," *Scientific American*, December, 1979, p. 12.
4. Personal conversation with Robert Ayres, scientist, December, 1994.
5. Personal conversation with Fred Leavitt, Council for Chemical Research, September, 1993.
6. Personal conversation with Ralph Merkle, Xerox Company, October, 1993.
7. Personal conversation with George Casheau, November, 1994.
8. Personal conversation with Joe Hladky, November, 1994.
9. "Benzene," *Environmental Writer Monthly Backgrounder*, September, 1994, p. 8
10. K.M. Draths and J.W. Frost, "Environmentally Compatible Synthesis of Adipic Acid from D-Gluscose," *Journal of the American Chemical Society*, Volume 116, #1, pp. 9725-9726.
11. Personal conversation between Dr. John Frost and researcher Jude Proctor, February, 1995.
12. Personal conversation with Jennifer Haley, interior designer, July, 1994.
13. Personal conversation between Anthony Bernheim and researcher Jennifer Haley, August, 1994.

Chapter 4

1. Personal conversation with Randall Swisher, American Wind Energy Association, December, 1994.
2. Personal conversation with Frank McQuerry, Aermotor Windmill Company, November, 1994.
3. Personal conversation with Robert Thresher, National Renewable Energy Laboratory, November, 1994.
4. Ibid.
5. Ibid.
6. Personal conversation with Dick Curry, Kennetech Windpower Company, November, 1994.
7. Personal conversation with avian expert Thomas Cade, November, 1994.
8. Personal conversation with Cynthia Struzik, U.S. Fish and Wildlife, September, 1994.

9. Personal conversation with Robert Thresher, National Renewable Energy Laboratory, November, 1994.
10. Personal conversation with Hap Boyd, Kenetech Windpower Company, November, 1994.
11. Ibid.
12. Personal conversation with lighting expert Nancy Clanton, August, 1994.
13. Personal conversation with Brad Davids, E-Source Company, August, 1994.
14. Personal conversation with Steve Selkowitz, Lawrence Berkeley Laboratory, August, 1994.
15. Ibid.
16. "Energy and Resource Efficiencies," Part I of the three-part video teleconference *Building Connections,* January 14, 1993.
17. Personal conversation with Greg Franta, AIA, April, 1993.

Chapter 5

1. John Perkins and Nordica Holochuck, "Pesticides: Historical Changes Demand Ethical Choices," *The Pesticide Question: Environment, Economics and Ethics,* edited by David Pimental and Hugh Lehman, Chapman and Hall, New York, 1993.
2. Ibid.
3. Nebraska Sustainable Agriculture Society newsletter, September, 1987.
4. Michael W. Fox and Nancy E. Wiswall, *The Hidden Costs of Beef,* Humane Society of the United States, Washington, D.C., 1989.
5. Personal conversation with Paul Faeth, World Resources Institute, July, 1991.
6. Personal conversation with farmer Lewis Ashton; interview for "Sustaining America's Agriculture: High Tech and Horse Sense," a video for U.S. EPA and U.S. Department of Agriculture, 1992.
7. Ibid.
8. Personal conversation with Bob Curtis, Campbell's Soup, August, 1993.
9. Personal conversation with farmer David Taylor, August, 1993.
10. G.A. Sturgeoner and W. Roberts, "Reducing Pesticide Use by 50% in the Province of Ontario: Challenges and Progress," *The Pesticide Question: Environment, Economics and Ethics,* edited by David Pimental and Hugh Lehman, Chapman and Hall, New York, 1993.
11. David Pimental et al., "Environmental and Economic Impacts of Reducing U.S. Agricultural Pesticide Use," *The Pesticide Question: Environment, Economics and Ethics,* edited by David Pimental and Hugh Lehman, Chapman and Hall, New York, 1993.
12. Personal conversation with farmer Paul Buxman; interview for "Sustaining America's Agriculture: High-Tech and Horse Sense," a video for U.S. Environmental Protection Agency and U.S. Department of Agriculture, 1992.
13. Ibid.
14. Ibid.
15. Personal conversation with farmer Tom Frantzen, July, 1992.
16. Personal conversation with agronomist Richard Cruse, July, 1992.
17. Wendell Berry, "What Are Communities For?" *Audubon Magazine,* March/April 1993.

18. Wes Jackson, *Becoming Native to This Place*, University Press of Kentucky, Lexington, Kentucky, 1994.
19. Personal conversation with ecologist Jon Piper, September, 1994.
20. Ibid.
21. Personal conversation with geneticist Wes Jackson, September, 1994.

Chapter 6

1. *Designing with Vision: Public Building Guidelines for the 21st Century*, Stafford Architects, Seattle, Washington, 1992.
2. Peter Calthorpe, *The Next American Metropolis: Ecology, Communities and the American Dream*, Princeton Architectural Press, New York, 1993.
3. Ibid.
4. Peter Calthorpe, "The Post-Suburban Metropolis," *Whole Earth Review*, Winter, 1991, p. 44.
5. Steve Weissman and Judy Corbett, "Land Use Strategies for More Livable Places," The Local Government Commission, Sacramento, California, June, 1992.
6. Peter Calthorpe, *The Next American Metropolis: Ecology, Communities and the American Dream*, Princeton Architectural Press, New York, 1993.
7. Personal conversation with John Clark, July, 1993.
8. Ibid.
9. Ibid.
10. Personal conversation with Dan Slone, July, 1993.
11. William Browning, "Green Development: Determining the Cost of Environmentally Responsive Development," Master's thesis, MIT School of Real Estate Development, 1991.
12. Ibid.
13. Personal conversation with Virginia Thigpen, Village Homes resident, July, 1994.
14. Personal conversation with Tom Gougeon, Stapleton Redevelopment, August, 1994.
15. Ibid.
16. Personal conversation with Terry Minger, Center for Resource Management, August, 1994.
17. Susan Peterson, "Alternatives to the Big Pipe," *Oceanus*, Spring, 1993.
18. Personal conversation with horticulturalist Russ Vernon, September, 1994.
19. Ibid.
20. Bernadette Kosar, *Building Connections*, an American Institute of Architects teleconference, March 4, 1992.

Chapter 7

1. Personal conversation with Terry Minger, Center for Resource Management, February 6, 1994.
2. Personal conversation with William Fields, Wal-Mart, February, 1994.
3. Personal conversation with Meredith Miller, Center for Resource Management, February, 1994.

4. William McDonough, quoted from documentation tapes of the Eco-Mart design charette process.
5. Personal conversation with Richard Miller, Forest Partnership, October, 1993.
6. Michael Wagner, "Visionary Architect," in *Interiors Magazine*, March 1993, p. 54.
7. Personal conversation with Berne Broudy, October, 1993.
8. Personal conversation with Steve Brown, BSW Architects, October, 1993.
9. Amory Lovins, from documentation tapes of "Building to Save the Earth," a symposium at Ball State University, Muncie, Indiana, September 11 and 12, 1992.
10. Ibid.
11. Ibid.
12. "The Relationships Between Halons, Chlorofluorocarbons and the Ozone Layer." *The Building Official and Code Administrator*. September/October 1992.
13. Personal conversation with C.L. Maurer, Landplan, September, 1993.
14. Personal conversation with Gary Rose, Engineered Air Company, January, 1994.
15. Personal conversation with Art Shelton, October, 1993
16. Personal conversation with C.L. Maurer, Landplan, September, 1993.
17. Ibid.
18. Personal conversation with Laura Bevilacqua, Wal-Mart, February, 1994.
19. Personal conversation with Meredith Miller, Center for Resource Management, February, 1994.
20. William McDonough, quoted from documentation tapes of the Eco-Mart design charette process.
21. Personal conversation with Patty Perez, Wal-Mart, September, 1993.
22. Ibid.
23. Personal conversation with William Fields, Wal-Mart, September, 1993.
24. Personal conservation with Patricia Morvain, September 7, 1994.
25. Personal conversation with Terry Minger, Center for Resource Management, February 6, 1995.
26. Jim McMahon, from *Warmer Bulletin*, Kent, United Kingdom, November, 1994.

Chapter 8

1. Werner J. Glantschnig, "Design for Environment and Its Role in Environmentally Sound Manufacturing," U.S.-Japan Center for Technology Management, Washington, D.C., March 25-26, 1993.
2. Joe Romm, for U.S. EPA, U.S. Small Business Administration, *Lean and Clean Management: Greening the Bottom Line while Reducing Pollution*, 1992, pp. 26-27.
3. Herman H. Goldstine, *The Computer from Pascal to von Nuemann*, Princeton University Press, New Jersey, 1972.
4. Hans Quisser, *The Conquest of the Microchip*, Harvard University Press, Cambridge, Massachusetts, 1988.
5. Donald Kevin Gordon, Peter Pocock, and Bruce F. Webster, *How Things Work*, chapter on computers, Time-Life Books, St. Remy Press, Alexandria, Va., 1990.

6. Pamela Weintraub, "Computers Redux," *Audubon*, May-June 1993, pp. 18-20.
7. Personal conversation with Kevin Allen, Hewlett Packard, July, 1994.
8. Ibid.
9. Brian Nadel, "The Green Machine," *PC Magazine*, May, 1993.
10. Personal conversation with Catherine Zoi, EPA, November, 1994.
11. Personal conversation with Pete Schneider, IBM, July, 1994.
12. Joseph S. Collentro, "CRT Disposal: Recycle or Pay the Cost," *Information Display*, January, 1993
13. Ibid.
14. Harry Freeman et al., *Industrial Pollution Prevention*, McGraw-Hill, New York, 1995, p. 621

Chapter 9
1. Personal conversation with energy liaison David Horne, January, 1995.
2. Wes Jackson, *Becoming Native to This Place*, University Press of Kentucky, Lexington, Kentucky, 1994.
3. Personal conversation with Michael Heller, Chesapeake Bay Foundation, June, 1991.
4. Paul Hawken, *Ecology of Commerce: A Declaration of Sustainability*, Harper-Collins, New York, 1993.

Index

About the Author

David Wann is a writer, teacher, and video-maker. He works part-time at the Environmental Protection Agency on pollution prevention and is an adjunct professor in the University of Denver's graduate environmental program. Television programs he has produced include *Beyond Business as Usual: Meeting the Challenge of Hazardous Waste; Transportation 2000: Moving Beyond Auto America; Sustaining America's Agriculture;* and *Mega-Cities.* He is now at work on a series of "video vignettes" produced by Greening America that document innovative design in the home and community. He is author of *Biologic: Designing with Nature to Protect the Environment* and a poetry book, *Log Rhythms.* His family will soon move into an alternative community in Golden, Colorado, that is co-designed by its residents.

Island Press Board of Directors